# The History of Paris

## The Shaping of a Metropolis

**CRAFTED BY SKRIUWER**

# Dear Reader,

Imagine the scent of woodsmoke and damp stone rising from a 3rd-century Roman bathhouse, or the thunder of cannon fire during the 1871 siege. This history is built not on abstract dates, but on the lives of those who walked these streets. Hear the rhythmic chiseling of masons perfecting Notre-Dame's flying buttresses in Chapter 6. See the flickering candlelight illuminating a clandestine Enlightenment salon debating liberty in Chapter 13. Taste the coarse, scarce bread that fueled a revolutionary's anger in Chapter 14, drawn from a primary source's desperate diary entry. Each chapter reveals these intimate human struggles.

🔥 The themes that forged Paris—revolution, resilience, and rebirth—are the very embers that glow in our modern world. As you turn these pages, I urge you to brew a strong tea, find a comfortable chair, and let the centuries fall away. Trace the map of the past on the city of today, and you will find that every stone has a story waiting to be heard. A JOURNEY THROUGH THESE PAGES IS A JOURNEY INTO THE VERY SOUL OF HUMAN ENDEAVOR.

*Why this book?*

- *Gripping, unsettling storytelling that brings history's darkest moments to life*

- *Unflinching accounts of cruelty, survival, and the unknown*

- *Eerie connections between past horrors and modern fears*

# Warmly,

*Skriuwer*

Copyright © 2025 by Skriuwer.

All rights reserved. No part of this book may be used or reproduced in any form whatsoever without written permission except in the case of brief quotations in critical articles or reviews.

At **Skriuwer**, we're more than just a team—we're a global community of people who love books. In Frisian, "Skriuwer" means "writer," and that's at the heart of what we do: creating and sharing books with readers worldwide. Wherever you are in the world, **Skriuwer** is here to inspire learning.

**Frisian** is one of the oldest languages in Europe, closely related to English and Dutch, and is spoken by about **500,000 people** in the province of **Friesland** (Fryslân), located in the northern Netherlands. It's the second official language of the Netherlands, but like many minority languages, Frisian faces the challenge of survival in a modern, globalized world.

We're using the money we earn to promote the Frisian language.
For more information, contact : **kontakt@skriuwer.com** (www.skriuwer.com)

## Historical Research Methodology

This work synthesizes information from:

- **Primary Sources**
  - Government archives and historical records
  - Period correspondence and eyewitness accounts
  - Contemporary newspapers and publications

## Disclaimer:

The images in this book are creative reinterpretations of historical scenes. While every effort was made to accurately capture the essence of the periods depicted, some illustrations may include artistic embellishments or approximations. They are intended to evoke the atmosphere and spirit of the times rather than serve as precise historical records.

"History is the version of past events that people have decided to agree upon."

– Napoleon Bonaparte

# Unsilenced: The Defiant Voice of Paris

'Paris is well worth a mass.'
- Henry IV (1593)

'L'État, c'est moi. (I am the state).'
- Louis XIV (1651)

'Crush the infamous thing!'
 - Voltaire (1762)

'Let them eat cake.'
- Attributed to Marie Antoinette (1789)

'Terror is the order of the day.'
- Maximilien Robespierre (1793)

'I found a crown in the gutter and picked it up.'
- Napoleon Bonaparte (1804)

'We must run a blade through the belly of old Paris.'
- Baron Haussmann (1853)

'It is we, the workers, who built this city. Now we will claim it.'
- A Communard (1871)

# INDOMITABLE PARIS: THE UNFINISHED REVOLUTION

### 🏺 c. 250 BCE–52 CE: SEINE OF THE PARISII

*Foundations in Mud and Myth*

- Celtic Parisii tribe coins wealth on the Île de la Cité (c. 250 BCE, Ch 1)
- Roman legions conquer Gaul; Lutetia rises on the Left Bank (52 CE, Ch 2)
- Baths and forums impose Roman order on a Gallic town (Ch 2)

### ⛪ 508–1300 CE: SPIRES AND SCHOLARS

*The Medieval Forge*

- Clovis makes Paris seat of Frankish power, embracing Cross (508 CE, Ch 3)
- Notre-Dame's cornerstone laid, a century of stone and faith begins (1163 CE, Ch 6)
- University attracts minds like Abelard, challenging orthodoxy (Ch 5, 6)

### ♦ 1540–1789 CE: PALACES AND PLOTS

*Bourbon Ambition*

- Henri IV gifts a "green lung" to his people with Place des Vosges (1612, Ch 10)
- Louis XIV abandons the city for Versailles, a fateful retreat (1682, Ch 12)
- Enlightenment philosophes in salons brew the ideas for revolt (Ch 13)

## ⚔ 1789–1871 CE: BARRICADES AND BOULEVARDS

*The Revolutionary Furnace*

- Bastille falls, the people seize the narrative of power (1789, Ch 14)
- Napoleon's Arc de Triomphe glorifies the modern empire (1806, Ch 15)
- Haussmann's broad avenues cut through revolt's old arteries (1853, Ch 18)
- Commune's desperate stand ends in blood and fire (1871, Ch 19)

## 🗼 1889–PRESENT: MODERN METROPOLIS

*The Enduring Beacon*

- Eiffel Tower scoffs at tradition, ushering in a new age (1889, Ch 20)
- City of Light endures war, occupation, and liberation (1940-44, Epilogue)
- Perpetual reinvention as the world's stage for art and protest

## ● LEGACY: THE ETERNAL STAGE

*Enduring Foundations*

- The Gothic form, born here, defines our image of the sacred (Ch 6)
- Revolutionary cries of Liberté still fuel global struggles for rights (Ch 14)
- The modern city itself, a monument to the power of radical design (Ch 18)
- The café, the salon—eternal crucibles of art and radical thought (Ch 13, 20)

# *"To Paris! The city of transformations, the city of marvels."*

—Victor Hugo (1862, *Les Misérables*, Ch 18)

# BEFORE WE START: 50 SHOCKING, BEAUTIFUL, & DISTURBING PARISIAN SECRETS

*The City of Light... and Shadows*

### ✘ REVOLUTION & TERROR
● **The last prisoner in the Bastille** wasn't a political martyr but a degenerate aristocrat, the Comte de Solages, imprisoned by his own family for incest and insanity.
🔥 **During the Terror**, executioners couldn't keep up with beheadings, so a special "blood tax" was levied on spectators in the front rows to pay for sand to soak up the runoff.
● **The guillotine** was considered a humane advancement; its inventor, Dr. Guillotin, was horrified that his name became synonymous with the revolutionary slaughter.

### 🏛 ROYAL DECADENCE & SCANDAL
👑 **Louis XV's mistress**, Madame de Pompadour, had a room in Versailles with a mechanical table that rose through the floor fully set to avoid servants overhearing state secrets.
🍽 **A 17th-century royal** feast featured a live, fully-decorated pastry that was cracked open to release a dwarf riding a live turkey for the guests' amusement.
💎 **Marie Antoinette's** infamous "Let them eat cake" was never uttered by her; the phrase was propaganda, lifted from philosopher Rousseau's writings about a different princess decades earlier.

### 🕯 MACABRE RITUALS & THE OCCULT
🦴 **For decades, the remains of millions** of Parisians were dug up and meticulously arranged in the Catacombs; workers often got lost and died in the endless ossuary tunnels.
👤 **Napoleon Bonaparte** famously held a séance in the Tuileries Palace, using a "magic mirror" to try and commune with the ghosts of past emperors.
🪦 **Père Lachaise cemetery** was initially a massive failure; managers had to stage fake burials of famous figures like Abelard and Héloïse to make it a desirable address.

## 🏗 HIDDEN ENGINEERING & URBAN SECRETS

🪣 **The city's first water system** used a massive iron steam pump that citizens believed was a demonic device devouring children from the Seine.

🌉 **Baron Haussmann's** "modern" boulevards were designed not for beauty, but as wide firing lanes for cannons to prevent future barricaded revolutions.

🗼 **The Eiffel Tower** was built from 18,038 individually pre-riveted pieces; workers risked their lives assembling it like a morbid metal jigsaw puzzle without harnesses.

## ⛪ SACRILEGE & CHURCH SECRETS

👹 **Notre-Dame's gargoyles** aren't medieval; they are 19th-century additions by Viollet-le-Duc, who designed them based on Victor Hugo's Gothic nightmares.

💍 **The preserved, shriveled heart of Louis XVII**, the boy king who died in prison, was smuggled out inside a hollowed-out book and kept in a crystal urn for centuries.

🕯 **The Sainte-Chapelle was built** not as a public church, but as a colossal, jewel-encrusted reliquary to house what was believed to be Christ's Crown of Thorns.

## 🍷 DEBAUCHERY & VICE

🐒 **The Jardin des Plantes** once featured a "Nursing Zoo" where noblewomen could pay to watch semi-naked "savage" women from colonies breastfeed their babies for entertainment.

💃 **The original Can-Can was a violent**, athletic dance performed by working-class women in grimy bars, designed to mock the stiff, aristocratic dances of the upper class.

🍸 **19th-century absinthe** was so potent and hallucinogenic that it was blamed for a man murdering his entire family; it was banned for nearly a century.

## ⚕ MEDICAL MADNESS & DISEASE

💧 **Parisian doctors** once believed the city's stench caused disease, so they prescribed "Fumigation Therapy"—forcing patients to inhale the smoke of burning human excrement.

🧠 **A famous 19th-century** neurologist kept the intact, pickled brain of his patient, a prolific assassin, in a jar to study the biological source of evil.

⚫ **The 1832 cholera pandemic** killed so quickly that people collapsed mid-step; their bodies were piled in the streets and collected with meat hooks.

## 🖋 WAR, SIEGE & SURVIVAL
🐀 **During the 1870 Siege**, the zoo animals were eaten; the menu at Voisin restaurant featured Elephant Consommé, Kangaroo Stew, and Roasted Camel.
⚫ **Communards executed the Archbishop** of Paris, not with a bullet, but by using a bayonet to carve a hole in his throat to mimic a bloody "second mouth".
📞 **The French resistance during WWII** used the Eiffel Tower's elevator cables to string a clandestine radio antenna, right under the noses of the Nazi occupiers.

## 🎨 ARTISTIC REBELLION & SCANDAL
🖼 **The Louvre was once an artist's squat;** painters lived illegally in its abandoned halls, burning old frames for warmth and painting masterpieces by candlelight.
🎬 **The first-ever film screened** for a paying audience wasn't a narrative but a 50-second clip of female factory workers leaving a plant, causing a riot of excitement.
🦞 **Poet Gérard de Nerval famously** walked a lobster on a pale blue silk leash through the Palais-Royal, claiming it was a superior pet that "didn't bark and knew the secrets of the deep".

## ⚖️ TWISTED LAWS & SOCIAL ORDER
♟ **The first-ever police force** was created in Paris not to stop crime, but to spy on nobles and suppress any criticism of the Sun King, Louis XIV.
👅 **A common punishment for blasphemy** in medieval Paris was having your tongue nailed to a door in a public square for 24 hours.
🃏 **During the Revolution,** playing cards were re-issued with "Liberty, Equality, Fraternity" replacing the traditional Kings and Queens, who were sent to the guillotine.

## 🐾 FORGOTTEN INNOVATIONS & ODDITIES
☎ **The world's first ever public fax machine service** operated in 1860s Paris, sending images over telegraph lines years before the telephone was invented.
🎩 **A famous 18th-century conman sold "magic"** lanterns that projected ghostly images, convincing grieving widows he could summon their dead husbands for a fee.
🚗 **The first-ever automobile death occurred in Paris in 1771**, when a steam-powered tractor built to haul cannons crashed into a wall, killing its inventor.

### 🔊 CULINARY CURIOSITIES
🔊 **Hot chocolate was introduced** to France as a bitter, spiced medicine; Louis XIV's wife, Maria Theresa, was so addicted she had it delivered to her bedchamber in a silver kettle.

👑 **Napoleon III**, desperate to find a cheap, nutritious food for the poor, sponsored a contest won by a scientist who invented margarine in a Paris lab.

✋ **Swans on the Seine** were considered royal property; poaching one was a crime punishable by having your hand publicly severed on the very riverbank.

### 👗 FASHION & FOLLY
👗 **The corset was so violently restrictive** that it regularly caused women to faint; doctors called this condition "Swooning Malady" and blamed it on female hysteria, not the garment.

🎀 **During the Directory period,** a fashion called "Victim Ball" emerged where survivors of the Terror wore thin red ribbons around their necks mimicking the guillotine's cut.

🥼 **The iconic white lab coat** was invented in Paris because scientists, tired of being mistaken for cooks in their aprons, wanted a symbol of clean, rational authority.

### 🔑 SECRETS OF THE STONES
🗿 **The Pont-Neuf, "New Bridge,"** is now the oldest standing bridge in Paris, a paradox known to every Parisian who walks its worn cobbles.

🔍 **Built into the wall of a private apartment** building is the last surviving sign marking the maximum height of the catastrophic 1910 Great Flood, a ghost watermark from a drowned city.

💐 **The famous "I Love You" wall in Montmartre** contains the phrase written 311 times in 250 languages, a silent, sprawling monument to heartbreak and hope in the city of lovers.

## "Paris is a sphinx whose smile hides the scars of a thousand revolutions."

— *A 19th-century flâneur (Chapter 19)*

# TABLE OF CONTENTS

## CHAPTER 1: THE BEGINNINGS OF PARIS – PREHISTORIC TO EARLY CELTIC PRESENCE

- *Earliest human settlements along the Seine*
- *Influence of Celtic tribes and the emergence of the Parisii*
- *Geographical factors shaping early habitation*

## CHAPTER 2: THE ROMAN ERA & THE TRANSFORMATION INTO LUTETIA

- *Roman conquest and administration*
- *Introduction of Roman architecture and engineering*
- *Cultural and economic shifts under Roman rule*

## CHAPTER 3: THE EARLY MIDDLE AGES – MEROVINGIANS & CAROLINGIANS

- *Collapse of Roman power and the rise of Merovingians*
- *King Clovis and the significance of early Christianity*
- *Impact of Carolingian rule on governance and religion*

## CHAPTER 4: THE RISE OF THE CAPETIAN DYNASTY AND MEDIEVAL PARIS

- *Foundation of the Capetian line*
- *Expansion of Paris as a political and trade center*
- *The role of churches and fortifications in urban development*

## CHAPTER 5: URBAN GROWTH, UNIVERSITIES, AND LIFE IN THE 12TH CENTURY

- *Formation of early academic institutions*
- *Marketplaces, guilds, and everyday life*
- *Architectural developments and public works*

## CHAPTER 6: THE 13TH CENTURY – SCHOLASTICISM, ARCHITECTURE, AND SOCIETY

- *Rise of scholastic thought in Parisian universities*
- *Gothic cathedral construction and architectural innovations*
- *Social hierarchy and the role of the Church*

---

## CHAPTER 7: THE HUNDRED YEARS' WAR AND ITS IMPACT ON PARIS

- *Causes and main events of the conflict*
- *Sieges, shifts in power, and social unrest*
- *Long-term consequences for the city's structure and economy*

---

## CHAPTER 8: THE RENAISSANCE IN PARIS – ART, ARCHITECTURE, AND ROYAL INFLUENCE

- *Transition from medieval to Renaissance styles*
- *Patronage of the arts by French royalty*
- *Introduction of humanist thought and its effects on learning*

---

## CHAPTER 9: THE WARS OF RELIGION AND THE STRUGGLE FOR POWER

- *Catholic–Huguenot conflicts and key events*
- *St. Bartholomew's Day Massacre and its aftermath*
- *Rise of Bourbon influence and the path to stability*

---

## CHAPTER 10: THE BOURBON KINGS AND THE SHAPING OF PARIS

- *Henry IV's efforts to restore order*
- *Infrastructure projects and urban improvements*
- *Developments in trade and commerce during Bourbon rule*

## CHAPTER 11: THE 17TH CENTURY – LOUIS XIII, RICHELIEU, AND THE SEEDS OF ABSOLUTISM

- *Centralization of power under Cardinal Richelieu*
- *Growth of noble townhouses and cultural institutions*
- *Setting the stage for Louis XIV's absolute monarchy*

## CHAPTER 12: LOUIS XIV'S REIGN – THE GRAND TRANSFORMATION OF PARIS

- *Major building projects and urban planning*
- *Cultural life, the arts, and the court's influence*
- *Socioeconomic impact of prolonged wars and royal policies*

## CHAPTER 13: THE ENLIGHTENMENT AND SOCIAL CHANGE IN 18TH-CENTURY PARIS

- *Philosophical salons and the rise of intellectual debate*
- *Critiques of traditional authority and new social ideas*
- *Paris as a hub of print culture and public discourse*

## CHAPTER 14: THE FRENCH REVOLUTION – COLLAPSE OF THE OLD ORDER

- *Economic crisis, social discontent, and the spark of revolution*
- *The storming of the Bastille and key revolutionary events*
- *Radical changes in governance and the Reign of Terror*

## CHAPTER 15: THE REVOLUTIONARY AFTERMATH – DIRECTORY, CONSULATE, AND THE RISE OF NAPOLEON

- *Post-revolutionary factions and the Directory*
- *Napoleon's ascent to power and the establishment of the Consulate*
- *Administrative, legal, and cultural reforms impacting Paris*

## CHAPTER 16: THE RESTORATION AND THE SHIFTING POLITICAL LANDSCAPE

- *Return of the Bourbon monarchy*
- *Political tensions and the balance between old and new ideals*
- *Influence on everyday life and national identity*

---

## CHAPTER 17: THE JULY MONARCHY AND THE SEEDS OF FURTHER REVOLUTIONS

- *The 1830 revolution and rise of Louis-Philippe*
- *Urban protests, barricades, and political clubs*
- *Socioeconomic reforms and growing discontent among the populace*

---

## CHAPTER 18: THE SECOND REPUBLIC, THE SECOND EMPIRE, AND HAUSSMANN'S PARIS

- *Revolution of 1848 and the establishment of a republic*
- *Louis-Napoleon's coup d'état and the birth of the Second Empire*
- *Baron Haussmann's sweeping urban modernization projects*

---

## CHAPTER 19: THE SIEGE OF PARIS AND THE PARIS COMMUNE (1870–1871)

- *Franco-Prussian War and the devastating siege*
- *Social and political factors leading to the Paris Commune*
- *The bloody end of the Commune and its lasting effects*

---

## CHAPTER 20: THE LATE 19TH CENTURY – CULTURAL FLOURISH AND INDUSTRIAL CHANGES

- *Rebuilding the city and the emergence of new industries*
- *Artistic and literary movements shaping Parisian culture*
- *Foundations laid for Paris's evolution into a modern metropolis*

# CHAPTER 1

## THE BEGINNINGS OF PARIS – PREHISTORIC TO EARLY CELTIC PRESENCE

## Introduction

Paris, one of the world's most renowned cities, has a history that stretches back thousands of years before it became a center of culture and power. Long before the iconic monuments were built and long before it was even recognized as "Paris," people of different eras settled along the banks of the river Seine. The earliest traces of human habitation in this region date back to prehistoric times. This means that long before any written records existed, small groups of hunter-gatherers made use of the natural resources found in the area.

Over time, these human communities changed from nomadic bands to more settled groups. They began domesticating animals, cultivating land, and forming small settlements. The various prehistoric periods—Paleolithic, Mesolithic, and Neolithic—each contributed important steps in the development of human society. The environment played a big role in influencing how people lived. The wide river, fertile soil, and moderate climate in what would someday become the Paris region made it a favorable place to settle.

After the prehistoric era, Celtic tribes, especially one called the **Parisii**, took advantage of the natural benefits of the region. The Parisii are the group that ultimately gave the city its name. It was under their influence that this stretch of land began to shape into a recognizable community. In this chapter, we will explore the beginnings of human activity in this place. We will walk through the earliest evidence of human life by the Seine, the arrival of the Celtic peoples, and how these foundations laid the groundwork for the city's later transformation under Roman rule.

# 1) The Geographical Setting

### The Seine and Its Surroundings

The Seine River, flowing in a winding path across northern France, has always been a major geographical feature. In ancient times, it served as a source of fresh water, food, and an avenue for travel and trade. The gentle slopes around the river made the land easy to settle. Floodplains provided rich soil for the early farmers who came after the hunters.

During the Ice Ages, the climate in this region of Europe shifted multiple times. Glacial and interglacial periods had an impact on water levels, flora, and fauna. However, compared to more northern regions, the climate around the Seine was often milder, which encouraged human presence. Small animals, fish, and later farmland resources made life sustainable for the groups who wanted to settle down.

Even in the earliest times, the Seine would flood regularly, depositing nutrients and silt on the surrounding plains. This cyclical renewal turned parts of the riverbank into fertile patches of ground that early people could cultivate. In addition, the surrounding forests provided wood for shelter and fires, as well as wild game for food.

### Forests and Wildlife

Ancient forests covered much of what is now northern France. These woodlands were rich in oak, beech, and pine. Alongside these trees, early inhabitants found game such as deer, boar, and smaller animals like rabbits. The biodiversity of the area offered various options for food, clothing, and tools. Bones from animals could be carved into needles, fish hooks, or other utensils, and hides were used for clothing or shelter.

The forests were not just resources for hunting. They also offered a level of protection. Early communities often used naturally defensive locations—like higher ground surrounded by woods—to protect themselves from wild animals or rival human groups. Over time, however, as settlements grew, the forests started to get cleared for timber and farmland.

---

# 2) Traces of Prehistoric Inhabitants

### Paleolithic and Mesolithic Presence

Archaeological digs in and around the Paris basin have uncovered stone tools, cut bones, and cave art fragments that hint at human activity dating back tens of thousands of years. The Paleolithic period (often known as the Old Stone Age) ended around 10,000 years ago, giving way to the Mesolithic (the Middle Stone Age).

In the Paleolithic era, groups of hunter-gatherers roamed the region, following herds of animals and changing their habitat with the seasons. Caves and rock shelters in this part of France provide evidence of their presence. Tools like hand axes and scrapers have been found, showing that these early humans could shape flint and other stones into tools. These tools helped them hunt animals, cut meat, and prepare hides for clothing.

As the climate warmed and glaciers receded, the Mesolithic period introduced small but important changes. People began to use more refined microlithic tools—tiny stone blades that could be attached to wooden or bone handles. While the population was still mostly nomadic, we see signs of camps and seasonal settlements. Remnants of fire pits, middens (trash heaps), and basic huts suggest these groups were slowly adapting to a less mobile way of life.

**Transition to the Neolithic**

The Neolithic period (New Stone Age) brought about a major shift from nomadic hunting and gathering to farming and animal husbandry. This transition didn't happen suddenly. It was more of a gradual process that spread from other parts of Europe and the Near East. People learned that certain seeds could be planted and harvested, leading to consistent food supplies. Domesticated animals like goats, sheep, and later cattle became common, removing much of the uncertainty of hunting.

These developments allowed communities to stay in one place longer, and this steadiness led to the building of more permanent structures. Small villages began to appear. The quality of pottery improved, and new techniques for stone polishing emerged. Trade networks started to form as groups exchanged tools, pottery, and other items with neighboring communities.

In the region that would become Paris, evidence of Neolithic culture includes polished stone axes, pottery shards, and the remains of megalithic structures in nearby areas. While large-scale monuments like Stonehenge in Britain are more famous, France also has its share of menhirs (standing stones) and dolmens (stone tombs). Some of these can be found in the broader Paris basin, although not always in the direct heart of the city.

---

## 3) Early Tribal Groupings and Cultural Development

**The Role of Family and Clan**

In these prehistoric and protohistoric societies, family ties and clans played a crucial role. People survived together by sharing work, protecting each other from external threats, and organizing communal tasks such as farming and building. Over time, these kin-based groups grew bigger and formed tribal communities, each with its own leaders, religious practices, and social structures.

Leaders in these groups were often the individuals who possessed specialized knowledge, like how to find the best hunting grounds or how to perform religious rituals that might ensure a good harvest. Ritual and belief systems varied, but many were centered on the natural world. The sun, moon, and stars were often revered, as were animals that represented important elements of survival.

**Trading and Interaction**

As these communities grew, so did their need to interact with neighbors. Barter systems were common; surplus grain might be traded for flint or obsidian for tools, or for cattle and sheep from areas where livestock breeding was more advanced. The Seine became a key waterway, allowing goods to be transported more easily. Over generations, this network of exchange expanded, indirectly connecting small settlements to a larger regional economy.

By the later phases of the Neolithic, the increasing sophistication of trade had a strong influence on local culture. When metal use began to spread during the Chalcolithic (Copper Age) and later Bronze Age periods, the Paris basin saw the exchange of metal items—though the full Bronze Age and Iron Age transformations would take time to reach the region.

## 4) The Arrival of the Celts and the Birth of the Parisii

**Introduction of Celtic Culture**

The Celts were an Indo-European people who spread across much of western and central Europe, reaching regions that now include France, Spain, Great Britain, and parts of Germany. By around the first millennium BC, Celtic tribes were well-established in

Gaul (the Roman name for the region covering modern-day France and neighboring areas). Gaul was not a single unified state; rather, it was a patchwork of tribal territories, each with its own chieftains and councils.

Celtic society was known for its metalworking skills, especially in iron. The arrival of the Iron Age in this part of Europe had a big impact on tools and weapons, which became stronger and more effective. This technological edge helped some tribes consolidate power and influence. It also enabled better farming, since iron plows could till the soil more efficiently than earlier wooden or stone-based tools.

**The Parisii Tribe**

Among the Celtic peoples who settled in Gaul, the **Parisii** tribe made their home in the area along the Seine. While there were other tribes in the vicinity, the Parisii became particularly important because of their strategic location on a navigable river. They established a settlement on what are now known as the Île de la Cité and its surrounding banks. This would eventually grow into the city of Paris.

Historical sources about the Parisii from this time are limited, mostly because they did not have a strong tradition of written records. Most of what we know comes from archaeological findings and later Roman texts, which mention the Parisii when describing the conquest of Gaul. Still, we can infer that the tribe had a structured society with warriors, craft specialists, traders, farmers, and religious leaders known as druids.

**Lifestyle and Economy**

The Parisii's economy relied heavily on agriculture and trade. They grew crops like barley, wheat, and legumes. They raised livestock such as pigs, sheep, and cattle. The surrounding forests and the river provided fish, game, and other wild foods. The ability to navigate the Seine meant they could trade with neighboring tribes, exchanging goods like salt, pottery, cloth, and metal items.

The Parisii likely built small fortifications called oppida (singular: oppidum). These were large, enclosed settlements that served as administrative or defensive centers. Remains of such structures in other parts of Gaul hint that the Parisii also had some form of organized defense or at least a communal gathering place for trade and governance. Some oppida could be quite large, indicating a thriving community.

---

## 5) Religious Practices and Worldview

### The Druidic Order

Celtic society is often associated with druids—religious figures who also served as judges, teachers, and advisors. Though druids are famously connected with areas like Britain and Ireland, Gaul also had its share of druidic traditions. These individuals took on ceremonial roles during festivals, sacrifices, and community gatherings. They were deeply respected and sometimes feared because of their perceived spiritual powers.

Religious sites were usually in natural settings—sacred groves, springs, or clearings near the riverbank. Offerings to gods included food, weapons, or jewelry, thrown into rivers or left at certain trees. The Celts believed in a pantheon of deities associated with aspects of nature such as the sun, rivers, forests, and fertility.

### Funerary Customs

Burial practices provide insights into Celtic beliefs about the afterlife. Wealthier individuals or chieftains were often interred with their possessions: weapons, ornaments, and sometimes even chariots. For the Parisii, as for other Celtic tribes, such burials reflected a belief in some form of existence after death, where earthly goods could still be useful. Grave goods also signified status and wealth.

Some archaeological sites in the region show evidence of cremation, with ashes placed in urns. Over time, different burial customs existed alongside each other. This could hint at evolving religious practices or the influence of neighboring tribes.

---

## 6) Society, Art, and Craftsmanship

### Social Hierarchy

Despite the lack of extensive written records, we can guess that Celtic tribes in Gaul, including the Parisii, had social classes. Warriors often held a high status, as they protected the tribe and led raids or defenses. Craftsmen were also respected because they provided vital tools, weapons, and jewelry. Farmers and laborers formed the backbone of the community by producing food. Druids, as mentioned, were an intellectual and spiritual elite, handling religious rites and legal matters.

It's possible that a chieftain led the Parisii, advised by a council of elders or influential clan heads. This leader would likely have made decisions on alliances, warfare, and trade negotiations. In times of conflict, strong leadership was crucial for uniting the tribe against outside threats.

### Celtic Art and Symbolism

Celtic art is famous for its curves, spirals, and complex knotwork designs. Metalwork was a prime medium for expression, especially in weapons like swords and spears, as well as jewelry such as torcs (neck rings) and bracelets. The designs often featured animal motifs—birds, horses, and mythical beasts—that might have held spiritual or cultural significance.

The Parisii would have shared in this artistic tradition. While the objects we find can sometimes be plain, important items often showcased remarkable detail. Bronze and iron were common, but gold and silver were also used by higher-status individuals. Archaeological finds from around the Seine have included fragments of decorated pottery and metalwork that reflect these Celtic styles.

---

## 7) Daily Life of the Parisii

### Housing and Settlement Layout

Celtic houses in Gaul were often round or rectangular, made with wooden frames and walls of wattle and daub (woven wooden strips coated with clay or mud). Roofs were thatched with straw or reeds. Larger settlements might have had several of these houses grouped together, sometimes enclosed by wooden palisades or earthen ramparts.

Inside, living spaces were simple. A central hearth provided warmth, light, and a place for cooking. People slept on bedding made from straw or animal skins. Furniture was minimal—wooden benches, small tables, or woven baskets for storage. The entire household worked together on tasks like food preparation, tool making, and caring for animals.

### Food and Agriculture

Agriculture revolved around cereals like wheat and barley. These were ground into flour using hand mills, then baked into bread or used to make porridge. Beer and mead might have been brewed for local consumption, while meat came from domesticated animals such as pigs and cattle. Seasonal fruits and vegetables, as well as wild berries, nuts, and herbs, supplemented the diet.

The Celtic calendar included agricultural festivals to mark sowing and harvesting periods. Livestock were valuable assets, and skilled breeders tried to improve their herds. During the colder months, animals were sometimes kept in barns or enclosures attached to living spaces, for warmth and protection from predators.

### Clothing and Personal Adornment

Wool and linen were common materials for clothing. Garments could be dyed using natural pigments from plants and minerals. Men often wore tunics and trousers, while women wore dresses or skirts and tunics. Cloaks were fastened with brooches or pins. Both men and women might wear jewelry—armlets, torcs, and rings—to display status or clan affiliation.

Artistic decoration extended to the textiles, where patterns and colors indicated skillful weaving. Jewelry could also be tokens of loyalty or trophies taken in conflict. The focus on personal adornment underscores the importance of appearance in Celtic society.

---

## 8) Political Alliances and Rivalries

### Interaction with Neighboring Tribes

Gaul was full of tribes that sometimes cooperated and sometimes fought each other. The Parisii were surrounded by other Gallic tribes, such as the Senones to the southeast or the Aedui further south. Alliances could be formed for trade advantages or military support, while rivalries might arise over land or resources.

This complex landscape of alliances and rivalries kept power balances shifting. A strong leader might unify several tribes for a while, creating small confederations. On the other hand, if disputes over territory or trade routes occurred, alliances could break down quickly.

### Early Conflicts

Before the arrival of the Romans, the Parisii and other tribes faced threats not only from their Gallic neighbors but also from migrating Germanic tribes crossing the Rhine. Skirmishes and larger battles would have been part of life, as each tribe defended its territory and sought to expand or protect trade routes.

While we lack detailed accounts of these conflicts, we know from archaeological evidence—like discovered mass graves or hoards of weapons—that warfare was not uncommon. Defensive structures, such as fortified oppida, are another clue that tribes in this region needed to be ready for danger.

---

## 9) Early Trade Networks

### The Importance of the River

The Seine's role in trade cannot be emphasized enough. River transport allowed bulk goods like grain, salt, and metals to move more efficiently than overland routes. The Parisii could connect to coastal regions via the Seine, opening the possibility of trade across the English Channel or into the Atlantic.

Boats and barges of the time were relatively simple, often made of large dugout canoes or wooden planks bound together. Yet, these vessels were quite effective for moving goods along calm stretches of river. Landing sites along the banks gave traders easy access to settlements.

### Craft Specialization and Commerce

As Celtic society became more complex, specialization in crafts increased. Blacksmiths, potters, weavers, and carpenters produced goods that could be sold or traded. This specialization allowed for higher-quality items and contributed to a more diverse range of products.

Trading was not just about goods—it was also about ideas. Travelers and merchants carried news, cultural practices, and technological knowledge between different tribes and regions. Through this exchange, the Parisii might have learned about innovations happening in other parts of Gaul or beyond.

---

## 10) First Contacts with the Mediterranean World

### Greek and Phoenician Influence

Long before the Roman conquest, Greek and Phoenician traders sailed the Mediterranean, establishing colonies in the south of Gaul. Over time, their goods—and sometimes their cultural ideas—moved northward through trade routes. The Celtic tribes, including the Parisii, thus had indirect contact with advanced Mediterranean civilizations.

Items such as amphorae (ceramic jars used to transport wine or oil), refined pottery, and other luxury goods occasionally found their way up the Rhone River and then toward the Seine region. While not as common as local crafts, these foreign items were highly valued. They could signify status and power in Celtic circles.

**Early Roman Contacts**

Even before Julius Caesar began his conquest of Gaul in 58 BC, the Roman Republic had some economic ties to the region. Roman merchants might have traveled into Celtic territories, and Celtic mercenaries sometimes fought in Roman armies elsewhere. These initial contacts were a harbinger of bigger changes to come.

For the Parisii, who were geographically well-positioned, these early contacts likely brought new goods, coins, and perhaps diplomatic ties with Roman officials. Yet, the real turning point would arrive with Caesar's campaigns, which we will explore in the next chapter.

---

## 11) The Significance of the Parisii for Future Paris

### Cultural Legacy

The Celtic roots of Paris run deep. While the city that emerged under Roman rule would differ greatly from the early settlements, the name "Paris" itself is a direct legacy of the Parisii tribe. The Celtic people laid the foundations for future growth, showing that the spot on the Seine was prime real estate for trade, agriculture, and community building.

In the centuries to come, many layers would be added: Roman urban planning, medieval fortifications, Renaissance palaces, and more. But the fact that people had already recognized the potential of this location millennia ago is a testament to the foresight and adaptability of the Celtic communities.

### Transition to Roman Domination

The Celtic way of life, including that of the Parisii, would eventually clash with Roman expansion. Julius Caesar's conquests in Gaul culminated in the full incorporation of these territories into the Roman Empire. This brought massive changes, from new laws and governance systems to language and religion shifts. But it also introduced advanced engineering and architecture, as we will see in the next chapter.

For the Parisii, the arrival of Rome was both a challenge and an opportunity. Some aspects of Celtic culture continued under Roman rule, blending over time. Others disappeared as the new empire asserted its control. Nonetheless, the survival of the name "Paris" is a reminder that the Celtic roots were never entirely erased.

# CHAPTER 2

## THE ROMAN ERA AND THE TRANSFORMATION INTO LUTETIA

## Introduction

By the time the Romans arrived in the region, the Celtic tribes—including the Parisii—had already developed a robust culture. They had their own religious practices, trade networks, and social hierarchies. However, the might of the Roman Republic, followed by the Roman Empire, was unlike anything Gaul had ever seen. The process of Roman conquest began in earnest under Julius Caesar in 58 BC, and over the next decade, the Gauls found themselves gradually absorbed into the growing Roman domain.

In this chapter, we will look at how the settlement known by the Celts was transformed into **Lutetia** under Roman rule. Roman roads, bridges, forums, and baths would appear, changing the landscape forever. The local population, including the Parisii, adapted to Roman governance, law, and culture. Over time, Lutetia became an important city in the province of Gallia Lugdunensis. We will examine how daily life changed, how religion evolved under Roman influence, and how this period set the stage for the future city of Paris.

## 1) Julius Caesar's Campaigns in Gaul

### Conquest and Resistance

Between 58 BC and 50 BC, Julius Caesar led campaigns in Gaul that would result in Roman control over much of modern-day France. The Celtic tribes put up resistance, most famously under the leadership of Vercingetorix, a chieftain of the Arverni tribe. Even though the Parisii were not as famously documented in these campaigns, we know they were part of the general Gallic coalition that opposed Roman expansion.

The Parisii were known to have participated in some key battles. For example, they sent troops and supplies to support neighboring tribes who fought against Caesar. Yet, as the Roman military machine advanced, the fate of independent Celtic societies was sealed. By around 50 BC, Caesar had effectively subdued the region. The Celtic elites who cooperated with Rome often retained some local authority, while those who resisted faced harsh reprisals.

**Aftermath of the Conquest**

With Caesar's victory, Gaul was divided into provinces. While some pockets of resistance continued, the region generally settled into Roman rule. The Romans brought their administrative systems, taxation, and laws. They also introduced new infrastructure, building roads that connected Lutetia to other major cities in Gaul and beyond. This integration into a vast empire was both beneficial and disruptive to local tribes.

For the Parisii, life changed. Roman governors replaced local chieftains in many instances, although some Gallic nobles managed to keep positions of power by pledging loyalty to Rome. The tribe's identity did not vanish overnight; instead, it was gradually woven into the broader tapestry of Roman Gaul.

---

## 2) Naming and Early Development of Lutetia

**The Name "Lutetia"**

One of the earliest records we have of the city under Roman influence is its mention as "Lutetia" or "Lutetia Parisiorum." The exact origin of this name is unclear. Some historians suggest it might relate to a Celtic word meaning "marsh" or "mud," referencing the wet, swampy lands around the river. Others believe it might simply be a Romanized version of a local Gallic place name.

In any case, "Lutetia" became the official Roman name for what we now call Paris. Over time, the city grew under Roman administration. There was significant building activity, much of it concentrated on the left bank of the Seine, though the Île de la Cité continued to be a strategic location for defense.

**Initial Roman Structures**

Rome's first impact on Lutetia was the establishment of basic infrastructure for governance and military control. A fortified camp or administrative outpost would have been among the earliest constructions. Roads branching out from Lutetia connected it to other Roman towns—like Lugdunum (Lyon) to the southeast.

Archaeological finds have revealed traces of a Roman road network, some of which still influence the layout of modern Paris. Wooden bridges spanned the Seine, replacing or supplementing earlier Celtic crossings. Within a generation or two, Lutetia began to look more and more like a typical Roman settlement, complete with grid-like streets and planning that took into account Roman urban norms.

---

## 3) Political and Administrative Organization

### From Tribal Governance to Roman Administration

Under Celtic rule, tribal chieftains and councils had made local decisions. Now, Roman magistrates and provincial governors took charge. Lutetia was part of the province called Gallia Lugdunensis, with its capital in Lugdunum. The Roman Empire was highly organized, with taxation, census taking, and administrative offices ensuring that resources flowed to Rome efficiently.

Local Celtic elites often adapted by serving as intermediaries. They collected taxes, administered Roman law, and sometimes became Roman citizens themselves. This process of "Romanization" allowed the empire to govern vast territories. People who cooperated were rewarded with status and economic benefits; those who resisted found themselves isolated or punished.

### The Curia and Local Government

Most Roman towns had a local council known as the *curia*, made up of *decuriones* (council members). These officials were responsible for city finances, building projects, and local religious ceremonies that honored the Roman gods and the Emperor. The curia in Lutetia helped guide public works and saw to the upkeep of roads, aqueducts, and markets.

Roman law also introduced a new approach to justice. Written laws and formal courts replaced or overshadowed Celtic customary rules. While local traditions did not vanish completely, the structure of Roman administration took precedence in official matters.

---

## 4) Urban Planning: Streets, Water, and Public Buildings

### The Roman Grid

One hallmark of Roman towns was their organized layout. Streets followed either a grid or a structured plan focused on two main roads: the *cardo maximus* (north-south) and the *decumanus maximus* (east-west). In Lutetia, this principle was somewhat adapted to the local geography, but the general concept of an orderly arrangement still emerged.

As the population grew, so did the number of buildings. Residential areas, or insulae (apartment-like blocks), housed ordinary citizens. Wealthier Romans and Gallic elites lived in domus (houses) with courtyards and elaborate decorations. Public buildings, such as basilicas (for administrative and judicial uses) and temples, were placed in central areas.

### Aqueducts and Baths

A defining characteristic of Roman civilization was its advanced approach to public water supply. In Lutetia, the Romans built aqueducts to bring fresh water from springs located miles away. Parts of these ancient aqueducts can still be traced in certain areas of Paris, though much has been destroyed or buried over time.

Baths (thermae) were central to Roman social life. They weren't just places to clean oneself; they also acted as social hubs where citizens could gossip, make business deals, and relax. Lutetia had its own public baths, complete with heated rooms (caldarium), warm rooms (tepidarium), and cold rooms (frigidarium). Some of these bath complexes also included spaces for exercise and lounging.

---

## 5) The Forum and Entertainment

### The Forum

Every Roman town had a forum—a marketplace and public square that served as the heart of political, economic, and social life. In Lutetia, the forum was located on the left bank, though its exact layout is pieced together from scattered archaeological evidence. Here, merchants sold goods, politicians held speeches, and citizens gathered to hear announcements.

Stalls and shops lined the edges of the forum, offering items like pottery, textiles, imported wine, and local produce. The forum would have also been decorated with statues, perhaps of the Emperor or local dignitaries who had donated money for public works.

## The Amphitheater (Arènes de Lutèce)

One of the most striking signs of Roman culture in Lutetia was the construction of an amphitheater, known today as the **Arènes de Lutèce**. Built in the 1st century AD, it could seat thousands of spectators. Performances included gladiator games, theatrical plays, and even naval mock battles (though these were more common in larger amphitheaters).

Having such a structure underscores Lutetia's importance within the Roman Empire. While it wasn't as grand as the Colosseum in Rome, the amphitheater gave local residents a taste of the empire's shared culture of spectacle and entertainment.

## 6) Religion: Blending the Old and the New

### Roman Gods and Imperial Cult

When the Romans conquered Gaul, they introduced the worship of Roman gods like Jupiter, Mars, and Venus. Temples dedicated to these gods appeared in and around Lutetia. Additionally, the imperial cult, which involved showing reverence to the Emperor as a divine or semi-divine figure, became part of public ceremonies.

Gallic inhabitants were not forced to abandon their gods. Instead, the Romans often practiced a form of religious syncretism, combining or equating Celtic deities with Roman ones. This approach helped maintain some local traditions while also asserting Roman control.

### Survival of Celtic Beliefs

Celtic spirituality did not vanish overnight. Some shrines, sacred groves, or small altars dedicated to local gods continued to function, especially outside the main urban centers.

Over time, many Gauls simply merged aspects of their religion with Roman practices. This blending is evident in inscriptions and dedication stones that use both Roman and Celtic names for deities.

Druids, however, lost much of their authority under Roman rule. The Romans were suspicious of druidic practices, partly because of their influence among the local tribes and partly because some druidic rituals (such as possible human sacrifice) clashed with Roman law. As a result, the druidic order faded into the background.

---

## 7) The Changing Economy of Lutetia

### Trade and Commerce

Under Roman rule, commerce in Lutetia expanded. The improved road network and navigable Seine made it simpler to import goods from as far as Spain, Africa, and the Eastern Mediterranean. Items like olive oil, wine, spices, and luxury goods became more common. Roman coins (denarii, sesterces, etc.) replaced the barter-based system or local Celtic coinage. This monetized economy further tied Lutetia to the rest of the empire.

Local industries also flourished. Pottery workshops, metalworking facilities, and textile production all found a market, not just locally but across other provinces. The city's strategic position made it an attractive point for merchants traveling through Gaul.

### Agriculture and Rural Life

Outside the urban center, many inhabitants continued to farm. The Romans introduced new techniques, including better plows and more systematic crop rotation. Villas—large estates owned by wealthy Roman or Gallo-Roman families—sprang up in the countryside. These estates could produce surplus grain, wine, and livestock for trade.

The city itself benefited from the produce of these surrounding villa estates. Fresh vegetables, meat, and grain were transported by cart or boat into Lutetia's markets. The robust supply chains kept the urban population fed and kept the rural economy connected to the city.

---

## 8) Daily Life in Roman Lutetia

### Housing and Neighborhoods

In Roman towns, housing ranged from simple insulae (apartment blocks) for poorer citizens to lavish domus for the wealthy. In Lutetia, the wealthy built homes featuring mosaics, underfloor heating (hypocaust systems), and private courtyards. Commoners lived in more cramped quarters, sometimes above shops or workshops.

Streets could be busy, with vendors shouting their wares, animals wandering about, and carts carrying goods. Public fountains were placed at intervals, providing clean water for residents. The city had to be kept relatively clean—Roman law imposed penalties for disposing of waste in the streets—but sanitation was still a challenge by modern standards.

**Social Structure**

Roman society in Gaul consisted of Roman citizens, some of whom were officials sent from Italy, along with Gallo-Roman elites who had adapted to Roman culture. Freedmen (former slaves) and slaves were also present. Slaves performed domestic tasks, labored in fields, or worked in public construction. Freedmen, once released, could run businesses and become part of the broader society.

Though the Celtic tribal ties still mattered to the local population, the main path to social and political influence now lay in aligning with Roman institutions. Education in Latin, knowledge of Roman law, and service in the Roman army could help local people advance.

**Food and Diet**

Roman cuisine in Lutetia was a mixture of local Gaulish products and imported goods. Bread, olives, cheese, and wine were staples for the middle and upper classes. Meat such as pork, beef, and lamb was eaten regularly by those who could afford it, while cheaper sources of protein—like fish or legumes—were common among the lower classes.

Markets sold fresh produce brought in daily. Street vendors offered quick snacks like bread dipped in sauce or roasted nuts. Wealthy banquets might feature exotic dishes like flamingo or imported fish, although these were more of a status symbol than regular fare.

---

## 9) Military Presence

**Garrison and Defense**

As part of the Roman Empire, Lutetia had to be defended from external threats and internal uprisings. A garrison of Roman soldiers was stationed in or near the city. At times, especially during later centuries when Germanic tribes threatened the empire's borders, the need for strong fortifications grew.

Walls were built or reinforced around the central areas. The Île de la Cité retained its importance as a fortified location due to the natural defensive advantage provided by the surrounding river channels. Soldiers patrolled roads to keep trade routes safe from bandits and potential rebellions.

**Veteran Settlements**

It was common Roman practice to grant land to retired soldiers in conquered territories. This served two purposes: rewarding military service and ensuring loyalty to Rome in potentially restive areas. Some of these veterans settled around Lutetia, contributing to the gradual Latinization of the region. They brought with them not only military discipline but also Roman customs and possibly families from other parts of the empire.

## 10) Cultural Life: Literature, Arts, and Leisure

**Roman Influence on the Arts**

Under Roman rule, Lutetia gained theaters, public art, and a more pronounced literary culture. While many major writers and poets of the empire resided in larger cities—like Rome itself—traces of a local literary scene existed. Intellectual life often centered around public spaces where educated citizens could discuss politics, philosophy, and culture.

Sculptures, mosaics, and frescoes adorned public buildings and private homes. These depicted Roman gods, mythological scenes, or scenes from everyday life. Gallic motifs sometimes persisted, merging with Roman styles. This fusion is visible in certain decorative patterns found in local ruins.

**Popular Entertainments**

Aside from the amphitheater, there were smaller entertainment venues like semi-circular theaters for plays. Chariot races typically required a large circus, which

Lutetia may not have had in the same grandeur as other cities, but smaller racing or sporting events could have been held on makeshift tracks.

Gladiator battles were popular, though they might have been less frequent compared to Rome or other large cities like Lugdunum. Nonetheless, these events drew large crowds eager for spectacle. Street festivals on religious holidays were also a regular occurrence, blending Roman religious rites with local traditions.

---

## 11) The Evolution of Gallo-Roman Identity

### Blending Cultures

Over a few generations, the people in Lutetia became what historians often call "Gallo-Roman." They still held on to some Celtic customs—especially outside urban centers—but were increasingly Romanized in language, dress, and social norms. Latin became the dominant language for administration, business, and the educated class, though local dialects likely persisted in everyday speech.

Intermarriages between Roman settlers and local women also helped blur lines between conquerors and conquered. Children born in these unions often enjoyed Roman citizenship if the father was a citizen. They could travel and do business across the empire.

### Economic Growth and Social Mobility

Roman trade networks offered new ways to amass wealth, and some local families took full advantage, becoming key suppliers of goods or crucial links in trade routes. Successful traders might donate to public projects—like a new temple or bathhouse—as a way to gain prestige and political influence.

At the same time, the social hierarchy remained strict. Many ordinary people lived modest lives, working farms or small workshops. Slavery was still a reality, supporting much of the economic system. Freed slaves could sometimes rise through the ranks, but this was not easy.

---

## 12) Christianity's Early Influence

### Introduction of Christianity

Christianity started as a small religious movement in the eastern provinces of the Roman Empire. It reached Gaul by the mid-2nd century AD, often traveling along trade routes. Initially viewed with suspicion by Roman authorities, Christianity spread slowly among urban populations, including in Lutetia.

Early Christian communities likely met in private homes. Over time, as the religion gained converts, it also gained recognition. By the 4th century, under Emperor Constantine's rule, Christianity began to enjoy imperial favor. This shift would have an impact on the religious life of Lutetia, leading eventually to the establishment of Christian churches and bishops.

**Coexistence with Traditional Beliefs**

Even after Christianity arrived, many people in Lutetia continued to worship Roman gods or follow lingering Celtic practices. It was not unusual for families to mix Christian and pagan elements in their daily lives. Full Christianization was a gradual process that would accelerate later, especially after the fall of the Western Roman Empire.

## 13) Economic and Political Challenges

**External Pressures**

From the 3rd century onward, Rome faced growing pressure from Germanic tribes that tested the empire's borders. Raids and migrations by peoples such as the Franks and Alemanni threatened Gaul. Lutetia's location in northern Gaul made it vulnerable to these movements.

To protect the city, Roman authorities reinforced walls and stationed extra troops. During times of crisis, local economies could suffer as trade routes became unsafe. Looting and disruption forced towns to become more self-sufficient.

**Internal Decline**

The Roman Empire itself struggled with internal problems—political instability, economic troubles, and leadership crises. Emperors came and went in quick succession.

Heavy taxation to support the army and bureaucracy put a strain on local populations. Over time, the unity of the empire weakened, and provinces had to fend for themselves more often.

In Lutetia, public building projects slowed. Maintenance of roads and aqueducts became harder as funds dwindled. Still, the city retained a level of importance within Gaul, partly due to its strategic location.

## 14) Transformations Leading Into the Early Middle Ages

**The Late Empire and Change of Name**

By the 4th century, Lutetia was commonly referred to as **Civitas Parisiorum** (the city of the Parisii), indicating a reemergence of the local tribal name. Latin references gradually began to shorten Civitas Parisiorum to just "Paris." This evolution shows how the older Celtic identity persisted beneath the Roman veneer.

Emperor Julian, who would later become known as "Julian the Apostate," was declared Emperor in Lutetia in AD 360. He spent significant time in the city, noting its comfortable climate. Julian's presence reflects the city's status as a military and administrative center in late Roman Gaul.

**Seeds of Medieval Paris**

As Roman authority in the West crumbled in the 5th century, Germanic tribes gained control of vast portions of Gaul. The Franks eventually seized northern Gaul, including Lutetia/Paris, setting the stage for the Merovingian dynasty. Despite the collapse of Roman central power, much of the Roman heritage in architecture, law, and language would remain. Over time, Latin evolved into early forms of French, and Roman roads continued to guide travel routes.

The Roman era left a deep imprint on Paris. Streets, building foundations, and cultural practices laid down during this time would influence the medieval city. Christianity would continue to grow, eventually shaping the spiritual and political life of future Paris.

# CHAPTER 3

## THE EARLY MIDDLE AGES – MEROVINGIANS AND CAROLINGIANS

## Introduction

The collapse of Roman power in the 5th century reshaped the face of Western Europe. In Gaul, Roman legions withdrew and left behind a blend of Roman culture and local Celtic traditions. Germanic peoples—most notably the Franks—took advantage of the power vacuum, gradually seizing control of significant portions of the region. Paris, known then as **Civitas Parisiorum** or simply **Paris**, became part of a new political landscape where the Frankish kings, particularly those of the Merovingian and later Carolingian dynasties, left their mark.

This chapter explores how Paris fared during the Merovingian period, beginning with King Clovis, who united much of Gaul under his rule. We will then look at how the city functioned in the centuries that followed—examining shifts in power, religion, and social order. Eventually, we will see how the Carolingians rose to prominence, setting the stage for further transformation of Paris as both a political and religious center.

## 1) The End of Roman Rule and the Dawn of the Frankish Era

After the decline of Roman authority, the region around Paris faced frequent incursions by various Germanic tribes. The Franks were one such group. They crossed the Rhine and established themselves in northern Gaul, gradually merging with local Gallo-Roman populations. When Roman officials left, many civic structures—administration, defense, and tax collection—either collapsed or adapted to new rulers.

In Paris, some remnants of Roman institutions stayed in place: city walls, roads, and aqueducts did not vanish immediately. However, maintenance became inconsistent. The local elites, many of whom were Romanized Gauls, had to negotiate with emerging Frankish warlords. Some aristocratic families sought alliances through marriage, while others leveraged the support of the Church to maintain influence.

For a while, Paris was one among many cities in northern Gaul, contending with places like Soissons or Reims for regional significance. It was not yet the unquestioned capital of a centralized monarchy, as it would become in later centuries. Instead, the city found itself at a crossroads—both literally, given its geographic position, and figuratively, as new political orders took shape.

---

## 2) The Merovingians: King Clovis and His Legacy

### Rise of the Merovingian Dynasty

One of the most pivotal figures of the Early Middle Ages in Gaul was **Clovis** (c. 466–511). He was from the Merovingian family of Frankish rulers, taking power around 481 AD when he succeeded his father, Childeric I. Although Clovis did not immediately establish Paris as the heart of his kingdom, his reign profoundly influenced the city's future.

Clovis is often credited with uniting a large portion of Gaul under his rule. He defeated rival Germanic kings and subdued various Roman remnants. Historians view his victory at the Battle of Soissons (c. 486) as a turning point because it ended Roman rule in northern Gaul. By incorporating the Gallo-Roman aristocracy into his administration, Clovis consolidated his power.

### Conversion to Christianity

One of the most famous events in Clovis's life was his **conversion to Christianity**. According to tradition, his wife, Clotilde, was a Christian who urged him to adopt her faith. Clovis eventually agreed, especially after a significant military victory that he attributed to the Christian God. He and many of his warriors were baptized, a symbolic act that cemented the bond between the Frankish monarchy and the Church.

This conversion impacted Paris profoundly. Though Christianity had been in Gaul since Roman times, Clovis's adoption of the faith elevated its status. Bishops became critical political advisors, and churches gained influence. The Church would remain a stabilizing force in Paris, preserving knowledge and offering spiritual guidance as the region faced ongoing turbulence.

**Establishing Paris as a Royal Residence**

Though not initially his sole capital, Clovis recognized Paris's strategic advantages. The Seine River, combined with surviving Roman fortifications, made the city defensible. Over time, Clovis chose Paris as one of his main residences, and he died there in 511 AD. This decision signaled that Paris was becoming an important seat of power, a status that would grow in subsequent generations.

After Clovis's death, the Merovingian kingdom was divided among his heirs according to Frankish custom. Yet, Paris remained a significant location, sometimes acting as a neutral meeting place in the frequent power struggles among Merovingian princes.

## 3) Merovingian Administration and Society

**Rule by Multiple Kings**

A defining characteristic of Merovingian governance was the practice of dividing the kingdom among the sons of a deceased king. This often led to **partible inheritance**, where each son received a portion of land. Such divisions caused internal conflicts and continually reshaped the map of Gaul.

Despite these fractures, the Merovingians shared common laws and customs, many of which were derived from a mix of Frankish tradition and Roman legal principles. The Salic Law—associated with the Franks—dealt with issues like inheritance, property rights, and criminal offenses. Over time, the law code influenced local governance in Paris and its surroundings.

### The Role of Bishops and the Church

During the Merovingian era, **bishops** in major cities, including Paris, became powerful figures. They oversaw not only religious matters but often served as local administrators or diplomatic negotiators. Since the Frankish kings often traveled, or had multiple seats of power, bishops provided continuity in the city. They maintained social services, supervised charity, and occasionally resolved disputes when secular authority was weak.

In Paris, the bishop's seat was a center of learning, storing religious texts and maintaining records. Monasteries emerged in the countryside around the city, where monks cultivated farmland and copied manuscripts. Although literacy was low overall, the Church became the guardian of whatever written culture survived.

### Social Strata

Merovingian society was hierarchical. At the top stood the king and the royal family. Below them were nobles, warriors, clergy, and then commoners—peasants and laborers who farmed the land. Slavery still existed in this period, although the Church sometimes encouraged the freeing of slaves as acts of Christian charity.

Daily life for ordinary Parisians centered on subsistence agriculture and artisanal trades. While urban life diminished compared to Roman times, Paris still had craftsmen and traders, and it continued to serve as a hub for nearby rural areas. The old Roman bridges and roads were used for commerce, though they often fell into disrepair.

---

## 4) Architecture and Urban Landscape Under the Merovingians

### Reusing Roman Structures

Many Roman buildings in Paris still stood, though they might have been partially ruined. The amphitheater (Arènes de Lutèce), the bath complexes, and segments of the city's walls were sometimes repurposed. Noble families or church authorities took over Roman villas, transforming them into Merovingian homes or monasteries.

Over time, new structures rose, often built with salvaged materials from Roman ruins. Stone, bricks, and even columns were reused to construct churches or fortified dwellings. This method allowed the Merovingians to preserve some of the older architectural legacy, even if inadvertently.

### Early Churches and Christian Buildings

Church construction was significant in shaping the city's landscape. One notable example was the Basilica of Saint-Martin, erected near the burial site of Saint Martin of

Tours (though outside Paris, it influenced the style of many Merovingian churches). Within Paris, churches dedicated to local saints emerged, often placed on or near Roman ruins for practical reasons—such as availability of building materials and defensible locations.

Baptismal chapels became important, symbolizing the spread of Christianity among the Franks. The architecture of these early churches was simple compared to the grand cathedrals of later centuries. Still, they served as focal points for both religious ceremonies and civic gatherings.

---

## 5) The Role of Queens and Noblewomen

### Influential Royal Women

Merovingian politics was not solely a male affair. Queens and noblewomen sometimes held significant power, acting as regents for their young sons or negotiating alliances between rival factions. Queen **Brunhilda** (or Brunhilde), from the late 6th and early 7th century, is a famous example—though she was more closely associated with the eastern part of the Frankish kingdom, she influenced events across Gaul, including Paris.

When a king died, his widow or the mother of his heir might step into a caretaker role. She could guide the young king's decisions, manage the royal household, and interact with bishops and nobles. In a time when the monarchy was often divided, a strong maternal figure could act as a unifying or disruptive force, depending on her alliances.

### Women in Noble and Ecclesiastical Circles

Outside the royal family, noblewomen and abbesses also wielded influence. Some founded monasteries, sponsored church construction, or corresponded with bishops and other religious leaders. Although women's roles were restricted by customs and laws, they found pathways to authority through religious patronage and land ownership.

These women's contributions to church life in Paris were particularly noteworthy. They might fund the building of chapels, donate land for monastic communities, or oversee estates that supplied the city's population with food and resources. Their involvement helped maintain social stability during frequent power struggles among male rulers.

---

## 6) Conflicts, Feuds, and the Influence on Paris

### Dynastic Struggles

Merovingian history is rife with **dynastic quarrels**. Sons of a king would split territories, but each one often tried to expand his share at the expense of his brothers. Civil wars between **Neustria** (the western part of the kingdom, which included Paris) and **Austrasia** (the eastern part) were common. Paris sometimes became a contested prize or a neutral meeting ground to sign treaties or host negotiations.

For the common people of Paris, these recurring conflicts led to instability. Armies marching to war needed supplies, and the city's inhabitants had to provide food or lodging. Occasional sieges or raids disrupted commerce. The bishop and local nobles tried to protect the population, but their power was limited if a major royal feud erupted.

### External Threats

In addition to internal wars, the kingdom faced threats from groups such as the Saxons or other Germanic tribes. These external dangers, coupled with internal divisions, meant that the Merovingian rulers had to balance military defense with political maneuvering. Paris's defensive walls, remnants of the Roman era, served as a crucial line of protection.

While Paris was never as exposed to maritime raids as coastal cities, it remained vulnerable to armies moving along the Seine or across northern Gaul. Local militias formed whenever the king's forces were absent. The city's location at a major crossroads meant it could not fully avoid the turbulence of the age.

---

## 7) The Gradual Shift from Merovingians to Carolingians

### The Rise of the Mayors of the Palace

As Merovingian kings squabbled among themselves, real power increasingly fell into the hands of the **Mayors of the Palace** (maior domus). Originally, these officials were managers of the royal household. Over time, they became the de facto rulers, controlling finances, military appointments, and day-to-day governance.

Notable mayors, such as **Pepin of Herstal** and later his son **Charles Martel**, carved out substantial authority. They often overshadowed the Merovingian kings, who were sometimes disparagingly called "do-nothing kings" (rois fainéants) due to their reduced political clout.

### Charles Martel and Defense of the Realm

**Charles Martel (c. 688–741)** is famous for his victory at the Battle of Tours (or Poitiers) in 732, which repelled an army from the Umayyad Caliphate advancing from Iberia. Although this event took place some distance from Paris, it elevated Charles Martel's status throughout the Frankish domains. He secured strong support from the nobility and the Church, both of which feared expansion by non-Christian forces.

In the aftermath, Charles Martel solidified control over large parts of Gaul. His leadership style, focusing on a strong military and alliances with bishops, set the stage for the Carolingian dynasty that would eventually replace the Merovingians.

**Pepin the Short and the End of Merovingian Rule**

Charles Martel's son, **Pepin the Short**, finally ended the Merovingian line. In 751, with the backing of the Pope, he deposed the last Merovingian king, Childeric III, and declared himself king. By doing so, Pepin officially founded the **Carolingian Dynasty**.

Paris took note: the city remained under the orbit of these emerging rulers, who saw the Church as an ally in legitimizing their new royal house. Pepin's coronation symbolized a shift in how kingship was understood. It was no longer merely a matter of lineage; it also required papal approval, enhancing the bond between church and crown.

## 8) Daily Life in Early Medieval Paris

**Homes and Streets**

During the Merovingian and early Carolingian periods, Paris was smaller and less urbanized than it had been under Roman rule. Houses were typically wooden or a mix of wood and stone, using leftover Roman materials where possible. Streets remained narrow, often following old Roman paths, but upkeep was inconsistent.

The Île de la Cité still served as a core area. Many people lived on the island or close to it, as the surrounding water provided some natural defense. Suburbs on the left bank and right bank existed but were less dense. The city's overall population was relatively small compared to later medieval or modern times.

## Trades and Crafts

Though agriculture was the main economic activity in the surrounding countryside, inside the city, specialized crafts still existed. Blacksmiths, tanners, bakers, weavers, and other artisans worked in small workshops. Trade with other cities in Gaul or beyond was modest but persisted along the Seine.

Coins minted under Merovingian and Carolingian authority circulated. Economic exchange was partly monetized, but barter was also common, especially in rural areas. Precious metals for currency were limited, making large transactions or long-distance trade somewhat challenging.

## Spiritual and Cultural Life

Religious practices centered on local churches. The bishop's influence reached into everyday life, from moral teachings to organizing charity during famines. Festivals followed the Christian calendar, merging local traditions with Church rites.

Education was mostly in the hands of the clergy. Monastic schools taught Latin to future priests or scribes, who maintained written records. A layperson might be literate if they were from a noble family, but the majority of commoners could not read or write. Oral tradition and storytelling flourished, passing down legends of saints, kings, and heroic battles.

---

## 9) Women and Family in Early Medieval Paris

### Marriage and Inheritance

Marriage arrangements among the noble classes were often political tools. Alliances cemented through marriage could stabilize the kingdom or spark feuds if a marriage broke down. Inheritance laws, guided by both Salic Law and local customs, generally favored male heirs. However, noblewomen could still inherit land in the absence of male relatives, although their control might be challenged by male guardians or relatives.

### Work and Daily Tasks

For common women, daily life involved spinning, weaving, cooking, caring for children, and working in fields or gardens. They also contributed to family crafts or small businesses in the city. Religious life provided another dimension, as some women joined convents. Nuns had the opportunity to study basic reading and writing, often surpassing the educational level available to most laywomen.

---

## 10) The Influence of Carolingian Kings: Charlemagne and Beyond

### Charlemagne's Ascension

Pepin the Short died in 768, leaving his realm to his two sons, **Carloman** and **Charles**. After Carloman's early death, Charles—who would become known as **Charlemagne**—ruled alone. His reign (768–814) oversaw an enormous expansion of the Frankish kingdom, transforming it into the Carolingian Empire.

Although Charlemagne primarily ruled from Aachen (in modern-day Germany), his policies impacted all of Gaul, including Paris. He fostered a cultural renaissance—often referred to as the **Carolingian Renaissance**—promoting learning, church reforms, and administrative efficiency. Scholars from across Europe were invited to his court. New script (Carolingian minuscule) made Latin texts more uniform and readable, indirectly influencing monastic scriptoria in Paris and elsewhere.

### Legal and Administrative Reforms

Charlemagne continued the tradition of dividing the kingdom into counties, ruled by **counts** who were responsible for justice, defense, and taxes. To keep them in check, Charlemagne sent **missi dominici**—royal envoys—to inspect local governance. In Paris, the count or bishop would receive such inspectors, ensuring that the city aligned with the emperor's decrees.

This was a step toward more centralized administration, but local identities remained strong. Paris was still not the empire's primary seat of power, but its strategic position along the Seine ensured that it remained significant as both a trading post and a defensible stronghold.

### Religious Patronage and Church Authority

Under Charlemagne, the Church gained even greater influence. Bishops, abbots, and abbesses were given lands and privileges. In return, they supported the emperor's policies, praying for the realm's well-being and educating future clergy.

In Paris, religious communities benefited from imperial or royal grants. Monasteries expanded their libraries, preserving classical and Christian texts. The seeds of future scholastic traditions might be seen here, although the full flowering of universities would come in later centuries.

# 11) Paris in the Later Carolingian Period

### The Viking Raids

After Charlemagne's death in 814, the empire was divided among his heirs, once again introducing fragmentation. By the mid-9th century, external threats—particularly **Viking** raids—became a pressing concern. These Norsemen sailed up the Seine, looting towns and monasteries.

Paris was a prime target. Records indicate that in 845, Vikings under the leadership of Ragnar Lothbrok (according to some accounts) besieged and plundered the city. Later raids in the 860s and 880s inflicted further destruction. While Paris's fortified positions on the Île de la Cité and the city walls offered some defense, the repeated Viking invasions tested the resilience of its people.

### Rise of Local Defenders

Faced with Viking threats, local leaders took on greater importance. One such figure was **Count Odo of Paris**, who led the city's defense against a major siege in 885–886. His bravery elevated Paris in the political sphere. When the Carolingian king, Charles the Fat, failed to effectively defend against the Vikings, discontent spread, and Odo was elected king by some Frankish nobles in 888.

This development marked a shift toward localized power structures. No longer would distant Carolingian emperors automatically command loyalty if they could not protect local communities from external threats. Paris's strong stand against the Vikings made it a symbol of resistance and a new center of leadership in West Francia (the western portion of the Carolingian Empire, roughly corresponding to modern France).

## 12) Cultural and Intellectual Life in the Carolingian Age

### The Carolingian Renaissance in Paris

Though the primary intellectual center was at Charlemagne's court in Aachen, the ripples of the **Carolingian Renaissance** reached Paris. Monasteries and churches in the region received copies of Latin manuscripts and learned from the scholars the emperor had assembled. Some local clergy traveled to Aachen for education, then returned to spread new ideas about literacy, theology, and governance.

Latin was the official language of administration and the Church, but spoken dialects of early French (often called the **langue d'oïl**) became more distinct in daily life. Scribes in Paris might have produced or copied manuscripts with more standardized scripts, making texts easier to read.

### Artistic Expressions

Carolingian art was influenced by Roman, Byzantine, and Germanic traditions. Illuminated manuscripts showcased intricate designs, biblical scenes, and decorative lettering. While many of the most famous manuscripts came from other regions, some were kept in Parisian religious institutions. Metalwork—particularly for reliquaries and church vessels—combined precious materials with Christian symbolism.

Architecture advanced too. Stone churches with distinctive Carolingian elements—such as westworks (large, towered entrances)—were constructed. Though few purely Carolingian structures survive intact in Paris today, their foundations and partial remnants lie beneath later medieval buildings.

---

## 13) Shifts in Power and the Emergence of the Robertians

### The Robertian Family

During the Viking invasions, the **Robertian** family—ancestors of the future Capetian dynasty—gained prominence in defending Paris and other regions. **Robert the Strong** was a notable figure, and his descendants would continue to hold influence in and around Paris.

With the waning authority of Carolingian monarchs, local lords who proved their ability to protect land and people grew in power. Paris, thanks to its defenses and strategic position, became a sought-after base for these rising lords. This set the stage for the eventual transition to the Capetian line in the late 10th century.

### Count Odo and the Seeds of Change

As mentioned, **Count Odo**—a Robertian—was elected King of West Francia in 888. Although his reign was short and marked by ongoing struggles, it demonstrated that

Paris could be at the heart of a new royal power. Odo's leadership showcased how local success in warfare, particularly against the Vikings, could overshadow the weakened prestige of the Carolingian house.

While the Carolingians returned to the throne for a time after Odo's death, the seeds were planted for a more permanent shift. By the mid-10th century, the Robertians (and their close allies) were strong contenders for the crown, steadily eroding Carolingian authority.

---

## 14) Nobles, Knights, and Feudal Structures

### Early Feudal Patterns

In the later Carolingian period, the foundations of **feudalism** began to appear. This is often described as a system where local lords offered protection to peasants, who in turn provided labor or a share of their produce. Lords also granted **fiefs**—plots of land—to knights in exchange for military service.

In Paris and its surroundings, feudal relations were complex. Some land was under the direct control of the king, known as the **royal domain**, while other regions belonged to powerful abbeys or secular lords. Knights began to emerge as a distinct warrior class, owing allegiance to their local lord or count.

### Castles and Fortifications

Though large stone castles became more common in the 11th and 12th centuries, the 9th and 10th centuries saw the beginnings of such fortifications. Motte-and-bailey structures (a wooden or stone keep on a raised earthwork called a motte, accompanied by an enclosed courtyard or bailey) were sometimes built to defend territory against Vikings or rival lords.

Paris itself was better fortified than many towns, with its Roman walls still partially standing and with additional defenses erected over time. Lords in the region often built smaller fortresses on the outskirts to protect farmland and watch over roads.

---

# CHAPTER 4

## THE RISE OF THE CAPETIAN DYNASTY AND MEDIEVAL PARIS

## Introduction

With the election of **Hugh Capet** in 987, a new era dawned for Paris. The Capetian dynasty would rule France—initially just a portion known as the royal domain—continuously for centuries, leaving an indelible mark on the city's development. Under their reign, Paris grew from a modest medieval town into a thriving center of royal and religious power.

In this chapter, we will explore how the Capetians consolidated power, how Paris benefited from royal patronage, and how new social and economic structures emerged. We will examine key aspects like the growth of religious institutions, the establishment of new fortifications, and the birth of a distinct Parisian identity. These transformations laid the groundwork for the city's eventual prominence in Europe's cultural and political spheres.

## 1) Hugh Capet and the Early Capetians

### Securing the Throne

When Hugh Capet took the throne in 987, his actual control was limited. He held lands mainly around Paris and Orléans, an area known as the **Île-de-France**. Much of the kingdom was ruled by powerful dukes and counts who paid little more than nominal respect to the new king.

To strengthen his position, Hugh Capet relied on **alliance-building** through marriages and by placing loyal bishops in key dioceses. Paris, as his stronghold, became the symbolic heart of his rule. While the city still faced challenges from regional magnates, the Capetians slowly expanded their influence by shrewd political maneuvering and by maintaining the support of the Church.

**The Coronation Tradition**

One important strategy that Hugh Capet introduced—or revived—was the practice of having his son crowned during his own lifetime. This aimed to ensure a smooth succession and reduce the risk of a power struggle after the king's death. Although the official coronation site was often Reims, the existence of a recognized heir gave the Capetian line a measure of continuity that previous dynasties had lacked.

The idea that the crown passed from father to son, blessed by God, gave the Capetian kings religious legitimacy. Paris, as the place where the royal family often lived and administrated, benefited from the prestige surrounding the monarchy.

---

## 2) Paris as the Center of Royal Power

**The Royal Domain and Governance**

The Capetians exercised direct control over the **royal domain** (domaine royal), a relatively small area of land. However, their authority within this domain was strong, and Paris was at its core. Over time, the kings sought to extend their domain by acquiring territories through inheritance, marriages, purchases, or feudal claims.

Within Paris, Capetian kings set up administrative bodies that formed the beginnings of a centralized royal government. Officials such as **prevôts** (provosts) oversaw local matters on behalf of the king—collecting taxes, maintaining order, and ensuring the enforcement of royal decrees. This structure allowed the king to exert more direct control over Paris than many other parts of France.

**The Symbolic Power of Paris**

Beyond practicality, Paris held symbolic significance as the seat of the new dynasty. It contained royal palaces, including one on the **Île de la Cité**, near the old Roman palace remains. By holding court there, the Capetians showcased their authority and connected themselves to a lineage that reached back through Carolingian and even Gallo-Roman times.

Ceremonial events—such as royal councils, important religious feasts, and the reception of foreign envoys—took place in Paris. While many nobles spent most of their time in their own territories, they recognized the king's domain as a place where major decisions were announced, particularly those involving the Church or royal succession.

## 3) Fortifications and Urban Development

**Strengthening the City**

During the 10th and 11th centuries, the threat of external raids—like those from the Vikings—gradually lessened. However, internal conflicts persisted, and the Capetian kings recognized the need to protect Paris. They refurbished existing walls and built new fortifications to secure the city's perimeter, especially around the Île de la Cité.

Strong defenses also served as a message of power. The walls were not just practical; they were a statement that Paris was a royal stronghold, safe from the feudal turmoil that still plagued much of the kingdom. This sense of security encouraged merchants and artisans to settle in the city, slowly revitalizing urban life.

**Growth of Suburbs**

As the population increased, new neighborhoods, or **bourgs**, sprang up around the older core. These suburbs developed on both the left and right banks of the Seine. They housed the growing population of traders, craftsmen, and laborers. Over time, some of these suburbs were incorporated within expanded city walls.

Streets remained narrow, and building materials were still largely wood, but the city was growing. Guilds began to form, bringing together artisans of similar trades. They regulated quality, set prices, and provided mutual assistance, foreshadowing the richer commercial life of later centuries.

## 4) The Church and Ecclesiastical Influence in Medieval Paris

### Emergence of Major Religious Houses

During the early Capetian period, religious institutions flourished in and around Paris. **Abbeys** like Saint-Denis (just north of the city) held significant land and wealth. Saint-Denis was especially important because it housed the relics of Saint Denis, an early Christian martyr believed to have been the first bishop of Paris. Over time, Saint-Denis also became the royal necropolis, where many French kings were buried.

The monastery of **Saint-Germain-des-Prés**, on the left bank, was another influential establishment. Such abbeys contributed not only to religious life but also to agriculture, as they managed large estates that supplied food to the city. Their scriptoria preserved and copied religious and classical texts, continuing the intellectual traditions of earlier centuries.

### Notre-Dame and the Cathedral Chapter

While much of the current **Notre-Dame de Paris** was built in the 12th and 13th centuries, the site had earlier churches dating back to Merovingian times. Under the Capetians, the **bishop of Paris** and the **cathedral chapter** gained increased prominence. They held ecclesiastical courts, managed cathedral lands, and maintained close relations with the royal court.

Church institutions shaped moral and social norms, overseeing marriage, moral offenses, and wills. The Church's power in education also grew; young men (especially those of noble birth) learned basic literacy and Latin through clerical schools, which would later pave the way for the rise of the University of Paris.

---

## 5) Economic Revival and the Emergence of a Commercial Hub

### Trade Fairs and Markets

In the 11th century, trade began to pick up again across Europe, spurred by improved stability and agricultural surplus. Paris became a conduit for goods traveling along the Seine. It hosted regular **markets** where local produce—grain, wine, livestock—was sold. Over time, it also participated in regional trade fairs, connecting Parisian merchants with those from Flanders, Normandy, and Champagne.

The king encouraged commerce by granting certain privileges and charters. He could levy taxes on trade, which became an important source of royal revenue. Meanwhile, merchants benefited from the growing reputation of Paris as a safe marketplace protected by the king's authority.

### Artisanal Guilds

As commerce grew, so did **guilds** for various crafts: bakers, butchers, weavers, and metalworkers formed associations. These guilds regulated the quality of goods, set prices, and established rules for apprenticeship. Guild membership provided a pathway for social and economic advancement, as skilled craftsmen could accumulate wealth and gain influence in their community.

Over time, certain districts of Paris became known for specific trades. For instance, tanners might cluster near the river, where they could easily wash hides, while cloth merchants might gather in a central market area. This specialization gave parts of the city distinct identities, an early sign of urban diversity.

---

## 6) The Rise of Feudal Nobility Around Paris

### Royal Vassals

While the Capetian kings directly ruled Paris, much of the surrounding territory was under the control of **vassals**—nobles who pledged loyalty to the king in exchange for lands (fiefs) and titles. These nobles built castles, administered local justice, and raised troops for the king when needed. In turn, the king relied on them to uphold royal authority in more distant regions.

The relationship was complex. A powerful noble could sometimes challenge the king if he felt his rights were threatened. Conversely, the king could seize a noble's lands if the noble was accused of treason. The delicate balance of power shaped how Paris remained central to the monarchy: a bastion of royal prerogatives surrounded by a web of feudal allegiances.

### Conflict and Cooperation

Nobles around Paris varied in their loyalty. Some, like the counts of Champagne or dukes of Normandy, were nearly as powerful as the king himself. The monarchy had to navigate alliances carefully. Strategic marriages, as well as small military expeditions, helped keep the peace—or at least limit open conflict.

Paris benefited when the king successfully subdued rebellious lords or integrated their territories into the royal domain. Each territorial gain expanded the crown's direct control and enriched the city, with more resources flowing in. Conversely, if a powerful noble threatened the city, the king would bolster fortifications or station additional troops there.

# 7) The Influence of Pilgrimage and Early Tourism

## Sacred Sites in and Around Paris

During the medieval period, **pilgrimages** to holy sites became a widespread phenomenon. While Rome, Jerusalem, and Santiago de Compostela were the most famous destinations, many smaller sites also attracted pilgrims. Churches in Paris claimed relics of saints that drew the devout from nearby regions.

Saint-Denis, just outside the city walls, was significant not only for royal burials but also as a place of pilgrimage, due to its relics of Saint Denis. Pilgrims stopping in Paris needed lodging, food, and sometimes medical care, boosting local businesses. Monasteries and churches benefited from alms and donations.

## The Growth of Hospitality

The influx of pilgrims spurred the development of **inns** and **hospices** (often run by religious orders). These establishments provided simple accommodations. Over time, some wealthier travelers demanded more comfortable lodgings, encouraging a rudimentary form of "tourism" economy. This demand also helped shape the city's neighborhoods, with certain streets or quarters becoming known for lodging houses.

The presence of pilgrims from distant lands exposed Parisians to different dialects, customs, and trade goods. While not as cosmopolitan as later centuries, medieval Paris had a growing awareness of regions beyond its immediate sphere, aided by these religiously motivated journeys.

## 8) The Early Development of Scholarly Life

### Cathedral Schools

By the 11th century, **cathedral schools** in major cities became centers of learning. In Paris, the school attached to Notre-Dame gained a reputation for excellence in theology and the liberal arts (grammar, rhetoric, logic, arithmetic, geometry, music, and astronomy). Students included future clergy, administrators, and occasionally sons of nobles seeking an education.

These schools were not yet full-fledged universities, but they laid the groundwork for the intellectual growth that would characterize Paris in the 12th and 13th centuries. The bishop supervised the curriculum and hired masters who gave lectures on doctrinal and scholarly topics.

### Monastic Scriptoria and Libraries

Monasteries like Saint-Germain-des-Prés and Saint-Denis maintained **scriptoria**, where monks copied manuscripts. These texts ranged from the Bible to classical works by authors like Boethius, Cicero, or even fragments of ancient Greek philosophy (translated into Latin).

Over time, some of these monasteries built libraries that became repositories of knowledge. Although access to these libraries was limited to the clergy and a few privileged laymen, the act of collecting and preserving texts ensured that Paris was a custodian of religious and intellectual heritage.

---

## 9) Daily Life and Culture in 11th-Century Paris

### Housing and Urban Layout

Medieval houses in Paris were typically narrow, tall, and timber-framed, a style that would persist for centuries. The ground floor often served as a workshop or shopfront, with living quarters above. Wealthier families might have stone foundations, but most structures relied heavily on wood.

The streets were uneven, sometimes muddy, and lacked sophisticated drainage. Citizens disposed of waste in local ditches or even the river. Street cleaning was haphazard, and while some regulations existed to maintain cleanliness, enforcement varied.

### Clothing and Diet

Men commonly wore tunics and cloaks, while women donned long dresses, often cinched at the waist. Cloth was woolen for most social classes, with richer individuals sporting finer fabrics like linen or even imported silk. Commoners might dye their woolen garments in simple colors, but bright or exotic dyes were expensive, reserved for nobles or wealthy merchants.

The diet centered on bread, vegetables, and occasionally meat. Fish was also common, especially on religious fasting days. Wine from nearby regions, such as the vineyards around the Île-de-France, was a staple. Ale and beer were also consumed, though perhaps more in northern parts of the kingdom.

---

## 10) Courtly Life and Chivalric Ideals

### Knights and Courtly Rituals

By the late 11th century, the notion of **chivalry** gained traction among the nobility. Knights dedicated themselves to martial prowess, loyalty to their lord, and the protection of the weak—at least in theory. The Capetian court in Paris hosted tournaments and feasts that showcased these ideals, though actual violence between nobles was still common.

Certain codes of conduct, such as respect for one's feudal oath and the veneration of noblewomen, shaped the social fabric of court life. Over time, these ideas would be refined, influencing medieval literature and fostering legends of gallant knights and virtuous ladies.

### Royal Ceremonies and Festivities

The Capetian kings held ceremonial events in Paris to display regal majesty. These included royal weddings, baptisms, and feasts on major religious holidays. Nobles from across the kingdom might travel to Paris to attend, bringing gifts and tributes. Such gatherings offered the king a chance to affirm his place at the top of the feudal hierarchy.

Minstrels and troubadours sometimes performed at court, telling stories of heroic deeds or singing ballads about love and war. While the full flowering of courtly poetry would come slightly later in provinces like Aquitaine, seeds of a courtly culture were present in the Capetian milieu.

---

## 11) Law and Justice Under the Early Capetians

### The King's Peace

One of the ways the Capetian kings tried to extend their authority was by proclaiming the **King's Peace**. This was a set of decrees that forbade violence at certain times (like Sundays or holy festivals) or in certain places (churches, pilgrimage routes). Violators were subject to royal justice, which positioned the king as a defender of public order.

Over time, as the Capetians grew stronger, their justice began to override local customary law. In Paris, the royal court could intervene in disputes that affected the city's merchants, clergy, or other royal subjects. The presence of the king in the city also meant that litigants from elsewhere might bring their appeals to Paris, expanding its judicial importance.

### The Role of Church Courts

Alongside royal justice, the **ecclesiastical courts** handled matters related to canon law: marriage, moral offenses, wills involving religious bequests, and disputes involving clergy. Bishops or their officials presided over these courts. Because Paris had a prominent bishopric, many such cases were heard in the city. This dual system of royal and church courts sometimes led to jurisdictional conflicts, but it also gave Paris a reputation as a place where important legal decisions were made.

---

## 12) Paris at the Turn of the 12th Century

### Consolidation of Capetian Control

By the end of the 11th century and into the early 12th century, the Capetians had consolidated their hold on the royal domain. Kings like **Robert II (the Pious)** and **Philip I** continued to strengthen ties with the Church, using religious patronage to legitimize their rule. They also attempted, with mixed success, to subdue recalcitrant vassals.

Paris benefited from the stability offered by a consistent ruling family. Gradually, artisans and merchants experienced fewer disruptions from feudal conflicts, enabling the city's economy to grow. Religious life deepened with the expansion of church building and monastic communities, while the seeds of intellectual life were about to bloom more fully in the next century.

### Emerging as a Cultural Focal Point

Although not yet the dazzling center it would become, Paris was starting to attract attention from scholars, clerics, and nobles. Its strategic location, enhanced by the stable presence of the royal court, made the city a place of opportunity. Craftsmen found patrons, students sought education, and pilgrims visited the relics in local churches.

No single factor can fully explain Paris's rise. Instead, it was a combination of geography, royal support, ecclesiastical patronage, and economic revival that propelled the city forward. By the early 12th century, Paris was on the cusp of its medieval golden age—though it would still face challenges from internal and external forces.

---

## 13) The Shaping of Medieval Identity

### The Role of Legends and Saints

During this period, legends surrounding saints and heroes played a key role in shaping the communal identity of Parisians. **Saint Genevieve**, revered for her role in protecting Paris from the Huns in the 5th century, was celebrated as a local patron. Churches and shrines dedicated to her attracted worshipers, and her story fostered pride in the city's resilience.

Stories of **Charlemagne** and **King Clovis** also contributed to a sense of historical continuity. Whether entirely factual or embellished, these narratives helped connect the new Capetian age with a storied Frankish past, solidifying the notion that Paris was an ancient seat of Christian kings.

### Language and Custom

While Latin remained the language of the Church and official documents, a burgeoning form of **Old French** was spoken among common people. Epic poems such as **The Song of Roland** might have circulated orally or in manuscript form, reflecting chivalric ideals and shaping the cultural imagination.

Customs like the daily ringing of church bells to mark the hours, the celebration of saints' feast days, and the observation of Lent gave a rhythmic structure to life in medieval Paris. These customs united people across social classes, fostering a collective identity that was increasingly tied to the city itself.

---

# CHAPTER 5

## URBAN GROWTH, UNIVERSITIES, AND LIFE IN THE 12TH CENTURY

## Introduction

By the dawn of the 12th century, Paris was emerging from the early medieval period with fresh momentum. The Capetian monarchy had consolidated its hold on the region around the city, slowly expanding royal authority. This relative stability, combined with population growth and a budding economy, led to a new phase in the city's development. Paris was still not the only major center in France—cities like Rouen, Reims, and Chartres also wielded influence—but it was becoming increasingly important.

In this chapter, we explore how Paris transformed over the course of the 12th century. We will look at the reigns of notable kings like **Louis VI (the Fat)** and **Louis VII**, who laid groundwork for both physical growth and intellectual pursuits. We will then delve into the major drivers of urban expansion—trade, construction, religious patronage, and the early stirrings of what would later become the world-famous University of Paris. This period set the foundations for Paris's later prominence as a center of culture, learning, and power.

## 1) The Capetian Context in the Early 12th Century

### Consolidation of Royal Power

At the start of the 12th century, the Capetian kings still ruled a relatively small domain directly, mainly centered on Paris and its surrounding territories in the Île-de-France.

Yet the monarchy managed to project influence through feudal ties, alliances, and the Church's support. King **Louis VI** (r. 1108–1137) was a key figure. Despite challenges from powerful lords—particularly in regions near Paris—he worked tirelessly to assert royal control.

Louis VI spent much of his reign battling local barons who resisted the king's authority. He also took steps to improve the governance of royal lands, appointing officials to oversee justice and collect revenues. Over time, these measures made Paris more secure and attractive to merchants, artisans, and scholars. It was during Louis VI's rule that people began seeing Paris as more than just another feudal town. Instead, it was recognized as the seat of an active and interventionist king.

**The Growing Importance of the Church**

The Church continued to play a major role in daily life and politics. Bishops and abbots had their own spheres of influence, often rivaling secular lords. However, the French crown increasingly sought to strengthen ties with ecclesiastical institutions in and around Paris. Monastic houses like **Saint-Denis** and **Saint-Germain-des-Prés** remained land-rich power centers, while the bishopric of Paris enjoyed royal favors that elevated its prestige.

In turn, these religious institutions supported the Capetians. They provided educated clerics to serve as royal advisors or scribes, legitimized the monarchy through liturgical ceremonies, and cultivated moral authority that complemented royal justice. This synergy between throne and altar was not always without tension—churchmen sometimes pushed back against kings they saw as overstepping—but on balance, the relationship remained mutually beneficial throughout the century.

---

## 2) The Reign of Louis VI (the Fat) and the Shaping of the City

**Military Campaigns and Defense**

Louis VI devoted significant energy to subduing rebellious barons around Paris. He built or strengthened fortifications near the city to protect royal lands, ensuring that banditry and feudal conflicts would not disrupt commerce. These defensive efforts often involved repairing or expanding older walls and watchtowers, many of which had roots in earlier centuries.

While Paris itself was not always directly attacked, its suburbs and trade routes could suffer if local lords turned bandits or feuded with each other. The king's interventions improved safety, making it easier for farmers to bring produce to market and for traders to travel. This, in turn, laid groundwork for urban growth, as a secure environment drew more people seeking opportunities.

**Royal Patronage and Construction**

Louis VI also supported religious institutions by funding church building projects, especially in the vicinity of Paris. Churches functioned not just as places of worship, but as communal spaces for gathering, education, and occasional shelter during raids. By endorsing construction, the king reinforced the city's spiritual and architectural fabric.

In the city center, older structures were repaired or upgraded—often with stone replacing wood. As the population grew, so did the need for new housing, markets, and workshops. A sense of renewal took hold, reflecting a broader shift in Europe toward re-urbanization after centuries of relative stagnation.

## 3) Louis VII, Eleanor of Aquitaine, and the Broader Stage

**The Marriage to Eleanor of Aquitaine**

Louis VI's son, **Louis VII (r. 1137–1180)**, continued his father's policies but also became entangled in major European events. Initially, Louis VII's marriage to **Eleanor of Aquitaine** in 1137 expanded the reach of the French crown, as Eleanor brought with her vast lands in southwestern France. This union briefly positioned Paris at the heart of a much larger realm, bridging northern and southern cultures.

However, the marriage soured over time, leading to an annulment in 1152. Eleanor then married **Henry Plantagenet**, who soon became King Henry II of England. This shift dramatically changed the balance of power, creating a long-standing Anglo-French rivalry. From a Parisian perspective, the city lost potential influence over Aquitaine, but remained a steadfast seat of Capetian authority.

## The Second Crusade and Religious Climate

Louis VII also led the **Second Crusade** (1147–1149) alongside Emperor Conrad III of Germany. Although the crusade ultimately failed to retake key territories in the Holy Land, it impacted Paris in smaller ways. Returning crusaders brought tales of distant lands, new tastes for exotic goods, and sometimes relics acquired abroad, which they donated to local churches. This infusion of international experiences subtly enriched the city's cultural outlook, even if the political gains from the crusade were negligible.

The ongoing crusading spirit in the 12th century also strengthened the Church's influence. Preachers and bishops in Paris organized prayer vigils and preached sermons encouraging support for these holy wars. The monarchy and clergy often used the crusades as a rallying point for unity, especially when domestic politics became turbulent.

---

## 4) The Expanding City: Physical Layout and Neighborhoods

### The Île de la Cité and Beyond

Throughout the 12th century, **Île de la Cité** remained the heart of Paris. It housed the royal palace and the cathedral (an older structure before the Gothic renovations of Notre-Dame began). The island's strategic location still provided defensive benefits, though the threat of large-scale invasions had lessened compared to Viking times.

On the **Right Bank**, trade and commerce thrived. Markets were held near the river, allowing goods to be easily shipped. Artisans and merchants clustered in districts devoted to specific trades—bakers, butchers, tanners, and textile sellers. While the Right Bank started out less populated than the Left Bank in earlier eras, it grew quickly in the 12th century, thanks to the bustling mercantile activity.

On the **Left Bank**, ecclesiastical institutions and schools began to attract students from various regions. Religious houses provided housing and education, setting an early pattern for what would later become the Latin Quarter. Over time, the Left Bank also developed its own markets and residential zones, though it retained a somewhat quieter, more scholarly feel than the Right Bank's commercial hustle.

### Wooden Houses and Narrow Streets

Despite gradual improvements in building materials, many homes were still made of wood and plaster, with thatched or wooden roofs. Streets were narrow and often poorly maintained. As the population density increased, fire hazards became a real concern. Occasional regulations tried to limit open flames or require more stone construction, but financial constraints meant many people stuck with cheaper wooden structures.

Sewers were rudimentary, and household waste disposal often involved simply tossing refuse into the street or nearby channels. The Church advocated for cleanliness in moral or religious terms, but large-scale sanitation systems were still far off. Even so, travelers often remarked on the energy and growing population of Paris, indicating that such inconveniences did not stop the city's rise.

## 5) Commerce, Guilds, and Economic Life

### Local Markets and Seasonal Fairs

With increased stability, **markets** in Paris multiplied. Local farmers brought vegetables, grains, and livestock for sale; nearby vineyards supplied wine; and fishmongers sold their catch fresh from the Seine or nearby waterways. Over time, the city also joined a broader network of regional fairs, notably in Champagne and Flanders, which created trade routes that passed through or near Paris.

Seasonal fairs brought merchants from distant regions, sometimes from as far as Italy or England. They brought luxury items such as fine cloth, spices, and metals. Parisian authorities imposed tolls and taxes on these goods, boosting royal and municipal revenues. This intersection of local and long-distance trade enriched not only the treasury but also the cultural mix of the city.

### The Rise of Guilds

In the 12th century, **guilds** became more formal. While earlier centuries saw loose associations of craftsmen, the 1100s gave birth to recognized guild charters for groups like bakers, goldsmiths, weavers, and parchment makers. Each guild regulated training through apprenticeships, guarded trade secrets, and controlled membership numbers to maintain quality and pricing.

Guilds also had social and religious functions: members supported each other in sickness, contributed to funerals, and funded chapels dedicated to patron saints. For instance, the guild of goldsmiths might sponsor a small altar in a local church, holding special masses on the feast day of Saint Eligius, their patron. These connections further integrated professional life with religious devotion.

**Monetization and Currency**

While bartering was still common, the 12th century saw more transactions in coin. Small silver deniers circulated widely, minted under royal authority. The king's right to coinage was a cornerstone of his power, symbolizing control over the economy. Counterfeiting was harshly punished.

Paris became a minting center, further reinforcing the city's role in national affairs. Reliable coinage encouraged trade; foreign merchants appreciated stability when exchanging their goods. Although the sums of money in circulation were modest by modern standards, the trend toward monetization helped Paris develop a more sophisticated economic structure.

---

# 6) The First Glimpses of the University of Paris

### Cathedral Schools and Early Scholars

Throughout the 11th century, cathedral schools around Europe had provided basic and advanced instruction in **Latin, theology, and the liberal arts**. In Paris, the school attached to Notre-Dame attracted talented masters and eager students. By the early 12th century, it was arguably one of the most respected educational centers in Northern Europe.

Notable scholars like **William of Champeaux** taught in Paris, developing curricula that included logic, rhetoric, and theology. Students began arriving from different parts of France, as well as England, Germany, and Italy, to study under famous masters. These early gatherings of scholars set the stage for a more formal academic community.

### Peter Abelard and Intellectual Debates

A key figure in the intellectual life of 12th-century Paris was **Peter Abelard (1079–1142)**. Known for his sharp intellect and controversial ideas, Abelard taught theology and dialectics, often challenging established authorities. He famously debated with other theologians, including Bernard of Clairvaux, pushing the boundaries of acceptable inquiry.

Abelard's love affair with Héloïse, a gifted student, further contributed to his legend. Their correspondence, partially preserved in letters, gives us a personal glimpse of medieval scholastic life. Abelard's bold questioning sometimes clashed with Church doctrine, leading to charges of heresy or censure. Yet his career exemplified the vibrant, if sometimes tumultuous, academic environment that was forming on the Left Bank of the Seine.

**The Formation of Student Communities**

As more scholars gathered, informal **student communities** emerged. These students typically lodged in simple rooms, sometimes near the schools or inside monasteries if they were clerics. Strict discipline was enforced in some establishments, while others were more loosely organized, giving rise to occasional rowdiness among student groups.

Many of these students were clerics in minor orders, meaning they were part of the Church's hierarchy but not fully ordained priests. This status gave them certain legal protections. They could be tried in ecclesiastical courts rather than secular ones, which sometimes led to tensions with city officials if students caused disturbances.

By the end of the 12th century, the concept of a formal **universitas** (or guild of masters and students) was emerging, though the University of Paris would not receive official recognition until the early 13th century. Even so, the seeds were planted, and Paris's reputation as a center of learning began to spread.

---

## 7) Religion in 12th-Century Paris: Everyday Faith and Great Projects

**Construction of New Churches**

The 12th century witnessed an evolution in church architecture. Romanesque styles—thick walls, rounded arches—were giving way to early **Gothic** elements by the end of the century. In 1163, under Bishop Maurice de Sully, the cornerstone of the **Notre-Dame Cathedral** was laid. While most of Notre-Dame's iconic features (flying buttresses, large rose windows) would come into prominence in the 13th century, its beginnings were firmly placed in the late 12th.

Smaller parish churches also sprang up, each serving the spiritual needs of specific neighborhoods. As the population grew, the Church worked to keep pace, building or refurbishing these local centers of worship. Some older wooden structures were replaced with stone, reflecting both the city's economic improvements and the desire for more durable, sacred spaces.

## Monastic Influence and Pilgrimage

Monasteries around Paris, such as **Saint-Denis** and **Saint-Victor**, continued to draw pilgrims and religious scholars. Saint-Denis, in particular, boasted the tombs of French kings and the relics of Saint Denis. Pilgrims arriving in Paris would often pray there before heading to other holy sites. Monastic communities supported these visitors with lodging and guidance.

The abbey of **Saint-Victor** became known as an intellectual center, producing theologians who contributed to the growing scholastic discourse. Figures like **Hugh of Saint-Victor** wrote influential works blending theology, philosophy, and mystical thought. These monastic scholars interacted with the emerging secular masters in the city, creating a dynamic interchange of ideas.

## Religious Festivals and Social Life

Religion remained deeply embedded in daily life. Church bells regulated the rhythm of the day—calling people to prayer, announcing feasts, and marking significant events. Major religious festivals drew large crowds to churches, with processions weaving through the streets. Guilds and confraternities organized special masses and charitable activities, reinforcing community bonds.

Fasting rules, observances of saints' days, and mandatory tithes shaped people's habits and finances. The Church also offered social services—like distributing alms to the poor—further anchoring it as the primary institution for both spiritual and practical assistance.

## 8) Royal Courtly Culture and the Influence of Eleanor of Aquitaine

### Eleanor's Patronage of Literature

Although Eleanor of Aquitaine's marriage to Louis VII was short-lived, her presence in the French court during the early years left cultural ripples. She introduced elements of the **southern French troubadour tradition**—poetry and music focusing on chivalry, love, and courtly manners. While Paris would not become the main hub of Occitan lyric poetry, these influences planted a seed of courtly culture that continued to grow under later rulers.

Eleanor's sophisticated tastes and experiences—she had traveled widely, even participating in the Second Crusade—impressed many at court. Noblewomen in Paris began to emulate her style of dress and her patronage of poets or minstrels. Though the king himself was more austere, the courtly atmosphere gained a new dimension.

### Tournaments and Court Festivals

Under Louis VII and the barons who surrounded him, **tournaments** became increasingly common. Knights from different parts of France and occasionally abroad would gather to display martial skills in jousts and mock battles. These events were as much about entertainment and politics as they were about military practice.

Tournaments brought money into the city, as knights and their retinues needed lodging, food, and equipment. Craftsmen who specialized in armor or horse tack found new patrons. At these gatherings, alliances could be formed or broken, and the social hierarchy was on public display. Parisian citizens, especially those from wealthier backgrounds, might come to watch the spectacle, blending aristocratic culture with more popular festivities.

---

## 9) Shifts in Law and Governance

### The King's Growing Judicial Role

Though feudal law was still dominant in much of France, the Capetian monarchs—starting with Louis VI and continuing through Louis VII—claimed an increasing right to act as arbiters of **justice**. Royal courts in Paris heard more cases, especially those involving significant disputes or crimes that affected the king's interests.

**Prevôts** (provosts) oversaw local administration in the city, handling smaller disputes and taxes. For more serious matters, litigants might appeal directly to the king's court. This growing royal judiciary was part of a slow centralization process, wherein Paris became the arena for important legal battles. The principle that "the king is the fountain of justice" gained traction, though it would reach fuller expression under 13th-century rulers.

## Canon Law and Ecclesiastical Courts

Alongside secular courts, **ecclesiastical courts** were active in Paris. They handled cases related to Church matters—marriage, wills involving religious bequests, and moral offenses. Students and clergy often enjoyed "benefit of clergy," meaning they could only be tried in these church courts. This dual legal system sometimes caused friction, especially when secular authorities felt the Church was being too lenient.

Nonetheless, the coexistence of two sets of courts contributed to the city's complexity. Legal scholars studied both **canon law** and **Roman law** (rediscovered in parts of Europe), fueling intellectual debates that would shape the future University of Paris.

---

## 10) Life for the Common People of Paris

### Housing and Daily Struggles

For ordinary people—artisans, laborers, small traders—life in the expanding city was a mix of opportunity and hardship. Work could be found more easily than in rural areas, but wages were low, and living conditions cramped. Many lived in simple wooden buildings with shared courtyards, lacking basic sanitation.

Commoners rose at dawn to start work. Artisans toiled in workshops attached to or near their homes. Women often helped with family trades or worked as laundresses, seamstresses, or midwives. Children contributed by running errands or learning basic skills from their parents. In busier neighborhoods, the noise of hammering, street vendors, and passing carts was constant.

### Food and Drink

The average diet revolved around **bread**, usually dark and coarse. Meat was a luxury for many, though fish appeared regularly thanks to the Seine and religious fasting rules (which encouraged fish consumption on certain days). Vegetables like onions, cabbage, and beans were staples, grown in small gardens around the city or in nearby farms.

Wine was increasingly common, even among lower-income households—diluted if necessary. Paris's proximity to wine-producing regions in the Île-de-France and the Loire Valley meant supplies were relatively cheap. Ale or beer was also consumed, but wine held cultural importance, reflected in tavern scenes and communal gatherings after church or market days.

### Social Gatherings and Entertainment

Despite hard work, Parisians found ways to socialize. Taverns and alehouses served as meeting spots, while religious feasts offered communal celebrations. During festivals, people enjoyed **street performances**, simple games of chance, or moral plays sponsored by the Church. Guilds might organize processions in honor of their patron saints, bringing a sense of pageantry to the streets.

Public punishments or executions also drew crowds—grim events that served as a reminder of the king's justice or the Church's moral authority. While macabre by modern standards, such spectacles were a part of medieval communal life and shaped people's understanding of order and punishment.

---

## 11) Women's Roles and Influences

### Noblewomen and Court Life

Women of noble birth had a better chance at literacy, especially if they joined convents or were educated by private tutors. Some, like Eleanor of Aquitaine, played pivotal roles in political alliances through marriage, dowries, and inheritance. Though many aspects of medieval society remained patriarchal, certain noblewomen wielded considerable influence, particularly as patrons of the arts or regents for underage sons.

### Women in Trade and Crafts

Among commoners, women worked in various trades—spinning, weaving, brewing, midwifery, or assisting in their husbands' shops. Some widows inherited guild memberships, running their own enterprises. However, societal norms still limited their independence. They often needed a male guardian for legal matters, and social mobility was scarce.

Religious life offered another avenue. Joining a convent could provide education, a stable environment, and sometimes a measure of autonomy for women who wished to avoid or leave marriage. Abbesses could direct entire communities, manage lands, and even hold moral authority over local lords.

---

## 12) Cultural Fusions and Influences

### Latin, Old French, and Vernacular Expression

Latin remained the language of scholarship, administration, and the Church. Yet, by the 12th century, **Old French** dialects were becoming increasingly common for everyday speech—and even for some literary works. Chansons de geste (epic poems) like **The Song of Roland** gained popularity, recited or sung by troubadours and jongleurs in noble courts.

Though The Song of Roland probably originated earlier, its oral circulation in the 12th century helped shape a sense of national identity. The poem dealt with heroism, loyalty, and warfare against non-Christian foes, themes that resonated with a society still mindful of crusades and feudal conflicts. Over time, these vernacular stories spread to Parisian audiences, bridging the gap between noble and common traditions.

**Influences from Abroad**

In addition to crusader stories, Paris felt subtle influences from other regions. Trade with England introduced certain goods and cultural exchanges, although tensions between the French and English crowns simmered after Eleanor's remarriage to Henry II. Italian merchants passing through might share tales of urban life in cities like Genoa or Venice, which were starting to flourish independently of feudal monarchs.

Architecture also saw small but notable outside influences. For example, some early Gothic ideas traveled from the region of Normandy or from further east, merging with local building techniques to create new styles. While the full flourishing of Gothic architecture would occur in the 13th century, the seeds of innovation were already present.

---

## 13) Tensions and Conflicts

**Noble Uprisings**

The Capetian kings, despite their growing power, had to contend with powerful vassals who resented direct interference. Some lords saw the monarchy's increasing hold on justice and taxes as an encroachment. Occasional rebellions flared up, though most were localized. Louis VI and Louis VII often responded by sending royal troops to quell these disturbances, relying on Paris as the administrative and logistical hub.

**Disputes with the Church**

While the monarchy and Church generally supported each other, they sometimes clashed over appointments to bishoprics or the extent of ecclesiastical immunity. If a royal official tried to tax church lands without permission, bishops might complain to the pope. Conversely, if a priest or monk committed a crime, city authorities might demand a trial in secular court, conflicting with the Church's claim of jurisdiction.

In Paris, such disputes were often negotiated carefully. The king needed the bishop and monastic communities for spiritual legitimacy, while church leaders recognized the king's protection was essential for security and economic well-being. These tensions rarely boiled over into large-scale conflict, but they foreshadowed bigger struggles in later centuries.

## 14) The Seeds of Future Expansion

### Plans for Notre-Dame

While the official commencement of Notre-Dame's Gothic construction occurred in 1163, the planning stages began earlier. Architects and bishops discussed designs that would surpass older Romanesque churches, both in height and luminosity. Early experiments in **ribbed vaults** and **pointed arches** signaled a new era of architectural ambition.

Once the cathedral was underway, it became a focus of civic pride. Workers, including skilled stonemasons, carpenters, and sculptors, flocked to Paris to be part of this grand project. Donations from wealthy families, guilds, and even modest parishioners funded different chapels or sections of the building. Although far from complete by 1200, the project itself symbolized Paris's upward trajectory.

### The Latin Quarter and Formalized Learning

By the late 12th century, the cluster of schools on the Left Bank was increasingly referred to as a unified body, though not yet with the official structure of a "university." Masters lectured on the liberal arts, theology, and, to a lesser extent, law and medicine. This area near **Montagne Sainte-Geneviève** was buzzing with youthful energy—students engaging in debates, copying manuscripts, and sometimes causing rowdy nights in local taverns.

A sense of camaraderie grew among students, many of whom were far from home. They formed **nations** (groups organized by geographic origin) that would later become part of the university's formal governance. The mixture of scholars from various lands fostered a cosmopolitan atmosphere, setting Paris apart from more provincial towns.

---

## 15) Concluding Reflections on 12th-Century Paris

### From Modest Town to Emerging Hub

The 12th century was a transformative period for Paris. Once a relatively modest city centered on the Île de la Cité, it was now spilling over onto the Right and Left Banks. Merchant activity boomed, guilds gained prominence, and the monarchy made strides in centralizing power.

Religious institutions—churches, monasteries, and an ever-growing cathedral—gave the city not only spiritual leadership but also economic and cultural vitality. Pilgrims, travelers, and students arrived in greater numbers, contributing to the diversity of daily life. The stage was set for even more dramatic growth in the following century.

# CHAPTER 6

## THE 13TH CENTURY – SCHOLASTICISM, ARCHITECTURE, AND SOCIETY

## Introduction

The 13th century is often regarded as a **golden age** for medieval Paris. Building on the foundations of the 12th century—greater social stability, robust trade, and the budding community of scholars—the city experienced a remarkable flourish. During this era, two Capetian kings left especially deep marks: **Philip II Augustus (r. 1180–1223)** and **Louis IX (Saint Louis, r. 1226–1270)**. Under their reigns, the city grew in size, wealth, and prestige.

In this chapter, we will look at the many facets of Paris in the 13th century: the expansion of royal authority, the formal establishment of the University of Paris, the apex of **Gothic architecture**, and daily life within a booming metropolis. We will also consider the social tensions that came with growth, as different classes and institutions jostled for influence. By the century's end, Paris would stand as one of Europe's most significant centers of culture, learning, and political power.

## 1) Philip II Augustus: Transforming the City

### Territorial Expansion and Royal Domain

Philip II Augustus, ascending to the throne in 1180, inherited a kingdom still overshadowed by the powerful Angevin Empire of the English kings. Through strategic wars, alliances, and political maneuvers (notably against Kings Henry II, Richard the Lionheart, and John of England), Philip II greatly **expanded the royal domain**. By seizing lands such as Normandy, Anjou, and parts of Aquitaine, he grew his realm into a more cohesive territory.

With these territorial gains, wealth poured into the royal treasury. Philip II invested heavily in **Paris**, aiming to make it the uncontested capital of his kingdom. Merchants found new security, as the king protected trade routes and insisted on uniform systems of justice and taxation in royal lands.

## The Wall of Philip II and Urban Development

One of Philip's most significant contributions to Paris was the construction of a new, much larger city wall—often called the **Wall of Philip II**—on both banks of the Seine. Built between roughly 1190 and 1210, these fortifications far surpassed earlier walls in scope, enclosing a bigger area to accommodate the city's growing population. This dramatic expansion signaled a new confidence in the city's future.

Inside these walls, Philip II also laid the foundations for the **Louvre**, initially built as a defensive fortress on the city's western edge. While it would later become a royal palace and, in modern times, a world-famous museum, its original purpose was to guard the Seine from potential invasions. By fortifying Paris, Philip II not only enhanced security but also spurred construction work that employed countless masons, carpenters, and laborers.

## Administrative Reforms

Beyond physical improvements, Philip II introduced **administrative reforms** that centralized governance in Paris. He appointed **baillis** (bailiffs) to oversee provinces, reporting directly to the king. This approach curtailed the power of local lords and ensured more consistent application of royal justice and taxes.

Paris itself became a hub for royal officials who managed the kingdom's finances, judicial matters, and diplomatic correspondence. The **Châtelet**, near the Pont au Change, served as a central courthouse and prison, symbolizing the king's justice. By the end of Philip II's reign in 1223, Paris had become unmistakably the political core of France, setting the stage for further cultural achievements.

# 2) The University of Paris: Formal Recognition and Growth

## Papal Recognition and Charters

While schools had flourished on the Left Bank throughout the 12th century, the 13th century brought formal recognition of the **University of Paris**. In 1200, King Philip II Augustus granted privileges to the scholars, offering them protection and defining certain legal rights. The pivotal moment came in 1215 and 1231, when papal bulls (notably from Popes Innocent III and Gregory IX) effectively recognized and regulated the university.

These charters solidified the university's structure as a **universitas**—a corporate body of masters and students. The institution was divided into **four faculties**: Arts, Theology, Canon Law, and Medicine. The Faculty of Arts served as the foundational level, after which advanced students specialized in the higher faculties.

## Nations and Governance

The student body was divided into **"nations,"** each grouping scholars by their geographic origin (e.g., French, Norman, Picard, and English/German). Each nation elected officers to represent its interests, resolving disputes and helping newcomers adapt. Overseeing everything was the position of the **rector**, typically elected by the masters of the Faculty of Arts, acting as a central figure for the entire university community.

These structures mirrored guild organization, reflecting the medieval inclination to form corporate bodies for mutual protection and to manage standards. The university's autonomy—and its direct link to the pope—occasionally placed it at odds with the bishop of Paris or royal officials, but it remained a cherished institution under royal patronage.

## Intellectual Currents: Scholasticism and Beyond

**Scholasticism**—the method of using logical analysis to reconcile classical philosophy (primarily Aristotle) with Christian doctrine—thrived in the University of Paris. Masters like **Thomas Aquinas** (born in Italy but teaching in Paris during the mid-13th century) and **Albertus Magnus** offered systematic theological and philosophical works that would influence Western thought for centuries.

Debates in lecture halls could be fierce. Students and masters engaged in **disputations**, where a thesis would be argued and countered, sharpening dialectical skills. While theology reigned supreme as the highest discipline, the faculty of Arts explored logic, grammar, rhetoric, and natural philosophy, laying the intellectual groundwork for Europe's later developments in science and humanities.

## 3) Notre-Dame and the Rise of Gothic Architecture

### Ongoing Construction

Building on the foundation laid in 1163, the **Notre-Dame Cathedral** rose in grandeur throughout the 13th century. The introduction of **flying buttresses** allowed for higher walls and larger stained-glass windows, flooding the interior with light. By around 1250, much of the main structure was complete, though decorative work continued for decades.

Notre-Dame's significance went beyond architecture. It was the seat of the bishop, the location for major religious ceremonies, and a symbol of urban pride. Pilgrims visited to see its relics, including a reputed piece of the Crown of Thorns (brought by Louis IX). The cathedral also stood as a spiritual anchor: local guilds funded chapels, wealthy patrons donated statues, and the city's inhabitants celebrated feast days in its expansive nave.

### The Sainte-Chapelle and Royal Patronage

Another Gothic masterpiece emerged under Louis IX: the **Sainte-Chapelle**, built between 1242 and 1248 within the royal palace on the Île de la Cité. Designed to house Louis IX's cherished relics of Christ's Passion (including the Crown of Thorns), the chapel became a pinnacle of Gothic elegance, renowned for its soaring stained-glass windows.

As a royal foundation, Sainte-Chapelle reinforced the bond between the Capetian crown and the Church. Louis IX—famed for his devout Christian faith—used the chapel to underscore his kingship's sacred character. This melding of royal and religious symbolism played a vital role in elevating Paris's status among European capitals.

**Influence on Lesser Churches**

Gothic innovations in Notre-Dame and Sainte-Chapelle inspired many other churches and chapels in and around Paris. Builders experimented with pointed arches, ribbed vaults, and tracery windows even in smaller parish churches. By the mid-13th century, Gothic architecture became the default style, symbolizing the city's alignment with contemporary artistic and spiritual trends across northern France.

---

## 4) Louis IX (Saint Louis) and the Height of Royal Influence

**King and Saint**

Crowned in 1226, Louis IX (commonly known as **Saint Louis** after his canonization in 1297) is often seen as the embodiment of medieval Christian kingship. Deeply pious, he attempted to model his reign on ideals of justice, charity, and devotion to the Church. He convened **royal courts** under the "Tree of Vincennes," as legend has it, seeking to appear accessible to commoners.

Louis IX's reign brought a sense of **moral authority** to the crown, building on the more pragmatic expansions of Philip II. Together, these two kings propelled Paris from a rising city to a commanding center of governance and culture.

**Legal and Administrative Reforms**

Under Louis IX, royal justice expanded further. He appointed **enquêteurs** (royal commissioners) to investigate abuses of power by local officials, including bailiffs. The king's court, or **Parlement**, took a more defined shape in Paris, becoming a permanent institution for hearing appeals.

Some historians see in Louis IX's reforms the foundations of a more modern state, where the king had direct authority over many aspects of his subjects' lives. Though feudalism was far from dead, the trend toward a centralized monarchy was unmistakable, with Paris as its administrative heart.

## Crusades and International Prestige

Like his predecessors, Louis IX engaged in **Crusades**. He led the Seventh Crusade (1248–1254) and the Eighth Crusade (1270), though both ended in difficulty. While these military campaigns strained the royal treasury and cost many lives, they also underscored France's role in global Christendom. Pilgrims and knights streamed through Paris, while the city's image as a devout capital solidified.

The presence of relics in the Sainte-Chapelle further bolstered Louis IX's international reputation. Foreign dignitaries visiting Paris would witness grand religious ceremonies and see the precious relics, reinforcing the notion that France was divinely favored—a notion the king used to strengthen his hand in European diplomacy.

## 5) Commercial Prosperity and Urban Life in the 13th Century

### The Growth of Trade and Guilds

By the 13th century, Paris was a busy commercial hub. Trade routes linked the city to Flanders, the Champagne fairs, and beyond. The construction of royal roads and bridges, along with the maintenance of the Seine as a navigable waterway, made it easier for goods to flow.

**Guilds** became more structured and powerful. Each major craft or trade had its own regulations, controlling apprenticeships, pricing, and quality standards. Some guilds, like the **Confrérie des Marchands de l'Eau** (the water merchants), held monopolies over certain types of commerce, especially river trade. The city administration, along with the king, recognized guild charters that balanced the crown's revenue interests with local economic freedoms.

### The Medieval Markets

Major **marketplaces** dotted the city. The **Halles de Paris** on the Right Bank became the premier market, bustling with stalls selling everything from fish and meat to textiles and spices. Over time, permanent structures replaced makeshift booths, creating a labyrinth of covered areas where merchants and customers haggled daily.

People from all social strata mingled in these markets. Nobles and clerics could buy fine imported goods, while commoners picked up everyday necessities. The markets formed a vibrant social center, with taverns and street performers catering to the crowds.

### Monetary Exchange and Banking

The 13th century saw the rise of **moneychangers** and rudimentary banking practices in Paris. While Italian bankers from cities like Lombardy were influential across Europe, local merchants and Jewish financiers also played roles in lending and exchanging currency.

Paris minted coins (such as the **gros tournois**, introduced under Louis IX) with higher silver content, facilitating larger transactions and international trade. Royal oversight of coinage was strict, as stable currency underpinned the economy and reflected the king's authority. Counterfeiting was severely punished, indicating the seriousness with which the crown guarded its monetary prerogatives.

---

## 6) Daily Life in a Flourishing Medieval Metropolis

### Housing and Sanitation

With population growth, **housing** in Paris became denser. Multi-story wooden houses loomed over narrow streets, sometimes leaning precariously. Fire remained a constant threat. Despite royal edicts encouraging stone construction, the expense remained prohibitive for many.

Sanitation was basic. While some streets were paved, others were dirt paths that turned to mud when it rained. People threw waste into gutters or the Seine, leading to foul smells and periodic outbreaks of disease. Efforts were made to keep main thoroughfares cleaner, but these regulations were not always enforced.

### Entertainment and Festivals

Parisians enjoyed a variety of **festivals**, tied both to the Church calendar and secular events. Religious processions during Easter, Christmas, and saints' days attracted large crowds. On the more popular side, the **Feast of Fools**, traditionally around New Year, allowed a brief inversion of roles where younger clergy parodied church rituals—though by the 13th century, Church authorities tried to curb its excesses.

Minstrels, acrobats, and animal trainers performed in streets or public squares. Tournaments, sponsored by nobles or the crown, added spectacle and color. In the evenings, taverns served as communal gathering spots for gossip, music, and sometimes rowdy brawls.

### Role of Women and Family Structure

Women of the merchant class or artisanal guild families participated in the family business, supervised apprentices, and sometimes conducted sales. Marriage alliances among guild families could bolster economic power. However, patriarchal norms persisted; women rarely held official positions in guild hierarchies unless widowed.

Noblewomen in Paris engaged in courtly culture, managing estates and patronizing religious or literary pursuits. Aristocratic marriages were frequently diplomatic, binding families and territories together. For lower-class women, labor ranged from domestic service to day labor in markets, with limited upward mobility.

---

## 7) Tensions and Conflicts in a Growing City

### Class Divisions and Urban Friction

The wealth flowing into Paris created stark contrasts: **nobles and top guild members** might live comfortably in houses of stone, while many poorer families shared cramped wooden buildings. Beggars and day laborers populated the streets, particularly near market areas where they hoped to find work or charity.

Social tensions could flare. Strikes or protests by apprentices were not unheard of. Some tried to form "unofficial" guilds to demand better conditions. While the crown and city officials usually suppressed open revolts quickly, the seeds of class consciousness were sown in this era of rapid change.

### Conflict with External Powers

Though Paris was less directly exposed to warfare in the 13th century than in some later periods, **English** claims to French lands led to periodic skirmishes and tension along the frontiers. Normandy, once controlled by England, was fully reclaimed by Philip II, but cross-Channel rivalry continued. Parisians remained aware of potential threats, but the city itself was rarely under direct siege during this century.

## 8) Intellectual and Cultural Landmarks

### The Expansion of the University of Paris

As the 13th century progressed, the University of Paris expanded in enrollment and prestige. Theology continued to dominate, but **Aristotelian philosophy**—interpreted through Scholastic commentary—made inroads. Figures like Thomas Aquinas, teaching at the Dominican house of Saint-Jacques, drew eager students to disputations on faith and reason.

Secular clergy (the cathedral chapter of Notre-Dame) and monastic orders (Dominicans, Franciscans, Augustinians) each maintained colleges. Over time, more specialized colleges were founded, creating a network of educational institutions. The ripple effect on the city was immense—booksellers and manuscript illuminators set up shop, taverns and lodging houses catered to students, and the intellectual milieu shaped a distinct **Latin Quarter** identity.

### Literature and Art

Alongside theological works, **vernacular literature** began to flourish. Poets and chroniclers wrote in Old French, narrating epic stories or commenting on contemporary events. Courtly romances gained popularity among the nobility, while historical writings documented the deeds of kings and saints.

Artistic production boomed. Sculptors, stained-glass artisans, and metalworkers found commissions in cathedrals and royal projects. Parisian style influenced neighboring regions, spreading Gothic motifs and refined craftsmanship across northern Europe. This synergy of art and theology culminated in majestic cathedrals, elaborate altarpieces, and intricately carved tombs.

---

## 9) Jewish Communities in 13th-Century Paris

### Economic and Cultural Contributions

Jewish communities had existed in Paris since at least the early Middle Ages, engaging in trade, moneylending, and scholarship. Some Jews studied Hebrew texts, contributing to broader intellectual discussions. Their presence in financial sectors often stemmed from restrictions that barred many Christians from charging interest on loans, giving Jewish moneylenders a niche but also exposing them to resentment.

### Persecution and Expulsions

Despite economic utility, the Jewish population faced **periodic persecution**. Rulers, under pressure from Church authorities or popular prejudice, sometimes imposed special taxes, forced conversions, or confiscations of property. Under **Louis IX**, policies tightened: Jews were forbidden to engage in certain trades, and public disputations were held to challenge Jewish texts.

In 1306—technically just beyond the 13th century—King Philip IV ("the Fair") would expel Jews from France, but the seeds of hostility were evident earlier. Tensions rose and fell in waves, overshadowing the community's valuable cultural and economic role.

---

## 10) Late 13th-Century Developments and the Road Ahead

### Philip III and Philip IV

After Louis IX's death in 1270, his successors **Philip III (r. 1270–1285)** and **Philip IV (r. 1285–1314)** continued to consolidate royal power from their seat in Paris. Philip IV in particular—known for his conflicts with Pope Boniface VIII and the Knights Templar—would push royal authority to new limits, sometimes straining relations with the Church and nobility.

The monarchy's ability to impose taxes, administer justice, and enact policies from Paris showed how far centralization had come since the early Capetians. The city thrived as an administrative capital, but also faced the complexities of a stronger state: more bureaucracy, heavier taxation, and political intrigues that would shape the coming century.

### Shifting Social Dynamics

By the end of the 13th century, **population estimates** for Paris range widely, but many historians suggest it was nearing 200,000 inhabitants—making it one of the largest cities in Western Europe at the time. This density created both economic vibrancy and social challenges. Overcrowding, limited sanitation, and class disparities were becoming more evident.

Wealthy nobles, high-ranking clergy, and prosperous merchants might live comfortably, but an underclass of laborers and the poor struggled daily. Still, the overall sense was that Paris was a place of opportunity—a magnet for merchants, craftsmen, and scholars seeking a better future.

---

## 11) The Legacy of the 13th Century for Paris

### A Flourishing Capital of Christendom

Through the combined legacies of Philip II Augustus and Louis IX, Paris emerged as one of the most influential cities in Europe. The **university** attracted students and scholars from across the continent, the **architecture** reached new heights with Notre-Dame and Sainte-Chapelle, and the **economy** supported thriving markets and guilds. Royal power, consolidated in the city, provided a framework for future monarchs to build upon.

At the same time, the city's identity was inseparable from its religious roots. The intense devotion of Louis IX—memorialized in the relics and chapels he introduced—underscored the unity of faith and kingship. Pilgrims, crusaders, and foreign dignitaries all perceived Paris as a spiritual beacon, exemplifying the Catholic world's grandeur.

**Tensions Beneath the Surface**

Despite its prosperity, Paris was not free of tension. Class divides widened, religious intolerance toward Jews marked a dark undercurrent, and the monarchy's growing power sometimes clashed with local liberties and church prerogatives. The seeds of future conflicts—both internal and external—were planted in these years of great expansion.

Moreover, Europe itself was on the cusp of monumental changes. Economic patterns, demographic shifts, and political rivalries would intensify in the 14th century, culminating in crises like the **Hundred Years' War** and the **Black Death**. Paris, for all its achievements, would not escape these upheavals unscathed.

# CHAPTER 7

## THE HUNDRED YEARS' WAR AND ITS IMPACT ON PARIS

## Introduction

By the early 14th century, Paris was a thriving city and the recognized seat of the French monarchy. Trade, guilds, and the Church had all helped the city grow into one of the most influential capitals in Europe. However, this era of relative prosperity was soon disrupted by a protracted conflict that would leave a profound mark on both France as a whole and Paris in particular: the **Hundred Years' War** (1337–1453).

This chapter explores how the Hundred Years' War began, why it lasted so long, and how it shaped life in Paris—socially, economically, and politically. We will look at key moments like the English invasions, the civil strife among French factions, the occupation of Paris, and the eventual revival that followed. Though the war was fought on many fronts, Paris often stood at its heart, symbolizing the kingdom's unity or, at times, its fragmentation. By the time the war ended, both France and its capital had changed in ways that would influence the late medieval and early Renaissance periods.

## 1) Origins of the Conflict

### The Question of Succession

The immediate trigger for the Hundred Years' War was a **dispute over the French throne** after the extinction of the direct Capetian male line. The last direct Capetian king,

Charles IV, died in 1328 without a surviving son. His closest male relative in the paternal line was **Edward III of England**, who claimed the French crown through his mother, Isabella (the daughter of King Philip IV of France).

However, French nobles rejected Edward III's claim, invoking traditional principles (later codified as the Salic Law) that prevented inheritance of the crown through the female line. Instead, they supported **Philip of Valois**, crowned as **Philip VI** in 1328. This set the stage for a rivalry between the House of Valois in France and the Plantagenets in England, intensifying tensions that were already high due to disputes over territories like Gascony in southwestern France.

**Political and Economic Tensions**

Beyond the succession issue, **economic** and **feudal** factors also fueled conflict. England relied on the export of wool to Flanders, while France had strong ties to Flemish cities. Control of trade routes, especially in the Channel, became a point of contention. In addition, certain French lords in regions close to the English territories maintained complex feudal allegiances, sometimes leaning toward English interests if it benefited their own wealth or independence.

As these tensions grew, Edward III ultimately **claimed the French crown** in 1337, marking the official start of what would become the Hundred Years' War. Although no one anticipated the conflict to last more than a century, it set in motion a series of military campaigns, political alliances, and upheavals that would repeatedly affect Paris.

---

## 2) Early Phases of the War and Paris's Initial Response

**Naval Clashes and Sporadic Invasions**

The early stages of the war (from around 1337 to the 1350s) involved mostly **naval battles** and localized fighting in regions like Aquitaine, Brittany, and Flanders. However, the English also tried to raid deeper into French territories. With each foray, there was anxiety in Paris about a possible assault on the capital.

Philip VI took measures to **fortify Paris**, ensuring that its walls and gates were well-guarded. The city had grown significantly since the reign of Philip II Augustus, and the more modern fortifications offered some confidence. Yet rumors of impending English attacks caused panic among merchants and commoners, sometimes leading to temporary flight to the countryside.

**The Black Death's Impact**

In the midst of these hostilities, the **Black Death** reached France in the late 1340s. This plague caused a massive death toll across Europe. Paris, with its dense population, suffered greatly. Historians estimate that the city may have lost a significant portion of its inhabitants within a short span of years (some suggest between one-third and half).

This sudden drop in population had immediate effects:

- **Economic Slowdown**: Trade slowed as merchants died or fled, and laborers were scarce.
- **Social Strain**: Survivors questioned divine judgment, with some blaming outsiders or particular communities.
- **Military Weakness**: With fewer men available, the kingdom's ability to field armies or collect taxes for war was severely hampered.

Though the plague briefly stalled major military campaigns, it did not end the war. If anything, the weakened state of France made Edward III's invasions more threatening in the years that followed.

## 3) The Battle of Crécy and the Road to Calamity

### English Tactics and French Defeats

One of the most famous early battles, **Crécy (1346)**, showed the formidable might of the English longbowmen against French cavalry. The French, under Philip VI, were decisively defeated, partly due to outdated tactics that relied heavily on charges by mounted knights. The English, well-disciplined and armed with longbows, inflicted terrible losses on French nobility.

Though Crécy was fought far from Paris (in northern France), news of the disaster reverberated in the capital. Morale plummeted, and tensions rose between the French crown and local nobles who felt leadership was lacking. Parisians grew concerned that the English might eventually approach the city if such defeats continued.

### Siege of Calais

Following the victory at Crécy, Edward III laid siege to **Calais**, a crucial port in northern France. This siege (1346–1347) ended with Calais falling to the English, who would hold it for over two centuries. While Paris was not directly attacked, the loss of Calais meant a significant English foothold on the continent, facilitating future invasions and raids deeper into French territory.

For Paris, the defeat damaged confidence in the monarchy. Philip VI's reputation suffered, and the ongoing war expenses grew heavier. Royal taxation in the city increased, fueling discontent among merchants and commoners already struggling with the plague's aftermath.

## 4) Civil Unrest in Paris: The Estates-General and the Rise of Étienne Marcel

### The Capture of King John II

Philip VI died in 1350 and was succeeded by his son, **John II (the Good)**. John's rule was marked by further catastrophic defeats, most notably at **Poitiers (1356)**, where he was captured by the English. With the French king held prisoner, political turmoil engulfed the nation.

In Paris, the **Dauphin Charles** (the king's son and heir) struggled to maintain order. Heavy ransoms were demanded by the English for the release of John II, putting immense financial pressure on the kingdom. Taxes soared, and critics began calling for reforms.

### Popular Discontent and Étienne Marcel

In 1357, **Étienne Marcel**, a wealthy Parisian merchant and provost of the merchants, took a leading role in challenging royal authority. Representing the city's merchants and the middle class, Marcel sought to reduce the influence of the nobility and push for economic and administrative reforms. He demanded that the Estates-General, an assembly of representatives from the clergy, nobility, and commoners, gain more say in running the kingdom.

Marcel's actions included:

- **Confronting the Dauphin**: At times, Marcel and his supporters even resorted to violence to force the Dauphin to accept reform measures.
- **Urban Militias**: Marcel organized militias in Paris to guard against both external threats (English raids) and internal ones (the nobility who opposed reforms).
- **Symbolic Changes**: He introduced distinctive red and blue caps for his supporters, making a show of unity and defiance against the royal court.

### The Maillotins and Further Tensions

The unrest peaked in 1358 with a revolt known as the **revolt of the Maillotins**, named after the iron mallets (maillons) used by insurgents. This uprising was fueled by anger over new taxes and the perceived incompetence of the royal government in defending the city.

Royal forces eventually suppressed the revolt, and Étienne Marcel was killed by opponents within Paris. The Dauphin, who would later become **King Charles V**, reasserted control. Although the rebellion failed, it was a sign that Parisians were willing to challenge royal authority if they felt their interests were ignored. The city's merchant class had shown considerable power, and the war's pressures only continued to fuel dissent.

## 5) King Charles V and the Recovery of Paris

**Strategic Reforms**

Crowned in 1364, **Charles V** (often known as "the Wise") oversaw a partial recovery from the chaos of the earlier decades. Learning from the mistakes of previous reigns, he favored cautious military tactics and strong fortifications. Under his direction, Paris witnessed:

- **Fortified Walls**: Charles V expanded and strengthened the city's defenses, building on the walls constructed by predecessors.
- **Bastille Foundation**: He commissioned the **Bastille** as a fortress on the eastern side of Paris, initially meant to protect against English incursions along the Seine.
- **Reorganized Finances**: Through the counsel of advisors like **Bureau de la Rivière** and **Nicolas Oresme**, Charles introduced fiscal policies that aimed to stabilize the currency and streamline tax collection.

**Cultural Revival**

Despite the ongoing war, Charles V had a deep interest in arts and literature. He built the **Louvre Palace** into a comfortable royal residence, stocked its library, and invited scholars to his court. This patronage set a tone of intellectual growth that resonated in Paris, even amidst the uncertainties of war.

Under Charles V, the capital also benefited from improved administration. Provosts and royal officials coordinated city life more effectively. While taxes remained burdensome, some measure of stability returned. Parisians, for a time, enjoyed relative peace, though the English threat never fully disappeared.

**Temporary Gains**

Charles V's reign saw French forces reclaim territory through tactical warfare and diplomatic maneuvers. The English were pushed back in several regions. Nevertheless, the war's nature remained unpredictable. When Charles V died in 1380, his son, **Charles VI**, was still a minor. This led to regencies and renewed power struggles at the highest levels of government—instabilities that would once again affect Paris.

---

## 6) Madness of Charles VI and the Rise of Factional Conflict

### Charles VI's Early Rule

Charles VI took the throne officially in 1380 but only came into his own a few years later. Early in his reign, he was known as "Charles the Beloved" for lowering taxes and making efforts to reconcile with various factions. However, from around 1392 onward, the king suffered bouts of **mental illness**, sometimes failing to recognize his surroundings or believing he was made of glass.

This condition, shocking to contemporaries, created a power vacuum. Princes of the royal bloodline vied for influence, especially the Dukes of Burgundy and Orléans. Their competition evolved into **open hostility**, and Paris became a stage for factional battles that would deepen the country's vulnerabilities during the war with England.

### Burgundians vs. Armagnacs

Two main factions emerged:

1. **Burgundians**: Led by the powerful Duke of Burgundy, they initially maintained a strong presence in Paris, enjoying support among certain guilds and noble families.
2. **Armagnacs**: Named after the Count of Armagnac who allied with the Orléans faction, they opposed Burgundian dominance and pushed for more direct confrontation with the English.

This internal feud often escalated into violence. Burgundian partisans at times held Paris, while Armagnacs tried to seize control by force. The king's madness prevented a firm resolution, leaving the capital subject to shifting allegiances and outbursts of brutality. Many Parisians were caught in the middle, longing for stability but forced to pick sides or risk persecution.

---

## 7) The English Occupation of Paris

### Henry V's Invasion and the Treaty of Troyes

Against this backdrop of internal division, **Henry V** of England launched a renewed offensive in France, culminating in the famous victory at **Agincourt (1415)**. The English inflicted another disastrous defeat on French forces, reminiscent of Crécy and Poitiers. In the years that followed, Henry V methodically conquered territories in northern France.

The Duke of Burgundy, seeking revenge for the murder of his father, John the Fearless, formed an alliance with Henry V. This culminated in the **Treaty of Troyes (1420)**. Under its terms:

- Henry V would marry **Catherine of Valois**, daughter of Charles VI.
- Henry V was declared **heir** to the French throne, disinheriting the dauphin (the future Charles VII).
- Paris effectively fell under English-Burgundian control.

When Henry V entered Paris in 1420, many Parisians had no choice but to accept English authority. The city's gates were opened without a major siege, partly because of the strong Burgundian faction inside who saw the English alliance as preferable to Armagnac rule.

### Life Under English Control

During the English occupation:

- **Regent Bedford**: Henry V died unexpectedly in 1422, leaving his infant son as the nominal King of France. Henry V's brother, **John of Lancaster, Duke of Bedford**, acted as regent in Paris, trying to establish efficient governance.
- **Tight Policing**: The English, aided by Burgundian loyalists, policed the city strictly to root out Armagnac sympathizers.
- **Financial Strain**: Taxes remained high to fund the war effort. Parisians resented paying levies to a foreign occupant.
- **Propaganda**: Churches and public proclamations cast the English king as the legitimate heir, while the dauphin Charles was painted as a rebel.

Though Paris did not suffer outright destruction during this occupation, the city's population lived under constant tension. Loyalty to the French royal lineage still ran deep, causing clandestine support for the dauphin. Meanwhile, markets functioned, and everyday life continued—but under the watchful eye of English soldiers.

# 8) Joan of Arc and the Turning Tide

## The Emergence of a Peasant Girl

In 1429, a young peasant woman named **Joan of Arc** (Jeanne d'Arc) appeared at the dauphin's court, claiming divine guidance to drive out the English and crown Charles VII as the rightful king. Although many nobles were skeptical, her conviction won supporters. She led French troops to relieve the Siege of Orléans, achieving a remarkable victory that changed the war's momentum.

Joan's presence revived French morale. Cities that had been neutral or loyal to the English began reconsidering their allegiances. The dauphin was crowned at Reims Cathedral in 1429, symbolically affirming his claim to the throne as **Charles VII**.

## Attempted Liberation of Paris

Buoyed by success, Joan marched towards Paris in 1429, hoping to liberate the capital from English-Burgundian control. However, the attack on the city's fortifications faltered. Joan was wounded, and French forces failed to break through. Paris remained in English-aligned hands, at least for the time being.

Nevertheless, Joan's campaigns fractured the English aura of invincibility. Over the following years, the French, rallying behind Charles VII, chipped away at English positions. Although Joan was captured by Burgundian forces in 1430 and later executed by the English in 1431, her role in galvanizing French resistance proved pivotal. By the mid-1430s, the tide was clearly turning in favor of Charles VII.

## 9) The Reconquest of Paris

### Internal Shifts and the Treaty of Arras

The alliance between the Burgundians and the English grew fragile over time. The Duke of Burgundy, Philip the Good, eventually moved toward reconciliation with Charles VII in a series of negotiations that led to the **Treaty of Arras (1435)**. This treaty ended the Burgundian-English alliance, a major blow to English ambitions in France.

With the Burgundians no longer supporting the English cause, Charles VII gained a powerful ally. The stage was set for a reconquest of lost territories, including Paris. By 1436, French forces, with Burgundian neutrality or support, approached the city. The English occupation was no longer tenable.

### Joyous Return of Charles VII

In April 1436, **French forces re-entered Paris**. The English garrison, recognizing its weakened position, withdrew. Citizens who had quietly longed for the return of a French king welcomed Charles VII. Some accounts describe jubilant crowds lining the streets, although others caution that not everyone was equally enthusiastic.

Charles VII's restoration in Paris was a significant emotional and symbolic victory. He established his court there, reasserting royal authority. Though the war continued in other parts of France, the loss of Paris severely dented English legitimacy. Over the next two decades, the French methodically recaptured most English-held territories, culminating in the official end of the Hundred Years' War in 1453.

---

## 10) Socio-Economic Consequences for Parisians

### Population Shifts

Prolonged war and recurring waves of plague had deeply impacted Paris's demographics. By the mid-15th century, the city's population was lower than at the start of the 14th century, though recovery was underway. Formerly vacant houses were reoccupied, and peasants from the countryside migrated to Paris seeking opportunities in trade and crafts.

### Economic Strains and Rebound

Years of conflict disrupted trade routes, reduced agricultural output, and caused inflation. However, once Charles VII re-established a more stable administration, commerce began to revive:

- **Guild Reorganization**: Some guilds restructured their leadership, acknowledging the new royal officials.
- **Tax Reforms**: The crown tried to implement more systematic tax collection, reducing arbitrary levies.
- **Infrastructure Repair**: Bridges and roads around the city were mended, encouraging the return of merchants.

By the late 1450s, Paris showed signs of renewed vigor. The monarchy's administrative machinery, including the **Parlement of Paris**, helped standardize laws and judicial processes, giving merchants and citizens greater confidence in the future.

**Cultural and Educational Developments**

Even during the war, Paris retained some intellectual life centered on the **University of Paris**. Scholarship in theology and law continued, though at times overshadowed by political unrest. After the war, the university's role expanded again, drawing students from across Europe. Churches and religious houses rebuilt or renovated their premises, sometimes incorporating the era's late Gothic styles.

---

## 11) Political Shifts and the Legacy of War

### The Strengthening of the Monarchy

One of the war's paradoxical outcomes was the **strengthening of royal power**. Initially weakened by defeat and internal strife, the French monarchy ultimately emerged with greater authority. Charles VII and his successors reformed the military, establishing a more permanent army (the Compagnies d'Ordonnance) and reducing reliance on feudal levies. They also reined in powerful nobles who had exploited the kingdom's chaos.

In Paris, these reforms were palpable. Royal officials enforced the king's peace more effectively, and the city's strategic importance made it a centerpiece of political life. No longer was Paris as vulnerable to factional takeover as it had been during Charles VI's bouts of insanity.

## Changing Identities

The war fostered a deeper sense of French identity among Parisians. Shared suffering from foreign occupation, combined with the heroic narrative of figures like Joan of Arc, strengthened a collective spirit. Although France was still a patchwork of local loyalties, the idea of a unified French kingdom became more tangible.

At the same time, the English departure—and the continued possession of only Calais—meant that cross-Channel tensions would linger. The war's end did not guarantee lasting peace, but it did mark a turning point in how the French monarchy and its capital perceived their role in Europe.

## 12) The Human Cost of Warfare

### Destruction and Rebuilding

Although Paris was spared the worst physical devastation compared to some towns in Normandy or Aquitaine, the city still experienced:

- **Periodic Looting**: Enemy soldiers occasionally seized supplies or valuables in the suburbs.
- **Refugee Waves**: People fleeing rural raids sought shelter in the capital, adding strain to resources.
- **Damaged Infrastructure**: Ramparts, gates, and roads needed constant repair after bouts of unrest.

Rebuilding took place slowly, funded by taxes and new forms of royal revenue (like the **taille**, a direct tax on commoners). Skilled laborers found employment in construction, but the city's overall wealth took time to fully recover.

### Trauma and Memory

Chroniclers of the era recorded not just military events but also the emotional toll on ordinary citizens. Plague outbreaks returned periodically, compounding the misery. The memory of the English occupation lingered, passing into local legends and cautionary tales. Some families retained resentment toward neighbors who had collaborated with the enemy, reflecting long-term social scars.

Yet, the city's resilience showed in its eventual revival. By the late 15th century, Paris was once again a bustling center, setting the stage for an even more dynamic transformation in the decades to come.

---

## 13) Shifts in Daily Life: Women, Guilds, and Social Structures

### Women's Roles

The war and the plague had opened certain opportunities for women in Paris. Some ran shops or workshops in the absence of male family members lost to war or disease. Wealthy widows sometimes managed estates. However, traditional gender norms persisted; legal and economic rights remained limited. The story of Joan of Arc, though extraordinary, did not translate into broad social change for women's status.

### Guild Adaptations

During the war, guilds had to adapt to fluctuating demand and labor shortages. When peace returned, many guilds reorganized:

- **Regulating Standards**: To ensure high quality, guild masters tightened rules on apprenticeships.
- **Collaboration with Royal Power**: Guild leaders often cooperated with the monarchy, providing financial support in exchange for charters or privileges.
- **Emerging Trade Networks**: With the reopening of trade routes, Parisian goods traveled more extensively, while foreign merchants returned to the city's markets.

### Class Divisions

Economic recovery also revealed stark class differences. Wealthy merchants and nobles who had weathered the war with enough resources emerged even richer, buying property at low prices from those in distress. Meanwhile, many urban laborers continued living in cramped quarters, reliant on daily wages. Occasional outbreaks of discontent reminded the crown that poverty and inequality remained unresolved.

---

## 14) Diplomacy and International Relations after the War

### The End of the Hundred Years' War

Although historians date the end of the Hundred Years' War to 1453 (when the English lost Bordeaux), no formal peace treaty immediately concluded the conflict. Instead, the

English retained Calais, and tensions remained. Still, for Parisians, 1453 effectively marked the war's close, allowing the monarchy to focus on internal reforms and diplomatic efforts to stabilize the realm.

**Shaping Europe's Balance**

The war reshaped Europe's political balance:

- **England**: Weakened by the protracted struggle, England soon faced internal conflicts (the Wars of the Roses).
- **France**: Emerging more centralized, with Paris recognized as its unchallenged capital.
- **Burgundy**: Continued as a powerful duchy, at times allying or opposing the French crown for its own benefit.

Diplomacy in the later 15th century often took place in or near Paris, as foreign envoys came to negotiate trade or alliances. The city's role in European affairs expanded, foreshadowing the centuries of diplomatic significance that lay ahead.

# CHAPTER 8

THE RENAISSANCE IN PARIS – ART, ARCHITECTURE, AND ROYAL INFLUENCE

## Introduction

As the 15th century gave way to the 16th, France emerged from the devastation of the Hundred Years' War with a renewed sense of optimism. Under the leadership of successive kings, Paris began to absorb new ideas and artistic influences from Italy and beyond, heralding the onset of the **Renaissance** in France. While the full flowering of the Renaissance in Italy was already underway in the 14th and early 15th centuries, Paris's embrace of Renaissance culture grew more pronounced in the late 15th and early 16th centuries.

This chapter explores how Paris transitioned from a war-ravaged medieval city to a center of art, architecture, and royal patronage during the French Renaissance. We will look at the monarchy's role in driving cultural change, the architectural transformations that reshaped the city's skyline, and the everyday impact on Parisians. By the end of this period, Paris would stand as a prominent European capital, forging its own distinctive style that blended medieval traditions with Renaissance innovation.

## 1) Setting the Stage: France after the Hundred Years' War

### Charles VII's Later Reign and Louis XI

The reconquest of French territories concluded around 1453, granting a measure of stability under **Charles VII**. He used the final years of his reign to strengthen royal administration, building on the centralized structures developed during the war. Upon Charles VII's death in 1461, his son **Louis XI** continued these efforts.

Louis XI is sometimes called the "Spider King" for his intricate web of political maneuvers. He favored Paris as a seat of administration but also traveled widely across the kingdom. Under his rule:

- **Royal Power Grows**: The king subdued powerful nobles and extended his domain, further solidifying Paris's position as the kingdom's administrative hub.
- **Diplomatic Ties**: Alliances and marriages connected the French court to Italy and the Holy Roman Empire, exposing court circles to Renaissance ideas.

### The Seeds of Cultural Exchange

Although the Renaissance is closely identified with Italy, commerce and diplomatic relations spread new ideas northward. In the 15th century, French mercenaries and nobles fought in Italy or traveled there, returning with stories of advanced architecture, humanist scholarship, and refined court life. These influences gradually filtered into Paris.

Wealthy merchants and bankers in the city also imported Italian luxury goods—textiles, jewelry, and art objects—that hinted at changing tastes. While the majority of Parisians remained focused on daily survival, an educated elite began to explore the humanist ideals of classical learning and individual potential.

---

## 2) Charles VIII, Italian Campaigns, and Early Renaissance Influences

### The Italian Expeditions

When **Charles VIII** inherited the throne in 1483, he was initially a minor, with regents ruling in his name. Upon reaching adulthood, Charles VIII launched an ambitious campaign in 1494 to assert claims in the Kingdom of Naples, leading a French army into the Italian peninsula. Although this military venture was short-lived and met with fierce opposition from Italian city-states and Spain, it had profound cultural repercussions.

French nobles and soldiers who participated in these campaigns were exposed to the splendor of Italian Renaissance courts in Florence, Milan, and Naples. They admired the palaces adorned with frescoes, the advanced fortification designs, and the lively humanist debates. Even though the campaign ended without lasting territorial gains, returning nobles brought back more than just stories—they brought artists, architects, and a taste for Renaissance aesthetics.

### First Wave of Artistic Exchange

After Charles VIII's death in 1498, some of the Italian artists, artisans, and scholars he had invited stayed on in France. While the king's own contributions to the arts were cut short by his untimely demise, seeds had been planted:

- **Italian Architects**: Skilled builders and designers introduced classical elements—columns, arches, and symmetrical layouts—to French construction projects.
- **Scholars and Tutors**: Humanist educators found patronage in noble households, teaching children the revived classical curriculum.
- **Court Fashion**: Silk garments and more intricate clothing styles, reflecting Italian influence, started appearing at French court festivities.

Paris, though not the only cultural center (the Loire Valley courts also played a key role), began to see architectural and intellectual shifts that hinted at the wider Renaissance movement.

---

## 3) Louis XII and the Consolidation of Renaissance Influence

### Peace and Governance

**Louis XII** (r. 1498–1515) continued the Italian claims of his predecessors, with mixed success in military terms. However, he displayed an appreciation for the arts and for the consolidation of good governance at home. While he sometimes resided in the Loire Valley castles, Paris remained essential for royal administration.

During Louis XII's reign:

- **Reduced Tax Burden**: He tried to lessen the financial strain on the populace, hoping to bolster economic recovery.
- **Nobles' Power**: He negotiated carefully with the aristocracy, ensuring their loyalty while gradually centralizing government structures.
- **Religious Harmony**: France largely avoided the early religious upheavals that were beginning to stir in other parts of Europe, leaving the monarchy and Church aligned.

### Architectural Projects and Noble Patronage

Noble families, influenced by the king's mild approach and stability, commissioned **new residences** in and around Paris. Some older medieval hotels (townhouses) were redesigned with more open courtyards, symmetrical facades, and refined decorations. Although still retaining Gothic elements, these buildings often featured Italianate details—a sign of evolving tastes among the elite.

At the same time, local artisans in Paris began experimenting with new forms of decoration. Stonework became more ornate, and interior furnishings reflected growing prosperity. Renaissance motifs—acanthus leaves, mythological figures, and classical columns—appeared in private chapels and salons.

## 4) Francis I: The Apex of the French Renaissance

### A New Vision for Kingship

The true flowering of Renaissance culture in France is often associated with **Francis I (r. 1515–1547)**. Taking the throne after Louis XII's death, Francis I was young, ambitious, and captivated by the splendor he had seen in Italy. He aspired to rival Italian princes like the Medici in Florence, aiming to make the French court—particularly in Paris—a center of artistic brilliance.

Francis I's early reign included:

- **Battle of Marignano (1515)**: A victory in northern Italy that momentarily secured Milan for the French crown, furthering direct contact with Italian artists.
- **Patronage of Art**: Francis I extended invitations to prominent Italian luminaries, including **Leonardo da Vinci**, who spent his final years in France (though not primarily in Paris, his presence symbolized the monarchy's commitment to Renaissance ideals).
- **Royal Building Projects**: While the king favored the Loire Valley for châteaux like Chambord, he did not neglect Paris, sponsoring building work that reflected classical influences.

### The Royal Court in Paris

Though Francis I divided his time among various residences, Paris remained central to French politics. When the king was present in the capital, he held lavish **court festivities**, tournaments, and banquets that displayed the monarchy's wealth and artistic taste. Noble families followed suit, refurbishing their Parisian townhouses to keep up with royal fashion.

This environment fostered:

- **Literary Circles**: Poets, playwrights, and scholars gathered in the city's salons, sharing humanist ideas.
- **University Growth**: The University of Paris encountered new streams of thought, though conservative theologians sometimes clashed with more progressive humanists.
- **Diplomatic Activities**: Ambassadors from across Europe arrived to witness the grandeur of the French court, forging marriages and alliances that further integrated France into the broader Renaissance network.

---

## 5) Renaissance Architecture and Urban Changes in Paris

### Blending Medieval and Classical Styles

Medieval Paris had been a maze of narrow streets, timber-framed houses, and Gothic monuments. The Renaissance introduced **classical symmetry**, columned facades, and decorative details inspired by ancient Rome. However, this transition was not abrupt. Many structures combined Gothic verticality with Renaissance ornamentation—an architectural hybrid unique to France's early 16th century.

Landmarks that showcased this blend included:

- **Hôtel de Ville (City Hall)**: Though original medieval structures existed, expansions and redesigns in the 16th century brought more Renaissance elements.
- **Private Townhouses**: Wealthy nobles or high-ranking officials commissioned residences with courtyards, gardens, and decorative portals. Some displayed medallions, pilasters, and carved mythological figures around doorways.

### Improved Streets and Bridges

Francis I and his successors recognized the need for better infrastructure in the growing city. They funded repairs and expansions to major **bridges**, crucial for connecting the Right Bank, Left Bank, and the Île de la Cité. Narrow medieval streets were widened in certain areas, though the city's overall layout remained crowded.

Some projects aimed to beautify the capital. Fountains, statues, and public squares added to Paris's charm, signaling the king's desire to rival the magnificence of other European courts. Though these improvements progressed slowly, they set a precedent for more ambitious urban planning in later centuries.

---

## 6) The Influence of Humanism and New Learning

### Shift in Education

Humanism, emphasizing the study of classical texts in Latin (and sometimes Greek), gained momentum in Paris during the early Renaissance. Prominent humanists included **Guillaume Budé**, who championed Greek studies and advised Francis I on cultural matters.

At the **University of Paris**, some scholars embraced these new approaches, focusing on grammar, rhetoric, and moral philosophy with direct references to ancient Roman authors like Cicero, Seneca, and Virgil. This shift was not without controversy; conservative theologians worried about the potential erosion of scholastic methods. Nonetheless, the king's patronage gave humanism official backing, gradually integrating it into the city's academic life.

### Printing Press and Book Culture

The spread of the **printing press**, introduced to France in the late 15th century, revolutionized the availability of books. By the 16th century, Paris housed several printing workshops that produced texts in Latin and French, ranging from Bibles to humanist treatises. The easier circulation of printed works meant:

- **Literacy Growth**: Urban elites and educated bourgeois families had more access to reading material.
- **Religious Debates**: Though we avoid focusing on later religious conflicts in detail here, the printing press helped circulate reformist ideas, setting the stage for future tensions.
- **Cultural Exchange**: Books from Italy or Germany reached Paris, and Parisian editions were sent abroad, enhancing the city's role in Europe's intellectual networks.

---

## 7) Courtly Life, Fashion, and Festivities

### Aristocratic Refinement

During the Renaissance, aristocratic fashion in Paris reflected Italian influence—richly embroidered fabrics, elaborate headpieces, and more fitted garments replaced the looser medieval styles. Silk stockings, lace collars, and slashed sleeves revealing contrasting linings were popular among nobles. Tailors in the city thrived, supplying the demands of court life.

Festivals and **court entertainments** grew more sophisticated. Masquerades, allegorical pageants, and elaborate banquets were staged to celebrate royal weddings or diplomatic visits. Music at court increasingly drew on polyphonic styles from Burgundy or Italy, performed by skilled court musicians.

**Women of the Court**

Royal and noble women played significant roles in patronizing the arts, hosting salons, and influencing fashion. Figures like **Margaret of Angoulême** (Francis I's sister) were known for literary salons that gathered poets and thinkers, encouraging a blend of social grace and intellectual depth. While male-dominated structures persisted, aristocratic women could wield cultural influence in these courtly circles, shaping the tastes of the elite.

---

# 8) Economic Changes and Middle-Class Aspirations

**Rise of a Prosperous Bourgeoisie**

The Renaissance period witnessed the rise of a more confident **bourgeois** (middle-class) sector in Paris. Merchants, lawyers, and officials in royal service accumulated wealth, fueling demand for:

- **New Housing**: Comfortable townhouses with limited but recognizable Renaissance flourishes.
- **Education**: Middle-class families sent sons (and occasionally daughters) to receive formal schooling, aiming for social advancement.
- **Cultural Participation**: Wealthy commoners sponsored local artists or attended theatrical performances, mirroring the aristocracy's patronage on a smaller scale.

**Guilds and Trade**

Guilds continued to dominate trades and crafts in the city. However, new trades emerged with the Renaissance, such as **bookbinding, printing, fine tapestry weaving**, and specialized goldsmithing. The monarchy supported this diversification, as it enhanced Paris's reputation for quality craftsmanship.

Increasing commerce also led to **banking services** and moneylending becoming more normalized, especially as large building projects and expanded trade routes demanded significant capital. While older prejudices lingered, a more complex financial system gradually took shape, reflecting broader economic shifts that accompanied Renaissance innovations across Europe.

## 9) Religious Life and Early Rumblings of Reform

### Traditional Devotion in a Changing Era

Despite the influx of classical ideas, the Church remained a major institution in Paris. Gothic cathedrals and churches still dominated the skyline, hosting processions and festivals that defined the city's spiritual calendar. Many Parisians held tight to **traditional forms of piety**, venerating local saints and attending Mass regularly.

Yet humanist thought subtly influenced sermons and theological discussions. Clergy members trained in classical languages read the Bible in Greek or Hebrew, encouraging more scholarly interpretations. Some praised the union of faith and reason, while others worried these methods would undermine established doctrines.

### Prelude to Religious Tensions

In the early 16th century, **reformist ideas** from Martin Luther or other thinkers began trickling into Paris via printed pamphlets. Though the monarchy and the University of Paris officially condemned "heresies," some intellectual circles entertained moderate reform proposals (such as the call for a more personal, scripture-centered devotion).

During Francis I's reign, religious dissent remained relatively contained, partly because the king valued religious unity to maintain political stability. However, the seeds of future conflict were sown, foreshadowing the **Wars of Religion** that would erupt in the late 16th century.

## 10) Women Beyond the Court: Work and Social Roles

### Artisan Wives and Merchants

While courtly women gained visibility, most Parisian women lived outside aristocratic circles. In the middle and lower classes, women contributed to family livelihoods:

- **Markets and Shops**: Many assisted in shops or sold goods at market stalls, especially if they were married to a merchant or craftsman.
- **Guild Participation**: In certain guilds, widows could inherit membership from a deceased husband and run the business.
- **Household Labor**: For many, daily work involved cooking, cleaning, child-rearing, and helping with craft production at home.

Though society remained patriarchal, the urban environment offered slightly more opportunities than rural settings, allowing some women to build modest independent incomes.

### Literacy and Education

A small but growing number of urban women learned to read and write, especially if their families were part of the burgeoning bourgeois class. Private tutors or convent schools provided rudimentary education. Some noblewomen, like Margaret of Angoulême, wrote poetry or spiritual reflections, proving that educated women could influence literary culture. These cases, however, were exceptions rather than the norm.

---

## 11) The Patronage Network: Artists, Writers, and Scholars

### Court Commissions

Kings Francis I and Henry II (who succeeded him in 1547) attracted artists from Italy and beyond, many of whom traveled through or settled in Paris. They received commissions to design royal palaces, tombs, and interior decorations. Although major building projects like **Château de Fontainebleau** overshadowed some developments in the city itself, Paris still benefited from the presence of these skilled individuals.

Italian-born artists introduced techniques such as **fresco painting** and more advanced geometry in architecture. French sculptors and painters combined these influences with the Gothic tradition, creating a distinct "French Renaissance" style.

### Literary Flourishing

Poets like **Clément Marot** and later **Joachim du Bellay** or **Pierre de Ronsard** found a receptive audience at court and among the literate bourgeoisie. While they were more fully recognized in the mid-16th century, their earlier works laid foundations for a French literary identity that balanced classical inspiration with the French vernacular.

In salons hosted by aristocratic or bourgeois patrons, authors read their latest works. The printed book trade in Paris ensured these poems, essays, and translations spread widely, elevating literacy and cultural conversation across social strata.

---

## 12) Festive Life in Renaissance Paris

### Public Celebrations and Royal Entries

When the king made a ceremonial **entry** into Paris—either after a military victory or a major royal event—the city erupted in elaborate street decorations, pageants, and allegorical displays. Artisans worked for weeks to create arches, banners, and sculptures that glorified the king's achievements and the city's loyalty.

These occasions blended medieval traditions of communal celebration with Renaissance flair for classical themes. Mythological figures, references to ancient Rome, and moral allegories abounded. For most Parisians, such spectacles were a rare chance to witness grand artistry for free, fueling civic pride.

### Theatrical Performances

Traveling troupes performed **mystery plays** in church squares, a holdover from medieval drama. But under the Renaissance spirit, new forms of secular theater emerged. Writers experimented with comedic plots drawn from Roman playwrights like Plautus or Terence. Although large, permanent theaters would come later, the city was already experiencing a taste of dramatic innovation.

---

## 13) Shaping Social Hierarchy and Monarchical Image

### Nobles in the City

Traditionally, French nobles owned estates in rural areas and castles along the Loire Valley. However, during the Renaissance, many spent more time in Paris to stay close to the royal court. They rented or built mansions within the city, forming aristocratic neighborhoods where lavish parties and courtly intrigues took place.

The monarchy, in turn, regulated noble privileges. The king bestowed titles and offices, creating a network of dependency that helped control potential rivalries. Ambitious nobles recognized that success hinged on favor from the crown, making them eager participants in the city's cultural life.

## Monarchical Authority

From Charles VII's reassertion after the Hundred Years' War to Francis I's grand vision, the French monarchy became increasingly **centralized**. In Paris, royal justice, taxation, and administrative offices flourished, managed by a cadre of professional bureaucrats. The king leveraged Renaissance ideals of enlightened rulership to project an image of a cultured sovereign—firm in authority yet open to artistic and intellectual pursuits.

This approach did not eliminate social tensions. Tax burdens still weighed heavily on peasants and urban poor, and the growing disparity between rich and poor would eventually fuel discontent in subsequent centuries. But in the 15th and early 16th centuries, the monarchy's strong image largely overshadowed these undercurrents.

---

## 14) The Later Reigns: Henry II and Further Italian Influence

### Continuity of Renaissance Patronage

After Francis I died in 1547, **Henry II** continued much of his father's patronage. Married to **Catherine de' Medici**, he maintained strong Italian connections. Though Henry II's reign (1547–1559) is slightly beyond the earliest Renaissance wave, his policies and tastes solidified what Francis I had begun.

Court festivities grew ever more lavish, featuring Italian dancing masters, sumptuous costumes, and architectural triumphs. Meanwhile, Catherine's presence brought additional Italian ladies-in-waiting and chefs, influencing everything from palace etiquette to culinary fashions in the city.

**Shifts Toward Religious Conflict**

Henry II also intensified measures against Protestant doctrines, reflecting the monarchy's stance on maintaining Catholic unity. The seeds of the **Wars of Religion** would soon germinate, overshadowing the cultural renaissance in later decades. For the moment, however, Paris was still primarily a stage for Renaissance splendor and unified Catholic piety—an image the crown was keen to preserve.

---

## 15) Conclusion: The Renaissance Legacy in Paris

By the mid-16th century, Paris had undergone a transformation from the war-torn city of the early 1400s to a recognizable **Renaissance** center. The transition was not abrupt; medieval characteristics lingered in architecture and traditions. Yet the influx of Italian artists, the enthusiasm for classical learning, and the monarchy's grand building projects all reshaped the city's identity.

Key legacies of the Renaissance in Paris include:

1. **Architectural Hybridity**: Gothic and classical elements coexisted, creating a unique Parisian style that paved the way for later architectural evolutions.
2. **Royal Power and Cultural Patronage**: Kings like Francis I leveraged Renaissance ideals to enhance their authority, making Paris the focal point of statecraft and cultural brilliance.
3. **Humanist Scholarship**: The University of Paris and private salons explored new ways of thinking, blending faith and reason, ancient texts, and contemporary debate.
4. **Social Mobility**: Middle-class families found some avenues for advancement through commerce, education, and patronage, though rigid hierarchies remained.
5. **Precursor to Conflicts**: Alongside the cultural flowering, religious and social tensions grew quietly, soon to erupt in the later Wars of Religion that would shake Paris once more.

The Renaissance in Paris was thus both a **flowering of art and intellect** and a time of brewing challenges. As the city stood on the brink of the 1560s, it carried forward the Renaissance's achievements but also approached a period of internal strife that would test its resilience yet again. In the chapters that follow, we will explore how these tensions culminated in the **Wars of Religion** and the further transformation of the French capital.

---

# CHAPTER 9

## THE WARS OF RELIGION AND THE STRUGGLE FOR POWER

## Introduction

As the Renaissance blossomed in France during the early to mid-16th century, not all developments pointed to peace and harmony. Beneath the cultural achievements, religious tensions were steadily growing. The spread of Protestant teachings, particularly among the Huguenots (French Calvinists), threatened the unity of a kingdom traditionally bound by Catholic faith. The French monarchy, focused on maintaining religious uniformity, struggled to contain these divisions.

Beginning in 1562, a series of violent conflicts—collectively known as the **French Wars of Religion**—would engulf the kingdom for decades. This chapter examines how these wars erupted, why they endured, and, most importantly, how they reshaped life in Paris. As the capital and symbolic heart of France, Paris became a central stage for massacres, power struggles, and shifting allegiances. The very fabric of the city—its social hierarchy, religious devotion, political authority—came under intense strain. By the time the wars drew to a close in 1598, Paris had endured trauma that would leave lasting marks on its identity and pave the way for a new royal dynasty to consolidate power.

# 1) The Religious Climate under Henry II and Catherine de' Medici

## The Late Reign of Henry II

Following the cultural flourish under Francis I, **Henry II (r. 1547–1559)** continued many of the same Renaissance policies—promoting art, encouraging architectural projects, and reinforcing royal authority. However, he was also deeply committed to upholding Catholic orthodoxy. During his reign, the monarchy took harsher measures against heresy, issuing edicts that punished Protestant teachings. In Paris, the Parlement (high court) worked closely with the crown to prosecute suspected heretics.

Despite Henry II's repression, the Protestant movement continued to gain followers in urban areas, including segments of the bourgeoisie. Some Parisians, attracted by ideas of scripture-based faith and simpler worship, met secretly in homes or small gatherings, avoiding the watchful eyes of the authorities.

## The Influence of Catherine de' Medici

Henry II's unexpected death in a jousting accident (1559) threw France into uncertainty. His widow, **Catherine de' Medici**, became a dominant political figure as regent for her young sons, Francis II (briefly king from 1559 to 1560) and Charles IX (r. 1560–1574). Italian by birth and schooled in Renaissance court intrigues, Catherine favored a balance-of-power approach. She recognized that the kingdom's fragile unity depended on managing both Catholic and Protestant factions.

Paris, as the seat of the Parlement and various religious institutions, became central to Catherine's policy-making. She vacillated between conciliatory edicts aimed at granting limited tolerance to Huguenots and severe crackdowns when Catholic fervor rose. These inconsistent policies, along with the ambitions of powerful noble houses (like the Guise family, staunchly Catholic, and the Bourbon-Navarre line, which leaned Protestant), created a volatile atmosphere primed for open conflict.

---

# 2) The Outbreak of War (1562) and Initial Implications for Paris

## The Massacre at Vassy

In March 1562, soldiers of François, Duke of Guise, attacked a group of Huguenots worshipping in a barn at **Vassy**, in Champagne. This tragic event left dozens dead or wounded and ignited widespread outrage among Protestants. Seen as a blatant assault on their right to practice faith, the massacre pushed France from simmering tension into outright warfare.

News of Vassy raced through Paris, inflaming the populace. Catholic Parisians hailed the Guise family as defenders of the true faith, while the city's hidden Protestant minority feared for their lives. Royal authority, divided between Catherine de' Medici and her young son Charles IX, struggled to contain the ensuing chaos. Protestant nobles raised armies in the south and west of France, while Catholic lords rallied around the Guise family and other fervent supporters of Catholicism.

## Paris Mobilizes

Fearing Protestant uprisings, the royal government worked with Parisian guilds and local militia to secure the city. Gates were monitored, suspected heretics were arrested, and Catholic clergy preached sermons condemning the Protestant "heresy." Many Catholic citizens, already wary of the new doctrines, turned aggressive toward neighbors suspected of harboring Huguenot sympathies. Some small-scale violence occurred in the streets.

Economically, the city felt the strain: trade routes were disrupted by local skirmishes, while traveling merchants avoided Paris. Noble families who owned property in rural areas diverted resources to support their private armies. The monarchy scrambled for funds, imposing emergency levies that fueled resentment among commoners. Within months of the war's outbreak, Parisians sensed they were entering a prolonged period of instability.

## 3) Catherine de' Medici's Attempts at Conciliation

### The Edict of Saint-Germain (1562)

Recognizing the dangers of civil war, Catherine de' Medici and her advisors sought compromises. One effort was the **Edict of Saint-Germain (January 1562)**, which granted limited freedoms for Huguenots to worship publicly outside of town walls and privately within them. However, the massacre at Vassy occurred shortly after, effectively undermining this edict before it could calm tensions. The breakdown of trust between Protestants and Catholics grew deeper.

**Shifting Power Balances**

Catherine's strategy to balance rival factions sometimes led her to form temporary alliances with the Huguenot leadership, including influential nobles like the Prince of Condé and Admiral Gaspard de Coligny. At other times, she sided decisively with the Catholic Guise family. Each shift aggravated one faction or another. Parisian officials, mostly Catholic, often resisted any policy that seemed too lenient on Protestants.

The monarchy's inconsistency was magnified by France's political fragmentation: large swaths of the kingdom were under partial control of local magnates who pursued their own interests. While Paris remained a royal stronghold, its stability depended heavily on preventing full-scale Protestant uprisings in the surrounding regions.

---

## 4) St. Bartholomew's Day Massacre (1572): The Darkest Chapter

**Prelude to the Massacre**

By the early 1570s, attempts at religious compromise yielded only temporary lulls in fighting. The Third War of Religion ended with the **Peace of Saint-Germain-en-Laye (1570)**, which again granted concessions to Huguenots. To solidify this fragile peace, a royal marriage was arranged between **Margaret of Valois** (the French king's sister) and **Henry of Navarre** (a leading Protestant prince).

This wedding, held in Paris in August 1572, drew many Huguenot nobles to the capital. Catherine de' Medici and King Charles IX hoped the union would symbolize reconciliation. However, tensions within Paris were palpable. Ultra-Catholic groups disliked the growing influence of Huguenot leaders near the royal family. When a failed assassination attempt targeted Admiral Coligny—a key Protestant advisor to Charles IX—the atmosphere turned explosive.

**The Massacre Erupts**

In the early hours of August 24, 1572—**St. Bartholomew's Day**—violence erupted against prominent Huguenot nobles in Paris. What began as targeted killings of Protestant leaders quickly spiraled into a general massacre, as mobs roamed the streets, attacking anyone suspected of being a Huguenot. Over several days, countless Protestants were slaughtered. Although the exact death toll is uncertain, estimates range in the thousands in Paris alone.

King Charles IX, possibly under pressure from Catherine de' Medici and extreme Catholic advisers, either authorized or failed to stop the killings once they began. Parisians who remained loyal to the crown or who harbored deep anti-Protestant sentiment joined the frenzy. The Seine was said to be filled with bodies, a horrifying symbol of the city's descent into religious violence.

**Aftermath and Trauma**

News of the St. Bartholomew's Day Massacre sent shockwaves across Europe. Catholic hardliners praised the purge, while most foreign observers condemned it as a brutal breach of trust. Henry of Navarre (the groom at the royal wedding) narrowly escaped death by renouncing his Protestant faith, at least temporarily, under duress.

For surviving Protestants, the massacre revealed the monarchy's inability—or unwillingness—to protect them in the very heart of the kingdom. Paris became synonymous with anti-Huguenot fanaticism. Internally, the event eroded the notion that the crown could balance religious factions. Fear and bitterness deepened on both sides, setting the stage for continued wars.

---

## 5) Renewed Conflicts and the Catholic League

**Heightened Polarization**

Following the massacre, any semblance of trust between Protestant leaders and the royal court collapsed. The next wave of conflict escalated into the Fifth and Sixth Wars of Religion, with even more radical factions gaining prominence. In Paris, the Catholic populace and clergy often pushed for harsher measures to eliminate Huguenot influence entirely. Meanwhile, pockets of Protestant resistance formed in various regions of France, led by experienced military nobles.

**Formation of the Catholic League**

By the 1580s, an ultra-Catholic organization known as the **Catholic League** emerged as a dominant force in Paris. Headed by Henry, Duke of Guise (a nephew of the infamous Francis, Duke of Guise), the League wielded enormous influence in the city. It had widespread support among artisans, guild members, and the devoutly Catholic middle class who feared Protestant infiltration of the capital.

The League effectively set up a parallel power structure, challenging the authority of King Henry III (r. 1574–1589). Although Henry III was himself Catholic, he was seen by the League as too weak—and too conciliatory toward the Huguenots. The king's attempts to broker peace deals were viewed with suspicion or outright hostility by League leaders in Paris.

## 6) The War of the Three Henrys and the Siege of Paris

### Three Rival Leaders

By the late 1580s, France was plunged into the "**War of the Three Henrys**," referring to:

1. **Henry III** (the reigning King of France, Valois dynasty),
2. **Henry of Guise** (leader of the Catholic League),
3. **Henry of Navarre** (the Protestant Bourbon claimant to the throne, future Henry IV).

Paris was a flashpoint of this triangular conflict. The Catholic League held power in the streets, while King Henry III struggled to assert royal authority. Henry of Navarre, commanding Protestant forces and allied nobles, aimed to secure his rightful claim to the throne if Henry III died without an heir.

### The Day of the Barricades (1588)

Tensions exploded in May 1588 during the "**Day of the Barricades**." When Henry III attempted to bring royal troops into Paris to subdue League influence, the city's populace, led by the League, erected barricades in the streets. They forced the royal forces to retreat. Emboldened, the Duke of Guise entered Paris in triumph, hailed by many as the city's protector against a king who was increasingly unpopular.

Henry III fled the capital. The League took de facto control of Paris, setting up committees to govern neighborhoods. Sermons in major churches denounced the king as a traitor to Catholicism. The monarchy appeared on the brink of collapse—stripped of its capital and overshadowed by the charismatic Duke of Guise.

### Royal Assassination and Renewed Chaos

In December 1588, Henry III orchestrated the **assassination of Henry of Guise** at the royal chateau of Blois. This act shocked Paris: Guise was deeply revered by the city's Catholic majority. In retaliation, the League declared Henry III unfit to rule, branding him an enemy of the faith.

With no way to retake Paris on his own, Henry III reluctantly allied with his former foe, Henry of Navarre, uniting Valois and Bourbon forces. Their combined army marched on Paris in 1589, hoping to break the League's grip on the city. But before they could succeed, Henry III was himself assassinated by a fanatical monk. This chain of events left Henry of Navarre as the last Henry standing—his claim to the crown now undisputed in theory, but fiercely contested in practice by the League-held Paris.

# 7) Henry of Navarre's Struggle for Paris

### Henry IV's Claim

Upon Henry III's death, **Henry of Navarre** became **Henry IV** (r. 1589–1610), the first Bourbon king of France. Many parts of the kingdom accepted his legitimacy. But Paris, under League control, refused to acknowledge a Protestant monarch. Pro-League preachers declared him a heretic unworthy of the throne. Armed clashes continued, and the capital remained defiant.

For Henry IV, winning Paris was essential. He reportedly declared, "Paris is well worth a Mass," implying he might convert to Catholicism to secure the loyalty of his kingdom's principal city. Although he retained his Huguenot convictions privately, the realities of uniting France under a single crown forced him to consider a strategic conversion.

### The Siege of Paris (1590)

In 1590, Henry IV led forces to **besiege Paris**. Lacking consistent external support, the city began to suffer acute shortages of food. Reports of starvation circulated, with inhabitants reduced to eating horses, dogs, or worse. Yet the League's leadership, supported by Spanish troops and funds, held out stubbornly. Religious zeal fueled the resistance: many Parisians saw themselves as defending the true Catholic faith against a heretical king.

Henry IV's siege did not break the city's spirit, and the arrival of Spanish relief forces forced him to withdraw. Over the next few years, Henry IV combined military pressure with diplomatic outreach. He recognized that relentless war would devastate the country further and hamper any chance of reconciliation.

## 8) Henry IV's Conversion and the Reconquest of Paris

**"Paris Is Worth a Mass"**

In 1593, Henry IV publicly **converted to Catholicism** at Saint-Denis. While some die-hard Protestants felt betrayed, the majority of war-weary French citizens welcomed this move. For Catholic Parisians, this act removed their primary objection to recognizing Henry as king. The Catholic League, losing credibility and foreign support, began to fracture.

The conversion, albeit politically motivated, allowed Henry IV to approach the gates of Paris with a renewed claim of legitimacy. He offered general amnesty to League supporters, pledging to preserve the city's Catholic identity. By 1594, many former League loyalists accepted Henry IV as their rightful monarch, and his entry into Paris was largely peaceful.

**Reconciliation and Recovery**

Henry IV's arrival in Paris, in March 1594, was met with cautious relief. The capital's citizens, exhausted by famine and conflict, saw the Bourbon king's presence as a chance to rebuild. Royal officials quickly took steps to restore order, reopen trade routes, and strengthen the city's administration under the monarchy.

Still, not everyone in Paris fully trusted Henry IV. Some Catholics remained suspicious of his sincerity; some Huguenots lamented his conversion. But the majority recognized that only a stable crown could restore prosperity. Over the next few years, Henry IV worked tirelessly to unify France, culminating in the famous **Edict of Nantes (1598)**, which granted limited toleration to Protestants while affirming Catholicism as the state religion.

---

## 9) The Edict of Nantes (1598) and Its Effect on Paris

**Terms of the Edict**

The **Edict of Nantes** ended the major religious wars in France by establishing:

1. **Catholicism as the official religion** of the kingdom, with the monarchy's support.
2. **Civil and religious rights** for Huguenots in specific strongholds and regions, allowing them to worship freely and hold public office.
3. **Mixed tribunals** to settle disputes impartially between Protestants and Catholics.

For Paris, the edict confirmed the city's Catholic character—no Protestant worship would be allowed within its walls. Yet it offered a framework for national reconciliation, leading many Protestants elsewhere to lay down arms and rejoin public life under royal protection.

### Reception in the Capital

Many conservative Catholics in Paris found the edict too lenient, viewing it as an undeserved privilege for heretics. Some clerics preached against it, but the monarchy enforced acceptance. For war-weary Parisians, the prospect of peace trumped lingering hostility. Over time, the edict reduced large-scale violence, though animosities remained.

Economically, the city benefited from renewed trade and decreased military expenditures. Merchants once again traveled more freely, taxes stabilized, and guilds resumed peacetime production. The monarchy gradually rebuilt its authority, using Paris as the administrative heart of a recovering kingdom.

---

## 10) Transformations in Urban Life during the Wars

### Social and Demographic Shifts

Decades of warfare and periodic outbreaks of plague had affected Paris's population. Many had fled the city during the worst fighting, while others perished in sieges or political violence. Once peace took hold, rural migrants and returning refugees spurred a modest population rebound. Newcomers filled labor gaps in guilds and workshops.

Class divisions also evolved. Some noble families lost fortunes in the conflict, while enterprising bourgeois individuals profited from supplying armies or mediating negotiations. A handful of these commoners leveraged newfound wealth to purchase offices or land, merging into the lower ranks of the nobility—an ongoing phenomenon in early modern France.

### Religious Tensions and Devotions

Though open war ended, religious tensions lingered. Certain neighborhoods in Paris kept a close watch for any sign of Protestant gatherings. Processions celebrating Catholic saints or royal events often emphasized the city's Catholic identity, reinforcing communal unity. Churches that had been damaged or neglected were repaired, sometimes adorned with more elaborate decorations as a sign of renewed devotion.

However, pockets of discreet Protestant presence persisted. Merchants or artisans who quietly adhered to Huguenot beliefs navigated the city with caution, mindful of the edict's limits. Many preferred to live in areas where they could practice more openly, outside the capital's jurisdiction.

## 11) Political Reorganization and the Rise of the Bourbon Dynasty

### The Bourbon Ascendancy

With the death of the last Valois kings, the Bourbon line, starting with Henry IV, became the ruling dynasty. This marked a significant shift: the monarchy increasingly embraced practical governance over intense religious partisanship. Henry IV's priority was healing a fractured realm, and he used Paris as his base to extend royal authority more evenly across the kingdom.

Key measures included:

- **Centralizing Administration**: Royal councils and financial offices in Paris gained professional staff to manage taxes, justice, and military matters.
- **Infrastructure Investment**: Henry IV launched projects to improve roads and bridges around Paris, facilitating commerce and ensuring loyal communications with the provinces.
- **Courtly Splendor**: Although overshadowed by the tumult of war, the Bourbon court still patronized the arts, reflecting a lingering Renaissance spirit tempered by the memory of conflict.

### The Politique Approach

Henry IV's style exemplified the **"politique"** stance—those who believed that civil peace and strong governance outweighed religious dogma. Many of his closest advisors in Paris shared this outlook, focusing on pragmatic solutions to restore prosperity. They sought to moderate extremist voices on both sides, forging a royal bureaucracy that prized loyalty over confessional identity.

Some devout Catholics in the capital resented these changes, yearning for the fervor of the Catholic League days. Yet the majority, exhausted by chaos, came to value the stability that Henry IV's rule provided. The king's personal charisma, sense of humor, and paternal approach earned him the affectionate title "Good King Henry" among many Parisians.

# 12) Cultural Shifts and Intellectual Life Post-Conflict

### A Sobering Effect on the Arts

The Wars of Religion disrupted the cultural momentum of the earlier Renaissance. Patronage declined during the height of conflict, as funds were diverted to military needs. The once-thriving court festivals in Paris became subdued or purely propaganda tools. Many artists and writers had fled the city or struggled to find sponsors amid the turmoil.

Yet after 1598, a gradual revival began. Henry IV and his successors drew on the traditions of Renaissance patronage while also reflecting the more sober climate. Architecture in Paris took a practical turn, with emphasis on fortifications, bridges, and essential civic structures. Overly lavish projects were scaled down, mindful of royal finances.

### The University of Paris and Religious Debates

At the **University of Paris**, theological discussions continued, shaped by the war's outcome. Conservative faculty who had supported the League found themselves adapting to a monarchy that insisted on outward religious harmony. Meanwhile, some humanist scholars advocated for a measured tolerance, seeing the war as proof of the perils of fanaticism. Intellectual life in the city thus became a careful balance between upholding Catholic orthodoxy and acknowledging the new reality of limited Protestant rights.

Printing presses in Paris churned out pamphlets celebrating Henry IV's reconciliation efforts, along with moral treatises warning against the "sins of fanaticism." A small but notable circle of writers documented the horrors of the war, providing future generations with firsthand accounts of the city's darkest days.

## 13) The Assassination of Henry IV (1610) and Its Immediate Impact

### A Shocking End

Henry IV's reign ended tragically on May 14, 1610, when he was assassinated in the streets of Paris by François Ravaillac, a fanatical Catholic. The king's death sent shockwaves through the capital. Many Parisians had come to see him as the architect of national healing, and his loss ignited fears of renewed instability.

Henry IV left behind a nine-year-old son, Louis XIII. A regency under his mother, **Marie de' Medici**, took the reins of government. Although the wars were over, the memory of conflict remained fresh, and the monarchy's future seemed uncertain without Henry IV's unifying presence.

### Funeral and Mourning

Henry IV was mourned lavishly. Funeral processions in Paris displayed the city's deep affection for the monarch who had ended the wars. Church bells tolled, guild representatives donned mourning attire, and preachers delivered sermons celebrating the late king's virtues. Yet beneath this shared grief lurked anxiety. Parisians worried about the possibility of factional resurfacings or foreign meddling during the child king's regency.

In practice, however, the Bourbon hold on the throne remained firm. The wars had taught the nobility and the urban elites the high cost of chaos. They were not eager to return to open conflict. Thus, Paris once again braced for a new chapter, with hopes that the monarchy, even under a minor, could preserve the hard-won peace.

---

## 14) Reflections on the Wars of Religion's Impact on Paris

### A City Scarred yet Resilient

The Wars of Religion drastically altered Paris. The city had seen internal revolts (like the Day of the Barricades), occupations by radical Catholics, assassinations of kings and dukes, and brutal massacres. Family ties were torn apart by religious loyalties, and commerce suffered repeated disruptions. Yet through it all, Paris survived. Its institutions—guilds, the University, the Parlement—reemerged, albeit in a changed social and religious landscape.

**Emergence of Religious Boundaries**

While the Edict of Nantes brought official toleration to Huguenots, Paris itself remained a predominantly Catholic stronghold. The monarchy had learned the perils of letting extremist factions take the city hostage, and future kings would be wary of allowing any group to dominate the capital's streets again. Parisians, for their part, carried the memories of brutal acts like the St. Bartholomew's Day Massacre and the prolonged siege by Henry IV. These events shaped collective identity, reinforcing the city's self-image as a powerful political stage where matters of religion and sovereignty collided.

**The Dawn of the Bourbon Era**

Out of the ashes of civil war rose the **Bourbon dynasty**, with Henry IV's pragmatic kingship charting a new course. Though his rule ended abruptly, the blueprint for a more centralized, modern monarchy was laid. Future Bourbon rulers—beginning with Louis XIII—would expand on these foundations, further shaping Paris as the heart of an increasingly absolutist state.

Thus, the Wars of Religion represented both devastation and a turning point. They ended the centuries-long Valois lineage, ushered in the Bourbons, and left Paris more cautious about religious zealotry. The stage was now set for the next transformation: under Bourbon kings, Paris would steadily become a grand royal capital—one in which the scars of war would slowly give way to new architectural projects, administrative reforms, and cultural achievements.

# CHAPTER 10

## THE BOURBON KINGS AND THE SHAPING OF PARIS

## Introduction

With Henry IV's rise to the throne in 1589, the **Bourbon dynasty** claimed leadership over a kingdom still reeling from decades of religious conflict. Following the Edict of Nantes in 1598, France entered a period of relative calm. This chapter examines how the Bourbon kings—starting with Henry IV and extending through the early 17th century—reshaped Paris both physically and politically. Through urban planning, economic reforms, and royal patronage, Paris evolved into a more modern capital, laying the groundwork for further transformations in subsequent reigns.

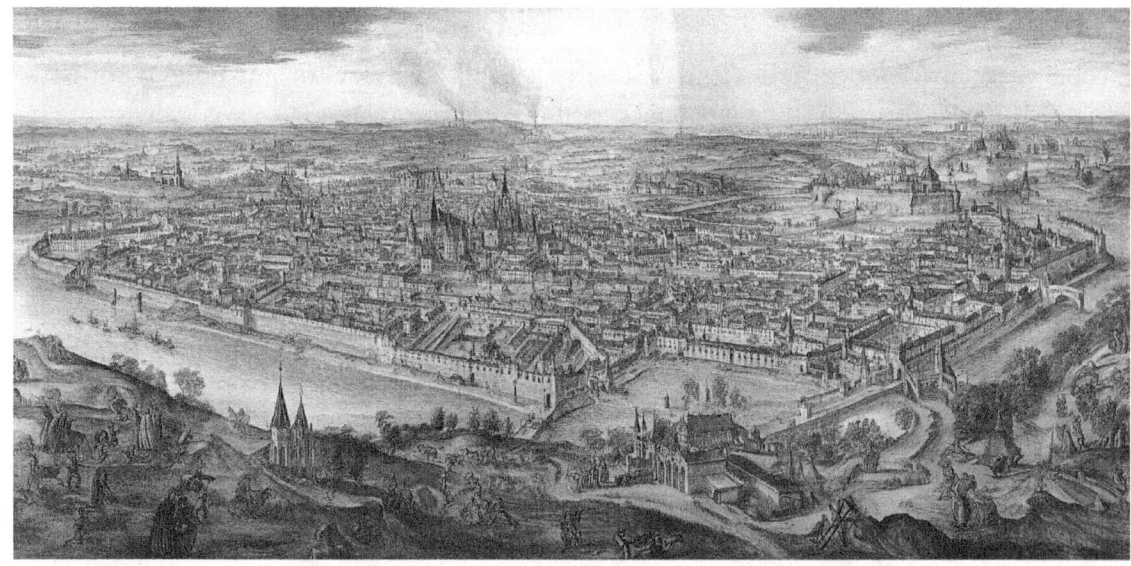

## 1) Henry IV's Reign: Healing a War-Torn City

### Stabilizing the Realm

When **Henry IV** re-entered Paris in 1594, he confronted a city still marked by siege and factional strife. Determined to heal wounds and restore prosperity, he enacted measures that balanced firmness and reconciliation:

- **Amnesty and Reconciliation**: Henry offered pardons to former Catholic League supporters, provided they accept his rule.

- **Maintenance of Catholic Character**: Despite his Protestant origins, Henry upheld Catholicism in Paris, honoring the city's majority faith.
- **Support for Commerce**: He lowered certain taxes, opened trade routes, and encouraged foreign merchants to return.

These initiatives helped quell lingering resentments. Parisians, weary of chaos, warmed to a monarch who demonstrated genuine concern for their well-being. Henry IV gained a reputation for strolling the city incognito, chatting with citizens—a stark contrast to the remote medieval kingship of earlier centuries.

**Economic Regeneration**

France had been economically devastated by the Wars of Religion. Henry IV appointed **Maximilien de Béthune, Duke of Sully**, as his chief minister to revitalize royal finances. Sully embraced mercantilist ideas: developing industries, promoting agriculture, and organizing state monopolies. Paris, as the kingdom's commercial hub, benefited from these policies:

- **Infrastructure**: Roads leading to the capital were improved, and the Seine's navigation was made more reliable.
- **Urban Markets**: With better supply lines, the city's markets stabilized in price and quantity, aiding guilds and artisans.
- **Population Growth**: Peace attracted rural migrants seeking opportunities, slowly boosting the city's demographic recovery.

While challenges persisted (poverty, high taxes, class disparities), Henry IV's consistent efforts fostered a more secure environment for Parisians. The monarchy's credibility recovered as well, fortifying the Bourbon claim to rule.

---

## 2) Transforming the Urban Landscape: Henry IV's Vision

**The Pont Neuf and Public Spaces**

Among Henry IV's lasting contributions to Paris was the construction of the **Pont Neuf** (begun under Henry III, completed under Henry IV). Despite its name meaning "New Bridge," it became the oldest existing bridge over the Seine in modern times. The Pont Neuf was revolutionary for having no houses built upon it, allowing open vistas of the river. It also provided convenient pedestrian paths and areas for vendors. Parisians quickly embraced it as a communal gathering spot—a place to stroll, gossip, and observe daily life.

Nearby, Henry IV commissioned improvements to surrounding quays, intending to enhance riverbank traffic and create more cohesive public areas. These open spaces hinted at a new appreciation for urban planning, contrasting with the congested, haphazard medieval streets in much of the city.

**The Place Royale (Place des Vosges)**

Henry IV also initiated the development of the **Place Royale**, later renamed the **Place des Vosges**. Built in the Marais district, it was among the first planned squares in Paris. Elegant houses with uniform facades surrounded a central public space. While some earlier squares existed, this project signaled a more structured approach to urban design, reflecting Renaissance ideas of symmetry and civic harmony.

The Place Royale became a fashionable address for nobility and wealthy bourgeois, setting a trend for future squares and boulevards. In time, these squares would serve as locations for markets, celebrations, and social gatherings. By shaping the city's public spaces, Henry IV's regime laid foundations for the more extensive transformations of the 17th century.

---

## 3) Fostering a Sense of Royal Authority

**Ceremonial Entries and Civic Rituals**

Just as earlier Valois kings employed grand entrances into Paris, the Bourbon monarchy refined these ceremonies to reinforce its legitimacy. Henry IV's triumphant arrival in 1594 was followed by periodic processions, often incorporating newly built landmarks like the Pont Neuf. Each spectacle reminded Parisians of royal power—yet with a new tone of paternal accessibility.

Royal baptisms, weddings, and visits by foreign dignitaries further displayed the king's central role in unifying the kingdom. The monarchy used these events to cultivate loyalty among guilds and local elites, who participated in elaborate pageants and gift-giving traditions.

**The King's Goodwill**

Henry IV was known for his down-to-earth manner. Parisians, especially the poorer classes, cherished anecdotes of him in disguise, visiting markets or conversing in taverns. While some stories may be embellished, they underscore a shift toward a more personal monarchy. This approach resonated well in a city still fragile from war. By appearing caring and involved, Henry IV kept potential unrest at bay.

Nonetheless, the monarchy did not cede any real authority. Paris remained the hub of royal administration: the Parlement enforced laws, financial officers collected taxes, and city officials answered to the crown. The monarchy's paternal style complemented, rather than replaced, centralized power.

---

## 4) The Assassination of Henry IV (1610) and Marie de' Medici's Regency

**A Shocking Event**

Henry IV's rule ended abruptly in 1610 when he fell victim to the assassin François Ravaillac. The king's death echoed the violent pattern that had haunted France for decades, though this time the impetus was less about wide-scale religious war and more about a fanatic's personal convictions. Still, the loss was deeply felt in Paris, where Henry IV had become a symbol of peace and reconstruction.

**Marie de' Medici's Regency**

Henry IV left behind a young heir, **Louis XIII**, only nine years old. His mother, **Marie de' Medici**, assumed the regency. Although her Italian background evoked memories of Catherine de' Medici's controversial influence, Marie attempted to maintain her husband's policies. She kept Sully on for a time, but political pressures soon led to his dismissal and increased reliance on favorites.

Marie's regency saw:

- **Noble Discontent**: High-born nobles resented her Italian advisors and questioned her authority.
- **Financial Strains**: War debts and lavish spending on court life required heavy taxation.

- **Continued Peace**: The kingdom did not descend back into religious war, thanks largely to the Edict of Nantes remaining in force.

Paris witnessed royal ceremonies that attempted to affirm the Bourbon line's legitimacy during Louis XIII's minority. However, many worried that factional rivalries could destabilize the city as in previous eras.

---

## 5) Louis XIII: Consolidation of the Bourbon Hold on Paris

### The King Takes Power

Louis XIII officially took control of government in 1617, ending his mother's regency. Initially, he struggled to assert himself against powerful nobles and influential ministers. Over time, with the aid of key advisors, he managed to stabilize his rule. The king's authority in Paris was reaffirmed through:

- **Symbolic Acts**: He demanded loyalty oaths from city officials.
- **Military Presence**: Small garrisons in and around Paris ensured that no single faction could seize the capital.
- **Centralized Administration**: Royal edicts continued to strengthen the chain of command from the king to provincial governors and city magistrates.

### Cardinal Richelieu's Emergence

The most significant figure to rise during Louis XIII's reign was **Cardinal Richelieu**. Appointed as the king's principal minister in 1624, Richelieu rapidly became the architect of royal centralization. Although his major reforms and conflicts (such as the siege of La Rochelle and the struggles with Habsburg Spain) are beyond the immediate scope of Paris's urban story, they indirectly shaped the city by:

- **Enhancing the Monarchy's Prestige**: Richelieu's diplomatic victories boosted Louis XIII's reputation, reinforcing Paris's status as the seat of a powerful kingdom.
- **Controlling Dissent**: Any potential rebellion in the capital was swiftly managed through Richelieu's network of spies and loyal officials.
- **Promoting Culture**: Richelieu understood the propaganda value of art and literature, sponsoring theatrical works and monuments that would eventually grace Paris.

Though the cardinal's influence will be more central in later chapters, his partnership with Louis XIII left an enduring mark, ensuring that Paris remained firmly under royal supervision rather than a battlefield of noble factions.

# 6) Infrastructure and Architectural Projects under Early Bourbons

## Continuity from Henry IV

Despite the political dramas of Marie de' Medici's regency and Louis XIII's early reign, the monarchy sustained some of Henry IV's urban projects. The Place Royale (Place des Vosges) was completed, offering a refined residential square. Streets near the Louvre and the Tuileries saw modest improvements to accommodate royal processions.

## Expansion of the Louvre

The Louvre, originally a medieval fortress transformed by Francis I and subsequent kings, continued its evolution under the Bourbons. Henry IV had initiated the **Grande Galerie**—a long wing connecting the Louvre to the Tuileries Palace. Work continued intermittently, reflecting the monarchy's ambition to forge a cohesive royal complex in the heart of Paris. Although progress was slow, each extension signaled the growing importance of showcasing the king's grandeur in architectural form.

## Religious Buildings and Restoration

The Catholic Church, still the dominant religious presence in Paris, also benefited from Bourbon patronage. Some parishes damaged during the religious wars received funds for restoration or new construction. Bishops and wealthy patrons sponsored altarpieces and chapels. French Baroque styles began influencing church interiors, foreshadowing the grand ecclesiastical structures that would later adorn the city.

However, these projects remained relatively modest compared to the monumental building sprees of later Bourbon reigns. The early 17th century was still a period of cautious consolidation, overshadowed by political maneuvering at court and the necessity of stabilizing royal finances.

## 7) Social and Economic Developments in Parisian Life

### Guilds and Market Revival

Peace brought renewed vitality to commerce. Merchant guilds flourished as foreign trade routes reopened. Paris's strategic location on the Seine once again attracted traders from Flanders, Italy, Spain, and beyond. Market halls, including Les Halles, bustled with produce and goods. The monarchy's tax reforms, though often burdensome, at least brought a semblance of predictability compared to the extortions of wartime.

Some artisans gained enough wealth to move into new neighborhoods or purchase small suburban estates. This period saw the slow emergence of distinct social strata within the bourgeoisie:

1. **Haute Bourgeoisie**: Wealthy merchants, financiers, and high-ranking royal officers.
2. **Petite Bourgeoisie**: Skilled craftsmen, shopkeepers, and lower-level officials.

### Aristocratic Presence and Noble Townhouses

Many nobles who had fought in the Wars of Religion or who were newly loyal to the Bourbons settled in Paris to remain close to the court. They built or renovated **hôtels particuliers** (private mansions) in districts like the Marais or near the expanding royal palaces. These aristocratic enclaves fostered a lively social scene—balls, literary salons, and court intrigues.

Over time, the city's layout started to reflect this socio-economic clustering. Wealthy quarters with broad streets, elegant squares, and refined architecture contrasted with crowded, poorer districts. The monarchy tolerated these social divides, provided the elites remained loyal and contributed to the kingdom's coffers.

---

## 8) The "Great Conspiracy" Fears and Policing the Capital

### Noble Intrigues

The Bourbon kings, mindful of how earlier monarchs lost control of Paris to factions, maintained rigorous surveillance. Occasional conspiracies by ambitious nobles or discontented courtiers reminded everyone of the capital's volatile potential. Spies and informants kept watch on taverns, public squares, and even church gatherings.

One such scare occurred in the early 1620s when rumors spread that certain nobles plotted to kidnap the young Louis XIII. Although evidence was thin, the crown cracked down quickly, detaining suspects and tightening restrictions on carrying weapons within city limits. Such measures underscored the monarchy's resolve to prevent another Day of the Barricades or a League-like movement.

**Reinforcing Public Order**

To bolster security:

- **City Militia**: The monarchy supported local militias, especially in high-risk neighborhoods.
- **Night Watch**: A more organized system of watchmen patrolled streets after dusk, reducing petty crime.
- **Legal and Judicial Reforms**: Courts were encouraged to deal swiftly with banditry or conspiracies. The Parlement of Paris, loyal to the king, served as a judicial backstop to enforce draconian sentences where necessary.

These actions contributed to the sense that Bourbon Paris was less tolerant of civil unrest than the city under the late Valois kings. Residents often welcomed stricter policing as a guarantee of stability, though it also reflected the monarchy's growing authority over daily life.

---

## 9) Cultural and Intellectual Life under the Early Bourbons

**The Legacy of the Renaissance**

While the Wars of Religion had dampened some Renaissance fervor, the thirst for knowledge and art did not vanish. Under Henry IV, modest patronage of artists and writers resumed. Louis XIII, though more reserved than his father, maintained a court culture that valued music, painting, and literature. The University of Paris continued to refine its curriculum, balancing scholastic traditions with limited humanist influence.

**Early Academies and Literary Circles**

Paris saw the emergence of small literary circles where nobles, clerics, and educated bourgeois met to discuss poetry, philosophy, and politics. A few informal **"academies"** formed, precursors to the more established academies that would appear later. Though overshadowed by Italy's flourishing academies, these gatherings represented the city's evolving intellectual scene.

Theater also took tentative steps forward. Public performances—some comedic, others moral or historical—drew crowds, though censorship was strict. Playwrights tested the boundaries of royal and religious tolerance, while the monarchy realized the potential of theater as a tool for shaping public opinion.

---

## 10) Everyday Life: Housing, Health, and Social Customs

### Housing Conditions

For the common people, the city's medieval structure remained largely intact. Many still lived in timber-framed houses, squeezed into narrow streets with limited sanitation. Water came from the Seine or communal fountains. Wealthier residents paid water carriers or had private wells. Fires were a constant worry, as were outbreaks of contagious disease.

Despite incremental improvements in some areas, Paris retained a patchwork feel. A grand new square or widened street might sit next to a maze of antiquated alleyways. Attempts to regulate building codes often fell short, hampered by corruption or reluctance to demolish older structures.

### Public Health Measures

The monarchy and city officials introduced sporadic measures to combat unsanitary conditions. After each serious plague outbreak, new ordinances required the removal of refuse from streets, the closure of certain markets to limit contagion, and the isolation of the sick. While these efforts had mixed success, they showed a growing awareness of public health's importance for a capital city.

### Social Customs

Religious observances remained central to public life. Processions on feast days brought neighborhoods together, while guilds often sponsored altars or chapels dedicated to patron saints. Festivals were moments of relief from daily struggles, featuring music, dancing, and sometimes comedic plays. For the lower classes, taverns and inns provided social outlets. Meanwhile, aristocrats and wealthy bourgeois hosted salon gatherings or attended court receptions.

---

## 11) The Catholic and Huguenot Dynamic in the Post-War City

### Edict of Nantes in Practice

Under Henry IV's successors, the **Edict of Nantes** remained legally in effect. However, in Paris specifically, Protestant worship was still prohibited within the city. Huguenots who chose to reside in the capital often had to keep a low profile or travel outside the walls to attend services. Despite these constraints, a small Protestant merchant class persisted, recognized for its role in trade and finance.

## Resentments and Toleration

Catholic preachers sometimes railed against the continued existence of Huguenot enclaves elsewhere in France, while more moderate voices urged unity and acceptance of the king's law. The monarchy generally upheld the edict, recognizing that revoking it could reignite civil war. Yet Protestants understood that their freedom remained conditional, resting on the crown's goodwill.

For many ordinary Parisians, religious unity felt natural after so many years of Catholic dominance and the trauma of the Wars of Religion. They focused on rebuilding communal stability. Over time, open hostility toward Huguenots waned, replaced by an uneasy coexistence maintained by Bourbon power.

---

# 12) Marie de' Medici's Legacy and the Rise of New Royal Favorites

## From Regent to Influential Queen Mother

Marie de' Medici remained a significant figure in Parisian politics even after Louis XIII assumed full power. She commissioned architectural works, most notably the **Luxembourg Palace**, inspired by her native Florence's palatial style. Although she often clashed with her son and Cardinal Richelieu, the queen mother's patronage helped develop a more ornate approach to building design in the capital.

## Court Factions and Favorites

As in all monarchical courts, factions jockeyed for influence over the king. Certain nobles or ministers gained the king's ear, shaping policies on taxation, foreign alliances, and city governance. Richelieu's ascendancy signaled a move toward more centralized control, but that did not eliminate smaller power struggles among courtiers. Gossip and intrigue remained staples of Parisian high society, occasionally sparking public scandals that the crown tried to hush.

---

# 13) Tensions Leading to the Later 17th Century

## Seeds of Future Conflicts

Though the Bourbon monarchy had largely pacified Paris by the mid-17th century, the concentration of power also sowed the seeds of future unrest. High taxes to fund wars in Europe weighed on merchants and peasants alike. Nobles who felt sidelined by Richelieu's policies or the crown's favoritism might consider stirring opposition, recalling the city's history of barricades and rebellions.

### The Shift Toward Absolutism

Louis XIII's reign, guided by Richelieu, laid important groundwork for **absolute monarchy**, where the king's authority would brook minimal challenge from nobles or religious factions. Paris was the stage for many symbolic acts cementing this principle. Ceremonies, arrests of dissenters, and the expansion of royal offices all signaled a monarchy less tolerant of opposition.

In practical terms, this meant that while Paris might occasionally grumble under heavy-handed governance, the prospect of overthrowing the crown seemed increasingly remote. The monarchy's control over the capital's militias, finances, and legal system fortified it against the kind of rebellions that once plagued the Valois. The city's experiences in the Wars of Religion taught both the monarchy and citizens the destructive cost of letting factional strife run rampant.

---

## 14) Assessing the Early Bourbon Impact on Paris

### Physical Evolution

From Henry IV's bold projects like the Pont Neuf and Place Royale to the incremental expansions of the Louvre and new aristocratic hôtels, Paris saw a significant facelift under the early Bourbons. These changes brought a measure of aesthetic cohesion, an emphasis on open spaces, and a taste for more refined facades—a departure from purely medieval design. While not a complete urban overhaul, these initiatives laid the basis for grander transformations in later reigns.

### Political and Social Stabilization

Perhaps the most crucial legacy was the **stabilization** of royal authority in Paris. The monarchy had learned from the Wars of Religion that losing control of the capital risked catastrophic consequences. Henry IV, and then Louis XIII with Richelieu, ensured that the capital stayed firmly under the Bourbon banner, employing a mix of reconciliation, strategic policing, and symbolic gestures of royal care.

Economically, the city rebounded enough to see growth in trade, guild activity, and population—though social inequalities persisted. Parisians generally appreciated the relative calm, recalling the horrors of the preceding century. The old nightmares of religious massacres and barricaded streets gradually faded into memory, replaced by a cautious acceptance of Bourbon rule.

---

# CHAPTER 11

**THE 17TH CENTURY – LOUIS XIII, RICHELIEU, AND THE SEEDS OF ABSOLUTISM**

## Introduction

By the early 17th century, France had emerged from the Wars of Religion with a new ruling dynasty, the Bourbons. Under Henry IV, the kingdom regained a measure of stability, and Paris began to rebuild from the chaos of previous decades. After Henry IV's assassination in 1610, his son **Louis XIII** inherited a realm still reconciling religious divisions and wrestling with powerful aristocratic factions. Over the next several decades, Louis XIII and his principal minister, **Cardinal Richelieu**, would lay foundations for what became known as *absolutism*—a form of monarchy in which the king wielded near-total authority over governance.

In this chapter, we examine how Louis XIII and Richelieu consolidated power, shaped Paris's political and cultural life, and planted the seeds of a highly centralized state. Their partnership would have lasting consequences for the French capital—reinforcing its role as the administrative heart of the kingdom and a symbolic seat of royal might. We will look at how the monarchy dealt with rebellious nobles, strengthened bureaucratic institutions, used culture and ceremony to promote authority, and navigated religious challenges. By the end of Louis XIII's reign, Paris stood on the threshold of an even grander transformation—one that his successor, **Louis XIV**, would bring to fruition.

# 1) The Early Years of Louis XIII's Reign

### From Regency to Personal Rule

When Henry IV died in 1610, his son Louis XIII was only nine years old. His mother, **Marie de' Medici**, served as regent. Chapter 10 briefly discussed the regency, but let us delve deeper into how it shaped Paris. Marie's reliance on Italian favorites, her sporadic conflicts with influential nobles, and her lavish court spending created an atmosphere of intrigue in the capital. Although she generally maintained her late husband's policies of religious toleration and economic revival, tensions simmered just beneath the surface.

In 1614, Louis XIII turned thirteen—technically old enough to rule in name—but real power still lay with Marie de' Medici and her advisers. Many Parisians watched anxiously, recalling how the monarchy's weakness had previously led to civil strife. Urban militias, guild leaders, and city magistrates were prepared to support the crown, but only if it kept the peace and protected trade. They recognized that stability in Paris hinged on avoiding another destructive factional conflict like the Wars of Religion.

By 1617, the young king seized a measure of control, orchestrating the **"coup of 1617"** in which he exiled or eliminated his mother's closest advisors. He placed key government functions in the hands of more trusted ministers. This step marked Louis XIII's initial move toward personal authority, even if he still lacked a commanding presence. Yet it foreshadowed the kind of strong rule that would become more evident later in his reign, especially once Cardinal Richelieu emerged as a guiding force.

### Challenges to the Crown

Despite a shift toward Louis XIII's personal governance, the monarchy faced recurring challenges:

1. **Noble Discontent**: High-born aristocrats, sometimes resentful of an adolescent king, sought to reassert their regional influence. They occasionally conspired to pressure the crown or even raised small armies.
2. **Financial Strains**: Henry IV's policies had boosted the economy, but war debts remained. Taxation weighed heavily on both rural peasants and the urban bourgeoisie, including many in Paris.
3. **Religious Tension**: While the Edict of Nantes (1598) still held, certain ultra-Catholic factions pressured the crown to revoke or undermine Huguenot rights. Huguenots, on the other hand, maintained their fortresses in some provinces, wary of persecution.

Paris was shielded from some of these immediate frictions because it was staunchly Catholic and loyal to the Bourbons. Nonetheless, the city's notables paid close attention to royal policy shifts, aware that a renewed outbreak of disorder would disrupt commerce and daily life. The monarchy needed a unifying direction—something that would come in large part through the genius and iron will of Cardinal Richelieu.

## 2) The Rise of Cardinal Richelieu

### Richelieu's Background and Entry to Court

**Armand Jean du Plessis, Cardinal Richelieu** (1585-1642) was initially a bishop of Luçon, then a secretary of state, before fully rising to prominence under the patronage of Marie de' Medici. He gained a reputation for political acumen, skillful diplomacy, and an unwavering sense of the crown's interests. In 1624, Louis XIII appointed Richelieu as chief minister, granting him broad authority to manage both domestic and foreign affairs.

Richelieu's ascension coincided with a period of heightened noble intrigues. Some aristocrats still hoped to exploit the king's perceived inexperience. Richelieu, however, saw these challenges as opportunities to strengthen the monarchy, systematically dismantling the feudal privileges that allowed nobles to raise private armies or defy royal orders. He recognized that controlling Paris—financially, militarily, and symbolically—was vital to success.

### Goals and Strategy

Richelieu's overarching strategy involved three pillars:

1. **Curbing Noble Power**: By centralizing royal authority, he aimed to prevent a recurrence of the factional violence that had torn France apart during the Wars of Religion. He demanded obedience to the king above all else.
2. **Undermining Huguenot Political Autonomy**: While not bent on religious persecution per se, Richelieu believed that Huguenot fortresses and independent enclaves posed a direct threat to the monarchy's unity. He sought to confine Huguenots to religious rights rather than political or military privileges.
3. **Elevating France on the European Stage**: He used alliances, war, and diplomacy to challenge Habsburg dominance (particularly in Spain and the Holy Roman Empire). This required a robust administrative state, funded by taxes and loyal to the crown, with Paris serving as the administrative hub.

Richelieu's motto—"Raisons d'État" (Reasons of State)—summed up his willingness to override local or personal interests for the sake of France's sovereign power. Within Paris, this translated to a rigorous extension of royal bureaucracy and an intolerance for subversive activities. He expanded the network of intendants (royal officials) and increased oversight of city governance, ensuring that no local or noble faction could seize control.

## 3) Transforming Governance in Paris: Centralization and Control

### Bolstering the Royal Bureaucracy

Paris, as the kingdom's capital, housed many of the central organs of administration:

- **The Parlement of Paris**: The highest court of justice in northern France.

- **Financial Departments**: Responsible for collecting taxes (including the gabelle on salt and the taille on land) and funding the crown's policies.
- **Provost and City Officials**: Managed day-to-day municipal issues like policing, markets, and basic infrastructure.

Richelieu systematically installed loyal personnel in these offices or coerced existing ones to serve royal agendas. He introduced or reinforced the role of **intendants**, who reported directly to the crown and could bypass local authorities. Although the intendants were more influential in the provinces than in Paris itself, they still impacted how funds and laws were administered in the capital, tying the city's financial life more tightly to state policy.

**Surveillance and Censorship**

Fearing conspiracies, Richelieu bolstered surveillance within Paris. Street informants, court spies, and *lettres de cachet* (sealed warrants) allowed swift action against suspected traitors. Press censorship tightened. Printers and booksellers in the city faced scrutiny, and any publication deemed seditious could lead to arrest. While the monarchy had exerted control over printing since the 16th century, Richelieu took this to new heights—particularly when it came to criticizing state policies.

Despite such constraints, Paris remained a vibrant center of pamphleteering, especially among intellectual circles. Some underground tracts criticized the cardinal's methods or called for greater aristocratic freedom. Richelieu responded with selective crackdowns, aiming to deter serious threats without suffocating the intellectual life that also contributed to France's prestige.

**Showcases of Royal Justice**

Richelieu understood the power of spectacle in reinforcing obedience. High-profile trials or executions of rebellious nobles occurred in Paris, underscoring that no rank was above the law (i.e., the king's law). One notable example was the arrest and eventual execution of **Henri de Montmorency** in 1632, though carried out in Toulouse. Parisians followed the case closely, seeing it as a stark warning. If a prestigious peer of France could be punished, lesser nobles had even fewer illusions of invulnerability.

---

## 4) Religious Policies: Eroding Huguenot Political Power

### Huguenot Strongholds and Rebellions

Though the Edict of Nantes granted Protestants specific protections, many Huguenot communities enjoyed semi-autonomous governance, especially in regions like

Languedoc, Béarn, and Saintonge. They maintained their own defensive fortifications and militias, a vestige of the Wars of Religion. Louis XIII and Richelieu deemed this unacceptable—arguing that all fortified places must bow to the king's unified authority.

The monarchy confronted Huguenot rebellions directly. Between 1621 and 1629, a series of campaigns targeted fortified towns that resisted royal directives. The most famous example was the **Siege of La Rochelle (1627–1628)**, a major Huguenot port. Richelieu personally oversaw the siege, which ended with the capitulation of La Rochelle's population, drastically reducing Huguenot political autonomy.

**Impact on Parisian Protestants**

Within Paris, Huguenot worship remained officially prohibited, as it had been since the Wars of Religion. The city's Protestant population was relatively small and cautious. Although the Edict of Nantes remained on the books, the monarchy's renewed emphasis on Catholic unity discouraged open displays of Protestant faith. Some wealthy Protestant merchants discreetly conducted business in the capital but traveled outside its walls for religious services.

Religious tensions in Paris were more subdued than in earlier decades. Most citizens, having endured previous conflicts, welcomed the monarchy's firm stance if it meant preventing another descent into civil war. In time, however, the monarchy's approach—particularly under Richelieu—paved the way for a more sweeping revocation of Huguenot rights under Louis XIV. For now, though, Paris essentially functioned as a Catholic stronghold, with minimal open Huguenot presence.

## 5) War and Diplomacy: France on the European Stage

### The Thirty Years' War Context

Under Richelieu's guidance, France played a complex role in the **Thirty Years' War (1618–1648)**, a massive conflict primarily centered in the Holy Roman Empire. Although initially hesitant to intervene directly, Richelieu recognized that weakening Habsburg power served France's interests. By allying with Protestant states in Germany (despite France's Catholic identity), he aimed to encircle and diminish Spanish and Austrian Habsburg influence.

Paris was the nerve center for these diplomatic maneuvers. Ambassadors from various European courts thronged the city, negotiating with Richelieu's envoys. The monarchy used propaganda in the capital's churches and printing presses to justify policies that might have seemed contradictory—like a Catholic kingdom supporting Protestant princes abroad.

### Financing Military Engagements

Waging war on such a scale required substantial funds. Richelieu raised taxes, levied new duties, and borrowed from wealthy financiers—many of whom were based in Paris. The city's merchants profited from government contracts to supply armies, though the general population felt the burden of increased taxes. Nonetheless, the expansion of war-related commerce boosted certain sectors, like armaments, textiles, and logistics. Over time, the monarchy's military successes in the 1630s and early 1640s enhanced its prestige, reaffirming Paris's position as the capital of a formidable power.

---

## 6) Cultural and Intellectual Climate under Richelieu and Louis XIII

### Royal Patronage of the Arts

Despite Richelieu's heavy focus on political and military affairs, he did not neglect cultural patronage in Paris. He recognized that a flourishing cultural scene elevated France's international status. Together with Louis XIII, he supported the arts in several ways:

1. **Founding the Académie Française (1635)**: One of Richelieu's lasting legacies was establishing an academy dedicated to standardizing and preserving the French language. This institution would gather prominent writers and scholars, shaping literary norms for centuries.

2. **Promotion of Theater**: Richelieu sponsored playwrights and built the **Palais-Cardinal** (later renamed the **Palais-Royal**) in Paris, which included a private theater. Encouraged by this patronage, dramatists like Corneille rose to prominence, heralding the beginnings of French classical drama.
3. **Support for Architecture**: In addition to major state projects, Richelieu financed building initiatives in the city, including expansions of the Louvre. He also constructed his own grand residence, which further exemplified the cardinal's taste and power.

Louis XIII himself had a passion for music and choral compositions, fostering the tradition of royal orchestras. These cultural expressions found receptive audiences among Paris's nobility and emerging bourgeois classes, who sought to emulate royal tastes. Over time, the city's identity as a cultural nexus took firmer root.

**Scientific and Philosophical Currents**

The 17th century was also an era of burgeoning scientific inquiry in Europe. Although the fullest flowering of the "Scientific Revolution" would appear more vividly later in the century, seeds were planted during Louis XIII's reign. In Paris, intellectual circles discussed new mathematical and astronomical ideas. Jesuit colleges and the University of Paris taught both Aristotelian and updated scientific concepts, albeit cautiously, mindful of Church orthodoxy.

René Descartes, a pivotal figure in French philosophy and mathematics, visited Paris on multiple occasions, though his major works and most radical ideas matured outside the capital. Nonetheless, the city's environment—shaped by Richelieu's emphasis on reason of state and subtle acceptance of intellectual diversity—allowed philosophical discourses to gather steam. While strict censorship sometimes suppressed unorthodox viewpoints, the overall intellectual climate was more curious than in earlier epochs of religious strife.

---

# 7) Urban and Social Developments in 17th-Century Paris

## Demographic Growth and Neighborhoods

During Louis XIII's reign, Paris's population continued to climb, recovering from the devastations of the Wars of Religion. Estimates vary, but many historians suggest the city housed over 300,000 inhabitants by the 1640s, making it one of Europe's largest urban centers. New arrivals came from rural areas seeking work, or from smaller towns hoping to participate in the capital's commerce and royal patronage system.

Neighborhoods began to reflect evolving social stratification. The **Marais district** housed many aristocratic mansions (hôtels particuliers), while merchants and artisans clustered near Les Halles, the Rue Saint-Denis, and other commercial thoroughfares. Working-class districts, often crowded and poorly maintained, spread on the outskirts of the old city walls. The monarchy, preoccupied with controlling strategic points, cared less about improving living conditions in poorer quarters, leaving them prone to fires and epidemics.

**Daily Life and Social Customs**

Parisian society was heavily influenced by rank:

- **Nobles**: Many frequented the royal court or built impressive residences in the city. Some engaged in elaborate social rituals, from formal receptions to masked balls.
- **Bourgeoisie**: This rising class encompassed wealthy merchants, financiers, lawyers, and royal office-holders. Their education and resources allowed them to emulate certain aristocratic customs, though true nobles often guarded their status jealously.
- **Artisans and Laborers**: They worked in guild-regulated trades—baking, tailoring, metalworking, carpentry—and formed the backbone of the city's economy.
- **Urban Poor**: Large numbers struggled to survive through precarious day-labor, peddling, or begging. The Church provided limited charity, but the monarchy's social safety net was minimal.

Religious feasts, public executions, and market days punctuated daily rhythms. Despite Richelieu's policing, petty crime and prostitution thrived in certain districts. On the other hand, open factional violence, such as that seen in the League era, was now rare. Citizens valued the stability that Richelieu and Louis XIII's governance provided, even if it meant accepting tighter royal control.

---

## 8) Noble Resistance and the Day of the Dupes

**Court Intrigues and Conflicts**

No matter how powerful a minister might be, aristocrats continued to maneuver for influence. Richelieu's concentration of authority and his sometimes-arrogant manner rubbed many nobles the wrong way. The queen mother, Marie de' Medici, felt sidelined and, at times, openly opposed the cardinal. Various aristocratic cliques formed to challenge Richelieu's dominance, believing they could sway Louis XIII to dismiss him.

One famous episode illustrating these tensions was the **Day of the Dupes (November 1630)**. Marie de' Medici attempted to convince Louis XIII that Richelieu was harming the kingdom. The king seemed initially receptive, causing rumors that Richelieu would be dismissed. However, the next day, Louis XIII reaffirmed his trust in the cardinal, effectively branding the opposition as dupes. Marie de' Medici was exiled, and Richelieu's position became more unassailable than ever.

**Consequences for Paris**

The Day of the Dupes showed how palace dramas could send ripples through Paris. Noble families who backed Marie de' Medici found themselves temporarily out of favor, losing privileges and possibly facing financial ruin. The monarchy's swift resolution of the crisis reassured many Parisians who feared that further aristocratic infighting might lead to unrest in the streets. Richelieu's victory cemented the image of a centralized government where the king and his minister would not tolerate factional sabotage.

## 9) Richelieu's Architectural Footprint: The Palais-Cardinal

**A Grand Personal Residence**

Though overshadowed by the Louvre or the Tuileries, Richelieu's own palace in Paris symbolized his stature. He constructed and expanded the **Palais-Cardinal** near the Louvre, replete with elegant gardens, galleries, and a private theater. Upon Richelieu's death, the building was bequeathed to the crown and renamed the **Palais-Royal**. It would become an important royal and later public space in the capital.

The Palais-Cardinal showcased Richelieu's refined artistic taste. Influences from Italian Baroque and French classicism merged in its architecture. Lavish receptions there not only expressed the cardinal's personal wealth but also served as an extension of state ceremony, reinforcing the monarchy's prestige. Foreign ambassadors who visited were impressed (or intimidated) by the cardinal's power, manifested in architectural splendor. This practice of using grand residences to project authority would greatly expand under future reigns.

**The Cardinal's Tomb and Legacy**

Richelieu's death in 1642, just a year before Louis XIII's own demise, prompted the creation of an elaborate tomb in the Sorbonne's chapel, a structure he had also helped restore and expand. Though not open for general public viewing in the same manner as royal tombs at Saint-Denis, it symbolized how an extraordinary minister could leave a lasting imprint on Paris's religious and cultural landscape. In time, historians and visitors alike would note the cardinal's influence not just on French statecraft but also on the capital's physical form.

---

## 10) The Final Phase of Louis XIII's Reign

**Health Decline and Succession**

By the early 1640s, Louis XIII's health was failing. He suffered from chronic illnesses, which, combined with personal austerity, gave him a somber demeanor. Yet the monarchy's success in consolidating power was clear. Richelieu's policies had weakened internal opposition, funded wars against the Habsburgs, and laid strong administrative foundations.

In 1643, Louis XIII died. His heir, **Louis XIV**, was only five years old. The monarchy faced yet another regency—this time under **Anne of Austria**, Louis XIII's widow. While the general structure of centralized governance remained in place, the transition could still be risky. Nobles might again test the monarchy's strength, and foreign conflicts demanded continued attention.

**Paris at a Crossroads**

Paris had grown accustomed to strong rule under Richelieu and Louis XIII. The city appreciated the stability that replaced the chaos of earlier decades, though heavy taxes and strict policing were resented. Culturally, the capital blossomed through theaters, academies, and architectural enhancements. Yet the monarchy's victory over noble challenges and religious dissent also meant a narrower path for political participation. Absolutism was on the rise.

As Parisians mourned Louis XIII, many wondered how a child king and a new regent would sustain the kingdom's momentum. The seeds planted by Richelieu—intendant-based administration, a strong central army, and subdued nobility—would soon face a trial by fire in the upcoming **Fronde** rebellions. But the basic blueprint for an absolute monarchy was set, ready to be inherited and perfected by the young **Louis XIV**.

---

## 11) Social Stratification and the Seeds of Discontent

### Deepening Class Divisions

While the monarchy showcased unity, stark inequalities persisted in Parisian society. The aristocracy and high-ranking bourgeois basked in new royal offices or profitable financial ventures, often enjoying splendid urban dwellings. Meanwhile, the lower classes struggled with food prices, wage stagnation, and outbreaks of plague. Overcrowding in poorer districts fostered resentment that could spark riots under the right conditions.

Religious charity and guild-based mutual aid offered some relief, but it was not enough to eliminate poverty. The monarchy's focus on maintaining order through policing and censorship rather than structural reform meant that social tensions smoldered. Some bourgeois individuals, irritated by taxes on commerce, quietly criticized the crown, but few dared open defiance under Richelieu's watchful eye.

### Rise of Office-Holding

An important phenomenon was the purchase of *venal offices*. Wealthy bourgeois families could buy hereditary positions in the judiciary or tax collection systems. This practice helped the crown raise funds but also blurred lines between nobility and bourgeois. Families that acquired offices gained prestige and partial exemption from certain taxes, fueling social mobility on one hand and nobiliary resentment on the other.

Such office-holding families often shaped urban governance in Paris. By the end of Louis XIII's reign, a new stratum of "nobles of the robe" emerged—legally noble due to offices in the Parlement or other royal councils. Traditional sword nobles, who prided themselves on military lineage, often disdained these upstarts. Despite the monarchy's attempt to unify them all under one loyalty, the friction between old and new elites would echo through future conflicts like the Fronde.

---

# 12) The Cultural Legacy of Louis XIII and Richelieu in Paris

## Literature and the Theatrical Scene

Theater had been part of Parisian culture for centuries, but Richelieu's patronage made it increasingly prestigious. Authors such as **Pierre Corneille** found favor, crafting dramatic works that often celebrated heroic ideals or probed moral dilemmas relevant to state power. Corneille's *Le Cid* (1637) famously stirred controversy over questions of honor, duty, and romantic love—topics resonant with the aristocracy's chivalric self-image. The public debates surrounding the play, including official judgments from the newly founded Académie Française, underscored how literary works intersected with state authority.

Meanwhile, smaller theater troupes entertained broader audiences in makeshift venues around the city. Farces, comedies, and religious plays coexisted, reflecting Paris's diverse tastes. Street performances and puppet shows drew commoners, while noble families attended refined productions in private halls. This vibrant scene planted the seeds for a thriving theater culture that would only expand under Louis XIV.

## The Académie Française and Language Prestige

Richelieu's founding of the **Académie Française** in 1635 aimed to guide and standardize the French language, promoting it as a refined tongue worthy of great literature and state affairs. Meeting in Paris, academy members discussed grammar, vocabulary, and style, laying the groundwork for a comprehensive dictionary. This project reflected the monarchy's desire to link linguistic unity with political centralization: one language, one law, one faith, all under the king's authority.

Although it would take decades to complete the dictionary, the academy's early sessions cultivated the idea of French as a language of diplomacy and high culture. This contributed to Paris's reputation as a hub of intellectual sophistication. In time, French would rival Latin as the language of European courts, thanks in part to these systematic efforts.

## Artistic Commissions

Beyond theater and language, painting and sculpture found renewed impetus during Richelieu's tenure. Royal or ministerial commissions funded altarpieces, portraiture, and decorative programs in palaces and churches. Influenced by Italian Baroque, French artists began developing a distinct style that blended classical restraint with dramatic flourishes. The monarchy and the cardinal recognized the value of visual propaganda, ensuring that images of the king or symbolic representations of the state appeared in key public and religious spaces.

## 13) The Looming Transition: Toward the Fronde and the Age of Louis XIV

### The Fronde's Seeds

Though the monarchy seemed strong, discontents brewed under the surface. High taxes to fund wars, aristocratic envy of Richelieu's centralization, and popular grievances all simmered. These issues would erupt shortly after both Richelieu and Louis XIII died, in a series of civil disturbances called the **Fronde (1648–1653)**. The absence of Richelieu's iron hand and the youth of Louis XIII's successor, Louis XIV, emboldened nobles and Parisian magistrates to challenge the regency of Anne of Austria and her chief minister, Cardinal Mazarin.

While the Fronde lies beyond Louis XIII's lifespan, it emerged directly from the centralized state that he and Richelieu had shaped. Their success in forging an absolute monarchy also galvanized opposition from powerful groups wanting to regain local or class-based privileges. Paris, as always, would become the main battleground for these competing visions of governance.

### Reflections on the Seeds of Absolutism

By 1643, the monarchy had developed robust levers of control: a disciplined bureaucracy, a centralized army, tight surveillance, and cultural institutions reinforcing the king's prestige. Richelieu's guiding principle of *Raisons d'État*—that the state's interest trumped all other loyalties—had sunk deep roots in the capital's political culture. While the label "absolutism" would be most famously tied to Louis XIV, the architecture of that system was largely in place by the end of Louis XIII's reign.

For Paris, this meant a deeper relationship with the monarchy. Civic leaders, guilds, intellectuals, and aristocrats found their fate increasingly linked to royal policy. The capital's corridors of power became more formalized, and the monarchy's presence in everyday life grew more palpable. Richelieu's imposing figure had left behind a city more uniform and more subservient to the crown's directives.

## 14) Conclusion

Louis XIII's reign (1610–1643), guided by the formidable Cardinal Richelieu, was pivotal in consolidating Bourbon authority and shaping the future trajectory of both France and its capital. From a delicate regency overshadowed by aristocratic plotting, the monarchy emerged more centralized than ever. Paris, once prone to factional uprisings, was now kept in firm check, its administrative and cultural institutions harnessed to reinforce royal power.

The monarchy's focus on strategic warfare, censorship, bureaucratic expansion, and cultural patronage all served the goal of forging a cohesive nation-state with Paris at its epicenter. Despite the cardinal's passing and the king's premature death, the structures they built endured. In the next chapter, we will see how these foundations enabled **Louis XIV**—the "Sun King"—to orchestrate an even more dramatic transformation of Paris, culminating in the age of royal splendor and near-absolute rule.

# CHAPTER 12

## LOUIS XIV'S REIGN – THE GRAND TRANSFORMATION OF PARIS

## Introduction

In 1643, a four-year-old **Louis XIV** ascended the throne upon the death of his father, Louis XIII. Over the next seven decades—one of the longest reigns in European history—Louis XIV would forge the image of an *absolute monarch* more powerfully than any ruler before him. While much of Louis XIV's reputation centers on the **Palace of Versailles**, his impact on Paris was equally profound. From grand architectural projects to administrative reforms and the revocation of Huguenot rights, Louis XIV placed the capital at the service of his vision of monarchy.

This chapter explores how Louis XIV reshaped Paris, analyzing the interplay between royal authority, aristocratic culture, and civic life. We will look at how the trauma of the **Fronde** rebellions in his youth influenced the king's distrust of Parisian crowds, yet did not prevent him from investing in the city's infrastructure and grandeur. We will see how court life, while largely headquartered at Versailles, still reverberated in the capital, fueling economic booms and cultural developments. By the time of his death in 1715, Louis XIV left Paris both enriched by architectural splendor and strained by the weight of absolute rule.

# 1) The Regency of Anne of Austria and Cardinal Mazarin

## The Fronde: A Troubled Childhood for Louis XIV

Before Louis XIV exercised personal power, the monarchy endured a turbulent regency (1643–1651) under his mother, **Anne of Austria**, and her principal minister, **Cardinal Mazarin**. Their rule faced immediate challenges from the **Fronde**—a series of civil revolts that erupted in Paris and across France (1648–1653).

The Fronde had two main phases:

1. **The Parliamentary Fronde (1648–1649)**: Magistrates of the Parlement of Paris, resentful of new taxes and Mazarin's authority, led protests. Crowds in Paris erected barricades, echoing events from earlier centuries.
2. **The Fronde of the Princes (1650–1653)**: Discontented nobles, including high-ranking princes, waged open warfare against the crown. They occasionally seized or threatened Paris, forcing the royal family to flee multiple times.

For the young Louis XIV, these experiences were formative. He witnessed the Parisians' capacity to defy royal power and the humiliations inflicted upon the monarchy when it lacked firm control. The memory of these uprisings would shape his future policies, fueling a distrust of the capital's populace and an inclination to rule from a secure, controlled environment.

## Mazarin's Resilience

Cardinal Mazarin, Richelieu's successor, weathered these rebellions by adept political maneuvering and leveraging the monarchy's still-intact administrative machinery. He managed to reconcile some of the Parlement's grievances and outmaneuver noble conspirators. While the Fronde ended in a royal victory, the monarchy learned a potent lesson: Paris could quickly become a crucible of revolt if taxes, legal reforms, or personal ambitions ignited old resentments.

When the Fronde concluded, many Parisians welcomed the restoration of stable governance. Commerce had suffered from barricades and uncertain rule. The city yearned for the monarchy to guarantee order, even as some families resented the regency's heavy-handed methods. Once Louis XIV reached his majority, he would begin to implement his own grand vision, taking cues from the tumult he had survived as a child.

## 2) Louis XIV Takes Personal Rule (1661) and Moves Toward Absolutism

### The End of Mazarin's Influence

Mazarin died in 1661, just as Louis XIV was poised to rule independently. Rather than appoint another "first minister," Louis XIV shocked the court by declaring he would govern alone, stating, "I am the State." This declaration signaled a new era in which the king himself would wield direct authority. He continued and expanded Richelieu's and Mazarin's legacy of centralizing power but made it even more personal and encompassing.

### Core Principles of Louis XIV's Governance

Under Louis XIV, the monarchy pursued several key objectives:

1. **Absolute Royal Authority**: Every major decision—from war to finances to culture—flowed from the king's will. Ministers like Colbert and Louvois carried out his policies, but ultimate responsibility rested with Louis XIV.
2. **Unification of Faith**: He believed that religious uniformity would enhance the state's stability. This stance would culminate in actions to restrict or eliminate Protestant rights, ultimately revoking the Edict of Nantes.
3. **Glorification of the Crown**: Through elaborate ceremonies, architectural projects, and patronage of the arts, Louis XIV sought to display the monarchy's magnificence. While Versailles was the apex of this display, Paris also benefited from—and was shaped by—these efforts.
4. **Economic Development**: Minister of Finance **Jean-Baptiste Colbert** promoted mercantilist policies, aiming to enrich the kingdom and fund the king's ambitions. Paris's trade networks, guilds, and workshops played vital roles in these plans.

Although Louis XIV eventually relocated the court to Versailles, he initially spent considerable time in Paris, overseeing key reforms, launching building projects, and ensuring the capital remained obedient. Let us see how these policies manifested in the city's physical and social landscape.

---

## 3) Architectural Grandeur: Paris under Louis XIV

### The Eastern Façade of the Louvre

One of Louis XIV's earliest major commissions was the **completion of the Louvre**. Richelieu and Louis XIII had expanded the old royal palace, but it remained inconsistent in design. Louis XIV employed notable architects, including **Louis Le Vau** and later **Claude Perrault**, to craft the *Colonnade* on the Louvre's eastern façade—an iconic structure that fused classical symmetry with French elegance.

Although Louis XIV ultimately chose Versailles as his primary residence, the Louvre's completion symbolized the monarchy's ongoing presence in Paris. When foreign dignitaries visited, the Louvre's grand court and stately colonnade impressed them, underscoring France's cultural ascendancy. The city's populace took pride in the site's transformation, seeing it as both a unifying civic landmark and a testament to the king's power.

**Les Invalides and the Dome Church**

In 1670, Louis XIV founded **Les Invalides**, a large complex to house wounded and retired soldiers, reflecting both his concern for the army and his desire to demonstrate royal benevolence. **Libéral Bruant** designed the initial structure, followed by the addition of the **Dôme des Invalides** by **Hardouin-Mansart**, completed in the early 18th century. With its impressive golden dome, Les Invalides became an architectural marvel in Paris—a statement of the king's gratitude to his veterans and a monument to French military might.

The site served a practical function, giving thousands of veterans a place to live, pray, and receive medical care. Its design also showcased Louis XIV's Baroque aesthetic preferences, blending grandeur with rational organization. Parisians appreciated the infusion of public works that offered social services, even if it was primarily for soldiers. Over time, Les Invalides would further anchor the southwestern side of the city, complementing expansions along the Seine.

**City Gates and Fortifications**

Mindful of the Fronde's lessons, Louis XIV invested in fortifying Paris's perimeter, though the city had outgrown many medieval walls. New gates and ramparts in the late 17th century helped regulate entry, manage trade duties, and monitor potential rebellion. While these fortifications were not as imposing as those used for frontier defenses, they symbolized the monarchy's vigilance. The king sought to prevent any future scenario where barricades could hold the city hostage.

Occasionally, these gates also featured decorative triumphal arches, celebrating military victories or the king's achievements. Examples include the **Porte Saint-Denis** (1672) and **Porte Saint-Martin** (1674), built to commemorate successes in the Dutch War. These arches became landmarks of civic pride. Yet they also underscored the monarchy's message: The city gates were not just practical barriers but platforms for glorifying Louis XIV's martial prowess.

---

## 4) The Transformation of Public Spaces

### The Place des Victoires and Place Vendôme

Building on the tradition of planned squares like the Place Royale (Place des Vosges), Louis XIV sponsored the creation of new royal squares in Paris. Two prominent examples are the **Place des Victoires** (1686) and the **Place Vendôme** (1699), both designed by **Jules Hardouin-Mansart**.

- **Place des Victoires**: Centered on an equestrian statue of Louis XIV, erected to honor victories in war. Aristocratic residences surrounded the circular plaza, evoking a grand stage for state pageantry.
- **Place Vendôme**: Characterized by uniform classical facades, it would later be known for high-end shops, jewelers, and prestigious hotels. Initially, it featured another statue of Louis XIV, though the monument underwent changes over time.

These squares symbolized the monarchy's aspiration for order and harmony. By imposing symmetrical designs and refined architectural codes, Louis XIV displayed a meticulous control over the urban fabric. Wealthy nobles and bourgeois office-holders eagerly purchased lots around these squares, reinforcing their status while expanding the city's fashionable districts.

### Bridges and Quays

While the **Pont Neuf** dated back to Henry IV's era, Louis XIV continued improving Paris's bridges and quays. Expanded stone embankments along the Seine facilitated commercial traffic, reduced flooding risks, and provided scenic promenades. Merchants benefited from easier loading and unloading of goods, while Parisians strolled the newly paved quays, enjoying views of the city's evolving skyline.

These developments also served as a subtle instrument of royal authority. By demonstrating a commitment to better infrastructure, the king aimed to win the goodwill of city dwellers and merchants. Yet each new construction also carried his imprint—coats of arms, inscriptions, or inscriptions praising the monarchy's generosity.

---

## 5) Social and Economic Dimensions

### The Role of Colbert's Mercantilism

**Jean-Baptiste Colbert**, Louis XIV's finance minister, played a key role in shaping Paris's economic life. His mercantilist policies emphasized:

1. **Manufacturing**: Establishing or expanding royal manufactories, including luxury textiles, mirrors, and tapestries. The **Gobelins Manufactory**, for instance, thrived in Paris, producing tapestries for royal palaces and foreign export.
2. **Trade Regulation**: Colbert streamlined guild structures, introduced protective tariffs, and maintained strict standards on product quality to boost exports.
3. **Taxation**: While pushing for economic growth, he also demanded higher tax revenues to fund Louis XIV's wars and building projects. This burden fell disproportionately on commoners, sparking periodic unrest.

Paris, as the administrative center, oversaw much of Colbert's apparatus. Guild masters had to comply with royal decrees, adjusting production methods or standards. On one hand, certain industries flourished due to state backing; on the other, smaller artisans complained about intrusive regulations and the cost of new licenses or inspections.

**Aristocratic Townhouses and Urban Expansion**

During Louis XIV's reign, the city's aristocracy continued building **hôtels particuliers**, especially near the new royal squares or along wide thoroughfares. Architects like **François Mansart** and **Jules Hardouin-Mansart** perfected the style now known as the **French Classical** or **Louis XIV** style—emphasizing clean lines, symmetry, and harmonious proportions. Interiors boasted grand salons, ornate ceilings, and Italian-influenced decoration.

Wealthy families competed to display their proximity to the king's tastes, erecting facades with sculpted reliefs or elaborate pediments. These projects spurred job opportunities for masons, carpenters, and decorators. Yet they also magnified social disparities: while the elite reveled in opulence, the city's lower classes endured cramped, aging housing in older quarters. The monarchy generally tolerated such imbalances, provided the aristocracy remained politically docile and the urban poor did not openly revolt.

## 6) Court Culture and the Decline of Paris as a Royal Residence

### The Lure of Versailles

Though Louis XIV invested heavily in Parisian projects, he increasingly spent his personal time at **Versailles**, roughly 20 kilometers from the capital. Initially a modest hunting lodge, Versailles evolved into a colossal palace with extensive gardens, all orchestrated by architects like Le Vau and Hardouin-Mansart, and landscape designer André Le Nôtre. By the 1680s, the king and his court effectively relocated there, turning Versailles into Europe's preeminent center of courtly life.

The decision to move away from Paris was partly informed by Louis XIV's memories of the Fronde—he never again wanted to be vulnerable to rebellious Parisians. Versailles also allowed him to carefully manage the aristocracy by compelling them to attend elaborate court rituals, thereby reducing their capacity to conspire.

### Impact on the Capital

While the royal court's departure might suggest Paris waned, the city remained indispensable for governance, finance, and culture. Key administrative bodies—the Parlement, major financial bureaus, guild headquarters—stayed in the capital. Ambassadors, traders, and artists frequently traveled between Paris and Versailles. In effect, the monarchy created a dual power center: Versailles for court life and personal rule, Paris for state machinery and economic vitality.

Yet some aspects of city life changed. Noble families seeking the king's favor began spending more months at Versailles, leaving their Parisian mansions quieter. High-end markets, salons, and theaters adapted to court schedules, often bustling when nobles visited the city or during official events. Despite occasional moaning about the king's absence, many Parisians saw benefits: with fewer aristocrats year-round, the city experienced slightly less congestion, while still profiting from the monarchy's major building initiatives.

---

## 7) Religious Uniformity: Revocation of the Edict of Nantes (1685)

### The Dragonnades and Intensifying Pressure

Louis XIV believed that a single faith—Catholicism—best served national unity. Though initially the Edict of Nantes still safeguarded Huguenot rights, the king grew increasingly impatient with Protestant enclaves and worship. Colbert's death (1683) removed a moderate voice who sometimes tempered royal zeal. Soon, **dragonnades** commenced, wherein soldiers were quartered in Protestant households to harass them into converting.

In Paris, official Protestant worship was already banned. Even so, Huguenot merchants and artisans had quietly maintained their faith. Now they faced heightened scrutiny, with the monarchy pressuring them to attend Catholic Mass or face imprisonment and confiscation of property. The city's climate of tolerance from the Henry IV era vanished, replaced by suspicion and forced conversions.

### The Edict of Fontainebleau (1685)

In October 1685, Louis XIV issued the **Edict of Fontainebleau**, revoking the Edict of Nantes entirely. All Protestant churches were ordered destroyed, pastors exiled, and open Protestant worship forbidden throughout France. While some Huguenots renounced their faith, many secretly continued, or fled abroad—often to the Netherlands, England, or Brandenburg-Prussia. Thousands left Paris, depriving the city of skilled artisans and entrepreneurs.

The Catholic majority in Paris generally endorsed the revocation, seeing it as a triumph of orthodoxy and loyalty to the Crown. Yet some moderate Catholics and pragmatic officials regretted the economic and intellectual losses. Over the long term, the departure of productive Huguenot families weakened certain trades. Nonetheless, from Louis XIV's viewpoint, the move solidified religious uniformity, aligning Paris more closely with his vision of an absolute Catholic monarchy.

---

## 8) Wars and Their Effects on Paris

### Funding Louis XIV's Military Ambitions

Throughout his reign, Louis XIV led France in multiple conflicts—the Franco-Dutch War (1672–1678), the War of the Reunions (1683–1684), the Nine Years' War (1688–1697), and the War of the Spanish Succession (1701–1714). These wars aimed to expand or defend France's borders, impose French influence on Europe, and secure advantageous dynastic claims. They also required vast sums of money.

Paris, as the seat of the royal treasury, felt the brunt of war financing. Taxes increased, hitting peasantry and urban poor the hardest, yet also affecting bourgeois merchants. The monarchy sold more venal offices to wealthy families, further complicating social hierarchies. While some entrepreneurs profited from supplying the army, the capital's broader economy experienced inflation and occasional shortages of goods, especially during prolonged conflicts.

## Military Parades and Celebrations

Despite hardships, Louis XIV staged grand celebrations in Paris to mark his victories or peace treaties. Processions showcasing captured flags, fireworks displays at night, and ephemeral triumphal arches thrilled city crowds. These events served as propaganda—glorifying the king's martial prowess and reassuring Parisians that sacrifices bore fruit on the battlefield. City leaders, mindful of the monarchy's wrath, cooperated with organizing these festivities, hoping the display of unity would stave off discontent.

Nevertheless, disillusion grew as wars dragged on. By the 1690s and early 1700s, many Parisians grumbled about the cost of endless campaigns. Tales of rural misery and famine circulated in the capital, prompting charitable efforts led by religious orders or philanthropic nobles. Louis XIV himself occasionally directed relief measures, but the fundamental strain remained.

# 9) Cultural Splendors and the "Great Century"

## The Age of Classicism

Despite the financial and social toll of Louis XIV's wars, French culture in the late 17th century soared to new heights—often termed the **Grand Siècle** or "Great Century." Paris was the intellectual and artistic engine behind many achievements:

- **Literature**: Playwrights **Molière** (Jean-Baptiste Poquelin) and **Racine** dominated the stage, while **La Fontaine**'s fables delighted readers of all ranks. Classicism demanded structured plots, moral clarity, and elegant language, mirroring the monarchy's emphasis on order.

- **Academies**: Beyond the Académie Française, new institutions arose: the Académie de Peinture et de Sculpture (founded 1648) and Académie des Sciences (founded 1666). They formalized standards in art and science, linking creativity with royal patronage.
- **Music and Ballet**: Composers like **Jean-Baptiste Lully** flourished under royal support, creating operas and court ballets. Parisian theaters introduced elaborate stage machinery and professional troupes, setting trends for Europe.

While Versailles hosted many premieres and court spectacles, Paris saw public performances, broader distribution of printed works, and bustling art salons. Aristocrats who maintained townhouses in the capital sometimes sponsored private recitals or reading circles, nurturing the city's creative scene.

**Public Institutions and the Arts**

Louis XIV also invested in grand public buildings for scientific and cultural endeavors in Paris. For instance, the **Observatoire de Paris** was established in 1667, reflecting the kingdom's growing interest in astronomy and navigation—both crucial for warfare and commerce. The monarchy recognized that demonstrating intellectual leadership bolstered France's reputation abroad.

These developments combined to position Paris as the leading cultural metropolis of Europe by the late 17th century. Foreign princes and scholars visited the city to learn from French academies, observe architectural marvels, and partake in the refined social world. The monarchy's cultural policies underscored a central principle: praising the king, extolling Catholic order, and testifying to the state's wealth and sophistication.

---

## 10) Daily Life and Social Realities

### Urban Challenges

Beneath the veneer of cultural splendor, everyday life in Paris could be harsh. The city's population likely exceeded half a million by 1700, crammed into areas still characterized by medieval street patterns. Housing shortages and rising rents forced many families into subdivided dwellings. Public sanitation remained primitive, with open sewers and refuse dumping in the Seine. Plague outbreaks, though less frequent than in earlier centuries, still occurred periodically, and smallpox or typhus inflicted regular tolls.

Yet the monarchy's absolute stance meant that city officials had limited autonomy to address these issues. Occasional royal edicts mandated street cleaning or building regulations, but enforcement was inconsistent. The priority remained maintaining public order and collecting taxes. Wealthy Parisians lived in relative comfort, while the masses juggled precarious incomes, high living costs, and the possibility of famine if harvests failed.

## Police Reforms

To better control crime and potential unrest, Louis XIV created the **Lieutenant General of Police** for Paris in 1667. This office, first occupied by **Gabriel Nicolas de La Reynie**, introduced more systematic policing—patrols at night, lighting of certain streets, and record-keeping on criminals. While these measures improved security somewhat, the system often targeted petty thieves or "undesirables," leaving the wealthy or well-connected relatively unscathed. Still, the monarchy touted it as a sign of progress and paternal care for the capital's safety.

---

## 11) The Later Years of Louis XIV's Reign

### Economic Hardships and the Burden of War

From the 1690s onward, the kingdom suffered under the weight of nearly continuous warfare. The War of the Spanish Succession (1701–1714) proved especially draining, as multiple European powers united against France. Food shortages and harsh winters, such as the **Great Winter of 1709**, led to mass suffering in Paris and beyond. The monarchy resorted to new taxes, forced loans, and currency manipulations—eroding public confidence.

The capital, though culturally vibrant, saw a decline in real wages for most workers. Bread riots erupted sporadically. The monarchy clamped down quickly, fearing any spark of revolt. Loyal troops and police suppressed demonstrations. Many Parisians endured silent misery or turned to religious confraternities for charity. Meanwhile, aristocrats adapted their lifestyles modestly or tried to profit from war contracts, though some fell into debt if their estates were ravaged by the conflict.

### Religious Tensions Resurface

After the revocation of the Edict of Nantes, Louis XIV further aligned the monarchy with Catholic orthodoxy. He also launched campaigns against **Jansenism**, a Catholic reform movement perceived as doctrinally rigid and critical of royal-laden ecclesiastical practices. Some Parisian convents and schools, like the **Port-Royal** establishments, were dissolved or reformed under the king's orders. This crackdown signaled that even within Catholicism, dissent was not tolerated if it challenged absolute authority.

Although these religious controversies did not spark major riots in Paris—since the city's population mostly supported the Crown's religious stance—they undermined certain intellectual circles. Fear of heresy or suspicion overshadowed theological debates at the Sorbonne, stifling some streams of thought. The monarchy's narrative of unity demanded minimal friction from any corner, be it Protestant or Jansenist.

# CHAPTER 13

## THE ENLIGHTENMENT AND SOCIAL CHANGE IN 18TH-CENTURY PARIS

## Introduction

By the dawn of the 18th century, Paris stood as a city shaped by royal absolutism and classical grandeur. Louis XIV's reign (1661–1715) had endowed it with iconic squares, expanded bridges, and a deep-rooted bureaucratic apparatus. Yet the city also faced social and economic challenges—heavy taxation, religious uniformity, and the strains of prolonged warfare. When Louis XIV died, his successors, notably **Louis XV** (r. 1715–1774) and **Louis XVI** (r. 1774–1792), inherited a kingdom whose outward display of power concealed mounting issues.

In this chapter, we explore the **18th century in Paris**, focusing on the period often referred to as the **Enlightenment** (roughly 1715–1789). This was a time when new philosophies about reason, individual rights, and human progress captured the imagination of Parisian intellectuals. Meanwhile, the city continued to grow—its streets bustling with merchants, artisans, and aristocrats, all maneuvering within a rapidly evolving social framework. We will look at how Enlightenment thinkers challenged traditional authority, how salons fostered debate, and how royal policies oscillated between reform attempts and the preservation of old hierarchies. By the end of the century, Paris was on the brink of a political earthquake that would shatter the old order forever.

## 1) The Regency of Philippe d'Orléans and Aftermath of Louis XIV's Death

**The Transition: Louis XV's Minority**

When Louis XIV died in 1715, his great-grandson, **Louis XV**, was only five years old. During the new king's minority, **Philippe d'Orléans** served as Regent (1715–1723). The Regent initially resided at the **Palais-Royal** in Paris, shifting the epicenter of power away from Versailles. Parisians welcomed this partial return of the royal court, hoping it might bring economic relief after costly wars and heavy taxes.

The Regency era was marked by:

- **Financial Experimentation**: The Regent worked with John Law, a Scottish economist, to implement radical monetary policies—creating a national bank, issuing paper money, and forming the Mississippi Company. This "System," headquartered in Paris, generated speculative frenzy before collapsing in 1720.
- **Relaxed Censorship**: The Regent, more open-minded than his late predecessor, allowed certain philosophical works to circulate. This gave a small boost to the early Enlightenment movement, as pamphlets critiquing absolute monarchy or established religion found readers.
- **Social Shifts**: Some aristocrats who had felt excluded under Louis XIV's rigid court etiquette found new freedoms in the capital. Lavish parties and gambling clubs thrived, giving the Regency a reputation for moral laxity.

The economic shock following John Law's failed experiment tarnished the Regent's popularity. When Louis XV assumed personal rule in 1723, many Parisians hoped for a more stable era. Yet the city's fundamental problems—income inequality, debt, and the tension between an enlightened elite and a conservative establishment—remained.

---

## 2) Paris under Louis XV: Stability and Underlying Tensions

**The Personal Reign Begins**

Louis XV began governing in his own right around 1723–1726. Initially, he maintained the structures of absolutism, leaning on ministers who favored continuity with Louis XIV's methods. Versailles stayed the principal royal residence, but Paris remained the core for administration, commerce, and intellectual life. Royal edicts issued from Versailles were registered by the Parlement of Paris, preserving the capital's formal role in legitimizing crown policies.

Despite some early popularity—Louis XV was dubbed "Le Bien-Aimé" (the Well-Beloved)—public sentiment wavered over time. The monarchy's prestige suffered from:

- **Costly Foreign Wars**: Conflicts like the War of the Austrian Succession (1740–1748) and the Seven Years' War (1756–1763) drained resources and ended in defeats that eroded France's status.
- **Financial Instability**: The monarchy continued to struggle with high debts and an outdated tax system that exempted much of the nobility and clergy.
- **Court Extravagance**: Courtiers lived in luxury at Versailles, prompting discontent among middle and lower classes who shouldered the fiscal burdens.

Paris itself was an arena where these contradictions played out. The city's prosperity depended on stable governance, but the monarchy's inefficiency and favoritism often stifled the kind of economic reforms needed to keep up with a modernizing world.

**Royal Projects and Urban Improvements**

Louis XV did sponsor some large-scale projects in Paris:

- **Place Louis XV (Place de la Concorde)**: Commissioned in the 1750s, designed by Ange-Jacques Gabriel, it was a grand public square honoring the king. Later, during the Revolution, it would be renamed Place de la Concorde.
- **Ecole Militaire**: Founded to train young nobles for military service, it reflected the monarchy's desire to bolster the army with more professional officers.
- **Hospitals and Charitable Works**: Some expansions of hospitals, like the Hôtel-Dieu near Notre-Dame, aimed to address public health. Though still rudimentary, these efforts signaled a partial awareness of social responsibility.

Nevertheless, the monarchy's debt constrained many ambitions. Much of the city's growth in the mid-18th century came from private initiatives—aristocratic mansions in the Faubourg Saint-Germain, new commercial buildings near Les Halles, and expansions along major boulevards. Paris thrived in certain respects, but the veneer of royal grandeur concealed deeper problems soon highlighted by Enlightenment critiques.

---

## 3) The Blossoming of the Enlightenment in Paris

**Philosophical Foundations**

The **Enlightenment** was an intellectual and cultural movement emphasizing reason, skepticism of absolute authority, and belief in human progress. Its origins lay partly in the 17th-century "scientific revolution," but by the early to mid-18th century, Paris served as a key hub for Enlightenment thinkers or *philosophes*. They questioned the monarchy's legitimacy, the Church's dominance, and the long-held feudal traditions that structured society.

Leading figures included:

- **Voltaire (François-Marie Arouet)**: Known for witty critiques of intolerance and calls for freedom of thought. He spent time in and out of Paris—exiled at points, but always influential.
- **Montesquieu (Charles de Secondat)**: His *Spirit of the Laws* (1748) argued for separation of powers, challenging the centralized monarchy.
- **Jean-Jacques Rousseau**: Though of Swiss origin, he found an eager audience in Paris. His works on social contract theory, education, and equality resonated widely, suggesting that sovereignty resided with the general will of the people.
- **Denis Diderot** and **Jean le Rond d'Alembert**: Editors of the **Encyclopédie**, a monumental project (1751–1772) that aimed to compile human knowledge, reflecting Enlightenment ideals of rational inquiry and secular learning.

**Salons and the Role of Women**

A vital institution of Parisian Enlightenment culture was the **salon**—regular gatherings hosted in private drawing rooms, often by aristocratic or wealthy bourgeois women. Salons allowed authors, philosophers, scientists, and artists to mingle, debate, and share ideas in a relatively free space. Influential salonnières included **Madame Geoffrin**, **Madame de Pompadour** (a favorite of Louis XV), **Madame du Deffand**, and **Madame d'Epinay**.

These gatherings helped bridge social and intellectual divides. Nobles and commoners, men and women, could engage in conversation about literature, science, and politics. While the monarchy maintained censorship, salons functioned with some autonomy, facilitating the spread of sometimes radical views. Eventually, salon conversations influenced public opinion beyond these elite circles, feeding a growing undercurrent of reformist sentiment in broader Parisian society.

**Censorship and Underground Publishing**

The monarchy and the Catholic Church monitored printed works through censors at the royal court and the Sorbonne's theological faculty. Nonetheless, Parisian booksellers found ways to smuggle or publish banned texts—sometimes printing them abroad in the Dutch Republic or Swiss cantons and importing them secretly. Banned pamphlets criticizing the king, mocking the court's decadence, or advocating religious tolerance circulated quietly in the city.

Authorities occasionally raided printing shops and imprisoned outspoken writers. Voltaire himself endured Bastille imprisonment. Diderot faced arrest for his subversive ideas. But these crackdowns had limited effect; they rarely halted the clandestine flow of literature, and in many cases, arrests simply elevated the philosopher's profile. This tug-of-war between censorship and free expression became a defining feature of the Enlightenment era in Paris.

## 4) Changing Social Structures: Nobles, Bourgeoisie, and the Urban Poor

**Nobles of the Sword vs. Nobles of the Robe**

Throughout the 18th century, Paris's elite was divided into:

1. **Traditional Nobles of the Sword**: Families claiming ancient lineage and military origin. They often resided near the court in Versailles or in elaborate Parisian mansions.
2. **Nobles of the Robe**: Wealthy bourgeois who had purchased judicial or administrative offices, thus acquiring noble status. Concentrated around the Parlement of Paris and royal councils, they formed a powerful bloc defending their privileges.

Rivalries between these groups festered, though both shared privileges such as tax exemptions, feudal dues, and seigneurial rights. Enlightenment criticism of inherited privilege or corruption sometimes targeted them collectively. Yet, ironically, certain nobles embraced Enlightenment ideas, hosting salons or penning treatises on reform.

### The Ascendant Bourgeoisie

Below the nobility, the **bourgeoisie**—merchants, financiers, industrialists, lawyers, and administrative officers—experienced significant growth. Buoyed by colonial trade, manufacturing, and government contracts, many families accumulated considerable wealth. Some aspired to nobility by purchasing offices or estates, while others remained content with their status, investing in city property and philanthropic endeavors.

Bourgeois cultural life thrived in Paris. They established private clubs, reading societies, and Masonic lodges, where participants discussed everything from new scientific findings to political philosophy. The monarchy tolerated these gatherings, hoping they would remain harmless. However, these associations became breeding grounds for reformist sentiment that would later shape revolutionary demands for representation and fairness.

### The Urban Masses and Subsistence Crises

At the lower end of the social spectrum, Paris's population soared beyond 600,000 by the late 18th century. Workers, artisans, and servants struggled to survive amidst rising rents and periodic grain shortages. The price of bread—Parisians' staple food—was subject to speculation and harvest fluctuations. When bread prices soared, resentment toward privileged orders and incompetent government policies intensified.

Charity and religion offered partial relief. Confraternities, parish networks, and philanthropic nobles funded soup kitchens or distributed alms. Yet structural inequalities persisted. Enlightenment calls for rational governance and social improvement sometimes trickled down to these masses, fueling an undercurrent of discontent that would erupt by the 1780s.

---

## 5) Shifts in Religious Climate: Jansenists, Jesuits, and Freethinkers

### The Jansenist Controversy

While Louis XIV had suppressed Jansenism, it did not vanish. In the 18th century, certain Parisian parishes and devout nobles quietly supported Jansenist ideas, emphasizing personal piety and Augustinian theology over the more worldly aspects of official Catholicism. The **Parlement of Paris**, frequently in conflict with the royal court, sometimes sided with Jansenists as a way to oppose monarchical decrees. This alignment gave the religious controversy a political dimension.

One famous flashpoint was the dispute over "Unigenitus" (1713), a papal bull condemning Jansenist propositions. The Parlement resisted registering the bull, framing the monarchy's push to enforce it as an overreach. This standoff occasionally sparked street demonstrations and pamphlet wars in Paris, merging questions of spiritual belief with broader issues of legal autonomy and protest against royal centralism.

### The Expulsion of the Jesuits

Another major event was the **expulsion of the Jesuits** from France in 1764. The Society of Jesus had been a stalwart ally of absolutism and Catholic orthodoxy under Louis XIV. However, under Louis XV, a complex web of political rivalries and financial scandals led the Parlement of Paris to champion calls for the Jesuits' suppression. Enlightenment philosophers viewed Jesuits as defenders of papal authority and hence opposed them. The monarchy, needing Parlement's cooperation, acquiesced.

The Jesuit ban signaled that even the monarchy's closest ecclesiastical supporters were vulnerable to shifting public and legal opinion. Many ordinary Parisians took note: The state's religious posture seemed less monolithic, more subject to political bargaining. This crack in the alliance between throne and altar would expand in the next reign.

### Growth of Religious Skepticism

Enlightenment critiques of religion also eroded the old Catholic monopoly on truth. While the majority of Parisians remained observant Catholics, an undercurrent of **deism** or outright atheism emerged among certain intellectuals. Private gatherings debated biblical contradictions, the concept of miracles, and the rational moral code. The monarchy generally frowned upon overt irreligion, but the infiltration of irreverent or satirical works into Paris's literary scene signaled a gradual secularization of elite thought.

---

## 6) Louis XVI and the Drift toward Reform

### A New King with Old Problems

In 1774, **Louis XVI** ascended the throne, inheriting a kingdom deeply in debt, a restless society shaped by Enlightenment ideas, and an aging administration ill-equipped for modern challenges. Initially well-intentioned, Louis XVI appointed reform-minded ministers, such as **Turgot** (Controller-General of Finances) and later **Necker**, hoping to fix the tax system and lighten burdens on the peasantry.

Paris reacted cautiously. Turgot's proposals to liberalize the grain trade or reduce feudal privileges faced resistance from nobles and guilds who feared losing their advantages. When bread prices spiked, street protests erupted, overshadowing Turgot's positive reforms. Under pressure, Louis XVI dismissed Turgot in 1776, signaling that entrenched interests still held great sway.

## The American Influence

Meanwhile, France's support for the **American War of Independence (1775–1783)** revived national pride but also exacerbated royal debts. Parisians celebrated American victories over Britain, identifying them with Enlightenment ideals of liberty and self-governance. Figures like **Benjamin Franklin** became popular in Parisian salons, fueling admiration for a republican experiment across the Atlantic.

This enthusiasm contained a paradox: the monarchy spent millions to help Americans gain freedom from British rule, yet at home it denied fundamental reforms. Parisian elites followed the war's progress avidly, generating more radical debates about political representation and the natural rights of man. By the 1780s, a new generation of thinkers and lawyers emerged in Paris, calling for a constitution, a more equitable tax system, and checks on royal power.

## 7) Cultural Evolution: Theater, Press, and Scientific Advancements

### Expanding Theatrical Scene

Paris's theater life flourished in the 18th century, catering to diverse tastes:

- **Comédie-Française**: Performed classical tragedies by Corneille, Racine, and new works from Voltaire.
- **Opéra**: Offered grand spectacles, often referencing mythological or royal themes.
- **Comédie-Italienne**: Featured comedic performances, sometimes improvised, appealing to popular audiences.

Playwrights like **Pierre-Augustin Caron de Beaumarchais** dared to incorporate satirical attacks on aristocratic privilege. His *Le Mariage de Figaro* (1784) famously ridiculed noble arrogance, hinting that commoners might outwit the ruling class. Such productions stirred controversy but also drew large crowds in Paris. The monarchy's censorship apparatus wavered—fearful of public backlash, it occasionally let subversive plays pass.

**The Rise of Periodicals and Literacy**

Newspapers and periodicals multiplied in Paris, though all required royal permissions. Some specialized in fashion, society gossip, and court news, feeding an appetite for scandal. Others, more serious, discussed science, commerce, or political happenings. By the late 18th century, literacy among the bourgeoisie had risen significantly, creating a robust reading market. Even in working-class neighborhoods, public readings in taverns or informal clubs spread ideas of reform.

This broadening literate culture amplified Enlightenment philosophies. Writers like **Mercier** produced vivid "tableaus" describing daily life in the capital, highlighting social inequalities and mocking outdated customs. Pamphlets mocking the queen, **Marie Antoinette**, or condemning ministerial corruption circulated widely, revealing that the monarchy's once-fearsome censorship had become patchy and less effective.

**Scientific Societies and Academies**

Alongside the Académie Française, other academies in Paris advanced the sciences—astronomy, natural history, chemistry, and medicine. Public lectures at the **Collège de France** or the **Jardin des Plantes** drew curious onlookers. Technological innovations, such as hot-air balloons (the Montgolfier brothers' flights), captured the city's imagination.

While these pursuits might seem apolitical, they contributed to a general climate of questioning and confidence in human reason. The monarchy often sponsored or tolerated scientific research, hoping it would enhance France's prestige. Yet the principle that reason could explain and improve society led many Parisians to wonder why governance was still so archaic and unequal.

---

## 8) Cracks in the Old Regime: Financial Crises and Calls for Reform

**Mounting Debt and Fiscal Deadlock**

By the mid-1780s, France's debt had reached critical levels, aggravated by support for the American Revolution and the monarchy's lavish expenditures. Ministers like **Calonne** tried to implement universal land taxes or provincial assemblies to broaden the tax base. However, the **Parlement of Paris** blocked such measures, defending noble privilege and demanding that only the Estates-General—a body not convened since 1614—could approve new taxes.

This stalemate exposed the monarchy's weakened authority. The old system of regional parlements, corporate privileges, and feudal dues clashed with the monarchy's need for revenue. Parisians watched as aristocrats, ironically, clothed themselves in the language of legal and historical rights to resist the crown's reforms. Meanwhile, middle-class voices demanded deeper structural changes to break the impasse.

**Public Opinion and Libelles**

The capital's reading public followed these events with growing disillusion. **Libelles**—short, scandalous pamphlets—mocked the royal family, especially Marie Antoinette, portraying her as extravagant or even treasonous. Others attacked Louis XVI's perceived indecision. While often sensational, these libelles shaped public sentiment by undermining respect for the monarchy's moral legitimacy.

Salon conversations turned openly critical of the "Old Regime," a term increasingly used to describe the outdated feudal and corporate structures. Even moderate thinkers believed some form of constitutional monarchy was necessary, with an elected body to represent the nation's will. The monarchy, cornered by financial meltdown, finally agreed to convene the **Estates-General** for May 1789—an event that would bring tens of thousands of representatives, pamphlets, and petitions to Paris, setting the stage for revolutionary upheaval.

---

## 9) The Estates-General of 1789 and the Hopes for Change

**Preparations in Paris**

As news spread that the Estates-General would meet at Versailles, electoral processes took place across France. In Paris, each of the three traditional orders—Clergy (First Estate), Nobility (Second Estate), and Commoners (Third Estate)—chose deputies. Citizens drafted **cahiers de doléances** (lists of grievances) enumerating demands: tax fairness, freedom of the press, an end to feudal dues, and respect for property rights. Enlightenment ideals permeated these documents.

Local gatherings in Paris revealed widespread dissatisfaction with corruption, favoritism, and censorship. The Third Estate deputies from the capital, many aligned with the legal or commercial bourgeoisie, arrived at Versailles determined to push for real constitutional reform. Meanwhile, many city dwellers believed the Estates-General would usher in an era of greater liberty and economic justice. High expectations ran rampant.

**The Tense Atmosphere in the Capital**

In the weeks leading up to May 1789, Paris crackled with anticipation. Skilled workers and journeymen expressed optimism that new representation might lower bread prices and lessen guild restrictions. Radical pamphleteers championed the "rights of man" and demanded a constitution. Nobles and high clergy, on the other hand, braced for potential threats to their privileges, fueling an undercurrent of aristocratic conspiracy theories.

Bread shortages in early 1789 exacerbated tensions. The monarchy tried to stabilize grain supplies, but speculation and poor harvests led to price surges. Street protests broke out sporadically, with some blaming hoarders or accusing the court of neglect. Royal troops ringed Paris and Versailles, hoping to maintain order. The monarchy's incomplete grip on the city meant that any spark could ignite deeper unrest.

# CHAPTER 14

### THE FRENCH REVOLUTION – COLLAPSE OF THE OLD ORDER

## Introduction

The year 1789 stands out in global history as the beginning of the **French Revolution**, an event that dramatically recast political power not just in France, but also influenced broader Western societies. At the heart of the revolution was **Paris**, where decades of Enlightenment thinking, financial crises, and popular unrest coalesced into a radical break from the Old Regime. Over the next decade, the city experienced moments of electrifying idealism—proclaiming liberty, equality, and fraternity—alongside episodes of intense violence and political upheaval.

In this chapter, we trace how Paris both **ignited and navigated** the French Revolution, from the summoning of the Estates-General to the fall of the monarchy, the Reign of Terror, and eventual transition into new political structures. We examine the role of various social groups—bourgeois deputies, radical clubs, sans-culottes, and the shifting alliances that defined revolutionary politics. By the time Napoleon Bonaparte seized power in 1799, Paris had undergone a profound transformation, leaving the monarchy in ruins and the future of France uncertain.

## 1) The Estates-General and the Birth of the National Assembly (1789)

### Deadlock at Versailles

On May 5, 1789, the **Estates-General** convened in Versailles for the first time since 1614. Each Estate (Clergy, Nobility, Third Estate) submitted a long list of grievances, with the Third Estate demanding fundamental tax reforms, an end to feudal dues, and broader representation. However, an immediate conflict arose over **voting procedures**: the Third Estate insisted on voting by headcount (giving them a numerical advantage), while the privileged orders insisted on voting by order (maintaining their veto power).

Parisians eagerly followed these debates. Newspapers and pamphlets flooded the capital, analyzing every speech. When weeks passed with no resolution, tension mounted in the city's streets. Bread prices remained high, and rumors circulated that reactionary nobles planned to dissolve the Estates-General by force. In mid-June, the stalemate broke when representatives of the Third Estate, joined by some liberal clergy and nobles, proclaimed themselves the **National Assembly**—the true voice of the nation.

### The Tennis Court Oath

On June 20, 1789, barred from their usual meeting hall, the newly formed National Assembly convened in a nearby indoor tennis court, swearing not to disband until they had given France a constitution. This **Tennis Court Oath** electrified Paris. Crowds in the capital hailed the deputies as heroes. Royal attempts at compromise stumbled; Louis XVI vacillated, recognizing the National Assembly but also summoning troops to the Paris region, ostensibly for security.

Such contradictory signals heightened popular suspicion. Many citizens feared the monarchy planned a coup against the National Assembly. Key orators in Paris championed the cause of the Assembly, calling for vigilance against rumored "aristocratic plots." In a city already brimming with discontent, these warnings stirred an even larger mobilization—leading to the events that would permanently mark 1789 in French memory.

---

## 2) The Storming of the Bastille and Popular Uprising

### The Militia Movement

As tensions grew, Parisians organized spontaneously to defend the National Assembly. On July 11, 1789, news spread that Louis XVI had dismissed his reformist minister, **Jacques Necker**, widely seen as sympathetic to the people's grievances. A wave of alarm gripped the city. Inflamed by radical speakers at the Palais-Royal, large crowds gathered, determined to arm themselves.

Local committees formed to coordinate a people's militia—soon known as the **National Guard**—to keep order and protect the revolution. They seized weapons from armories and shops, but needed gunpowder. Their target became the **Bastille**, a medieval fortress-prison seen as a symbol of royal despotism, rumored to store large amounts of gunpowder.

**The Fall of the Bastille (July 14, 1789)**

On the morning of July 14, thousands of Parisians marched on the Bastille, demanding its commander relinquish the gunpowder. Negotiations faltered. The crowd grew restless, cannons were brought in, and fighting erupted. By mid-afternoon, the fortress fell to the insurgents, and the Bastille's governor was taken captive and later executed. Only a handful of prisoners were found inside, but the fortress's symbolic significance was immense.

This moment reverberated across France. Louis XVI, upon hearing of the Bastille's fall, reportedly asked, "Is this a revolt?" and was told, "No, sire, it is a revolution." Paris had effectively seized power from the crown, launching a new era. The monarchy, stunned, recalled Necker and accepted the formation of the National Guard under the command of the liberal noble **Marquis de Lafayette**. On July 17, Louis XVI visited Paris and donned the revolutionary tricolor cockade, symbolizing reluctant recognition of the city's ascendancy.

## 3) The Great Fear and Abolition of Feudalism

### Rural Echoes and the Great Fear

The Paris uprising ignited uprisings elsewhere. In many provinces, peasants attacked manor houses, suspecting aristocratic reprisals. This wave of panic and rebellion, known as the **Great Fear** (summer 1789), combined rumors of brigands with genuine peasant fury at feudal dues. The National Assembly responded with a dramatic session on August 4, 1789, where deputies renounced feudal privileges—abolishing tithes, corvée labor, and seigneurial dues.

Parisians celebrated this triumph over feudalism, though the city itself was less affected by manorial obligations than rural areas. Still, local guilds questioned if the same liberal logic should apply to their corporatist privileges. The revolution's ideological momentum was accelerating: "liberty and equality" seemed unstoppable watchwords in discussions, newspapers, and public gatherings.

### Declaration of the Rights of Man and Citizen

On August 26, 1789, the National Assembly adopted the **Declaration of the Rights of Man and of the Citizen**, proclaiming universal rights—liberty, property, security, and resistance to oppression. It also declared the principle of equality before the law and the sovereignty of the nation. This text, heavily influenced by Enlightenment ideals, had a profound impact on Parisians.

Copies were posted on walls and printed in pamphlets. Philosophers recognized it as a victory for reason and natural rights. Commoners felt empowered, believing the old divisions of estate and privilege were morally void. However, the monarchy had not formally endorsed the document. Tensions simmered, especially as the king hesitated to sign key decrees, and bread prices remained high due to ongoing shortages.

---

## 4) The October Days: Women March on Versailles

### Food Crisis and Protest

By October 1789, Parisian markets were again beset by bread scarcities. The revolutionary municipal government (the **Commune of Paris**) struggled to stabilize supplies. As rumors spread that the king's banquet at Versailles mocked the tricolor cockade, indignation soared. On October 5, a large crowd of women—market sellers, housewives, and fishmongers—gathered at City Hall, demanding action on bread prices. Their call: march to Versailles and confront the king directly.

Encouraged by radical agitators, thousands of women (joined by some National Guardsmen) walked the 12 miles to Versailles in the rain. They petitioned Louis XVI for food relief and insisted the monarchy should move closer to Paris to monitor the people's needs. The king, startled, promised grain distributions.

**The Royal Family Moves to Paris**

Overnight, skirmishes broke out when palace guards clashed with some protestors. On October 6, the crowd forced the royal family to relocate to the **Tuileries Palace** in Paris. The National Assembly, too, moved to the city. Louis XVI, now effectively under the watch of the revolution's epicenter, lost further autonomy.

This event, known as the **October Days**, symbolized the irreversible shift of power from Versailles to Paris. The monarchy, physically embedded in the city, became vulnerable to popular pressure. Observers worldwide recognized that the French Revolution was no fleeting rebellion—it was fundamentally remaking the relationship between crown and capital.

---

## 5) The Restructuring of France: 1790–1791

### Administrative and Ecclesiastical Reforms

With the king in Paris, the National Assembly proceeded with sweeping transformations:

- **New Departments**: France was divided into 83 departments, replacing old provinces. This rational system aimed to eliminate feudal fragmentation. Paris itself became part of the Seine department, under a newly elected council.
- **Civil Constitution of the Clergy** (July 1790): The Church was reorganized. Clergy became salaried officials of the state, required to swear allegiance to the revolution. Many Parisians supported the idea of curbing Church wealth, but devout Catholics felt betrayed. Tensions flared when some priests refused the oath, creating a schism within the Church.

### Festive Unity and Growing Splits

On July 14, 1790, the revolution's first anniversary was commemorated with the **Fête de la Fédération** on the Champ de Mars in Paris. The king, Assembly members, and National Guard leaders took oaths of loyalty to the constitution. Hundreds of thousands of spectators cheered, hoping that a constitutional monarchy would unite the nation.

Yet, disagreements persisted beneath this veneer of fraternity. Radicals pushed for deeper reforms—expanded suffrage, full equality for all classes—while moderates and constitutional monarchists desired a stable parliamentary monarchy. The Court quietly resisted changes that reduced royal prerogatives, fueling suspicion. Meanwhile, economic issues like inflation, the decline of certain industries, and continued bread price volatility pestered the city's working poor.

---

## 6) Emergence of Political Clubs and Radicalization

### Clubs and Newspapers

Paris in 1790–1791 saw an explosion of **political clubs**, each with distinct ideologies:

- **Jacobins**: Originating as the Club Breton, they became a nationwide network of radical republicans, emphasizing centralized power to implement egalitarian reforms. Their Paris headquarters on Rue Saint-Honoré attracted middle-class and elite revolutionaries.
- **Cordeliers**: More populist, championing direct democracy and vigilance against tyranny. Figures like **Georges Danton** and **Camille Desmoulins** were prominent members.
- **Feuillants**: A faction of moderate constitutional monarchists who split from the Jacobins, aiming to preserve a weaker but still significant monarchy.

These clubs published newspapers and pamphlets, shaping public opinion in cafes and meeting halls. They debated issues from foreign alliances to the future role of the king. Street corners in Paris teemed with hawkers selling daily journals, fueling a culture of intense political engagement.

### The Flight to Varennes (June 1791)

In June 1791, Louis XVI and his family attempted to escape Paris in disguise, hoping to reach royalist strongholds on the eastern frontier. They were caught at Varennes and brought back to the Tuileries. This incident shattered lingering illusions that the king embraced the revolution. Many Parisians felt betrayed; confidence in a constitutional monarchy plummeted. A new wave of radical agitation insisted that an untrustworthy king could not safely remain in power.

The National Assembly, dominated by moderates, tried to cover up the flight by claiming the king had been kidnapped, to preserve constitutional monarchy. But the Jacobins and Cordeliers spread a different narrative: The king was an enemy of the revolution. As trust in the monarchy eroded, calls for a republic grew louder in certain quarters of the city.

# 7) From Constitutional Monarchy to the First Republic

### The Legislative Assembly and War

A new legislative body, the **Legislative Assembly**, replaced the National Assembly in October 1791. Composed largely of younger deputies, it faced mounting crises:

- **Clerical Schism**: Many priests refused the Civil Constitution, stirring religious discord.
- **Noble Emigrés**: Aristocrats who fled abroad lobbied foreign courts for intervention.
- **Threats of War**: Austria and Prussia menaced France, threatening to restore full royal power.

War hawks in the Assembly, led by **Brissot** and other Girondins, argued that conflict would expose traitors and unify the revolution. In April 1792, France declared war on Austria. The monarchy's ambivalent stance and occasional vetoes of radical decrees fueled suspicions that Louis XVI secretly favored the enemy. Paris braced for invasion rumors, intensifying radical sentiment.

### 10 August 1792: Overthrow of the Monarchy

As the Prussian army advanced, radical mobs in Paris demanded the end of the monarchy. On August 10, 1792, thousands of National Guardsmen and revolutionary federates stormed the Tuileries Palace. The Swiss Guards defending the king were massacred. Louis XVI sought refuge with the Legislative Assembly but was arrested. A **revolutionary Commune** seized control of city government, effectively overshadowing the Assembly.

This day marked the **fall of the monarchy**. Louis XVI was suspended from office, and a new body, the **National Convention**, was to be elected by universal male suffrage. Paris erupted in celebrations, though overshadowed by fear of foreign invasion. The monarchy's centuries-long presence in the capital ended in bloodshed, propelled by the city's radical fervor.

---

# 8) The September Massacres and the Birth of the Republic

### Fear and Vigilantism

In early September 1792, news that Prussian forces had captured Verdun sparked panic in Paris. Rumors claimed that royalist prisoners in city jails planned an uprising to support the invasion. Radical journalists incited crowds to preemptively execute suspected counter-revolutionaries. Over several days, mobs stormed prisons, killing over a thousand inmates—nobles, priests, and petty criminals alike.

These **September Massacres** horrified moderates yet found some justification among extremists who believed the revolution was in mortal danger. The National Convention, just elected, had limited means to prevent the violence. A sense of dread mingled with triumph as revolutionaries insisted necessity and suspicion validated such brutality.

**Proclamation of the Republic**

On September 21, 1792, the Convention declared France a **republic**, abolishing monarchy. The following day, it adopted a new calendar, designating 1792 as Year I of the Republic. Parisians hailed this as a watershed moment—severing all ties with royal tradition. Nonetheless, the question remained: What form would this republic take? Jacobins, led by **Maximilien Robespierre**, Danton, and Marat, pushed for a radical democracy that championed egalitarian laws. The Girondins argued for a more moderate approach.

Meanwhile, the war turned in France's favor after the **Battle of Valmy** (September 20, 1792). Patriotism soared in Paris, fueling the conviction that the Republic could survive foreign armies and domestic treason. Yet with the monarchy gone, the revolution's next steps hinged on how far the city's radical clubs would push for social and political transformation—and how violently they would act against perceived enemies.

## 9) The Trial and Execution of Louis XVI

**A Divisive Decision**

Louis XVI, now a prisoner known as "Louis Capet," stood accused of conspiracy against the liberty of the nation. The National Convention debated whether to try him. In

December 1792, the king was put on trial; evidence from secret documents and prior events painted him as colluding with foreign powers. The city was riveted by the proceedings, with newspapers providing daily updates. Tensions soared—royalists prayed for leniency, while radicals demanded swift punishment.

On January 15–17, 1793, the Convention found Louis XVI guilty. By a narrow majority, it sentenced him to death. Outside, Jacobin clubs and sections (local revolutionary committees) insisted no compromise was possible with monarchy. On January 21, 1793, the king was guillotined at the Place de la Révolution (formerly Place Louis XV, later Place de la Concorde). The event was staged as a public spectacle. Thousands crowded to see the final demise of the Bourbon monarchy.

**Aftermath and Impact on Paris**

The king's execution radicalized the revolution further. European monarchs condemned the regicide, and France braced for expanded war. Within the city, many felt a mix of triumph and foreboding. Royalists and moderate republicans were shocked. In the following months, the Convention would also execute Queen Marie Antoinette, aristocrats, and clergy who refused loyalty to the Republic.

With the monarchy gone, Paris took on a new symbolic role: the cradle of republican virtue and the front line of a global struggle against tyranny. Yet that same impetus fueled a culture of suspicion. The revolution, forging new ideals, also unleashed a capacity for systematic terror to enforce them.

---

## 10) The Reign of Terror and Its Grip on the Capital

**The Committee of Public Safety**

Facing war on multiple fronts (Britain, Austria, Prussia, Spain) and internal revolts (the Vendée, federalist uprisings), the Convention granted extraordinary powers to the **Committee of Public Safety** in mid-1793. Led by **Robespierre**, **Georges Couthon**, and **Louis Saint-Just**, it aimed to root out enemies, real or perceived.

In Paris, revolutionary tribunals tried suspects daily—nobles, clergy, Girondins, suspected hoarders, or anyone accused by local sections of "anti-revolutionary" sentiments. Many were executed on the guillotine. The city's political clubs like the Jacobins supported these measures, arguing that **Terror** was necessary to save the Republic.

### Economic Controls and Social Measures

To address popular demands, the Convention introduced the **Law of the Maximum** (September 1793), capping prices of essential goods to combat inflation and ensure Parisians had affordable bread. Sans-culottes—urban workers wearing long trousers—pressured the government to adopt more egalitarian measures, from wage regulations to punishing profiteers.

The city's radical mood soared. Festivals replaced Christian ceremonies, worshipping reason or the Supreme Being. Catholic churches were repurposed, culminating in the **Cult of Reason** or **Cult of the Supreme Being**. While some Parisians embraced these anti-clerical transformations, others practiced faith in secret. Tensions between the radical leaders and moderate believers grew, fueling a climate where any dissent risked labeling one an "enemy of the people."

### Height of the Terror

By 1794, guillotine executions in Paris peaked—filling days with grim processions. Factions in the Convention turned on each other. The enragés demanded even harsher policies; Robespierre, balancing multiple pressures, orchestrated purges of both radical Hébertists and moderate Dantonists. Fear reigned in the city's corridors: no one felt safe from denunciation.

At the same time, the French armies were winning battles abroad. Many Parisians wondered if the Terror was still necessary. Whispers against Robespierre's dominance multiplied. By mid-1794, the Terror's grip seemed excessive, ironically endangering the very unity it was meant to preserve.

---

## 11) The Fall of Robespierre and Thermidorian Reaction

### 9 Thermidor (July 27, 1794)

Sensing that Robespierre planned another purge, rival Convention members moved first. On 9 Thermidor Year II (July 27, 1794), Robespierre and his allies were arrested, declared outlaws, and executed without trial. Crowds in Paris offered little resistance—exhausted by mass executions and uncertain about Robespierre's moral high ground.

This **Thermidorian Reaction** ended the radical phase of the revolution. The Jacobin Club was suppressed, and many leading terrorists faced prison or the guillotine. A more conservative republican regime took shape, known as the **Directory** (1795–1799). Though the Terror ended, inequalities persisted, and the Directory was hampered by corruption, inflation, and ongoing war.

## Social and Cultural Shifts

After Thermidor, Paris saw a brief surge of relief. Prisons were emptied, and survivors reemerged. Fashion changed dramatically—**Incroyables** and **Merveilleuses** paraded flamboyant styles in reaction to the grim uniformity of the Terror. Political clubs lost influence, replaced by salon gatherings with less dogmatic conversation.

Religious life revived somewhat; churches reopened. Yet the revolution's legacy had profoundly transformed society. Nobles who survived found estates confiscated or sold. The monarchy and privileges were gone, replaced by ephemeral republican institutions. Many Parisians realized that stable governance would still be elusive in a city accustomed to intense political fluctuations.

---

# 12) The Directory and Onward: 1795–1799

## The Constitution of Year III

In August 1795, the **Constitution of Year III** established the Directory, a bicameral legislature, and a five-man executive board. Voting rights were property-based, limiting most working-class Parisians. This step marked a retreat from the universal male suffrage of 1793, sparking resentment among the city's radicals.

Economic troubles persisted. Bread prices soared again in 1795, provoking the **13 Vendémiaire** royalist insurrection (October 5, 1795), which General **Napoleon Bonaparte** crushed with artillery on the streets of Paris. The Directory was thus bound to the army for survival, ironically granting ambitious generals significant political weight. Meanwhile, royalists agitated for a return to the throne, countering the lingering Jacobins who demanded a more democratic constitution.

## Cultural Flourish Amid Political Instability

Despite turmoil, Paris in the Directory period saw thriving theater, music, and intellectual gatherings. The Louvre opened as a public museum in 1793, gradually expanding its collections from seized royal or émigré property. Cafés multiplied, hosting debates about art, science, and politics. The city's printing houses resumed relative freedom, though the Directory still enacted censorship when threatened.

Yet no faction fully commanded public loyalty. Many saw the Directory as corrupt or ineffective—too aristocratic for some, too revolutionary for others. In the provinces, petty rebellions flared, while the war in Europe continued. Bonaparte's Italian campaigns (1796–1797) fueled patriotic pride in Paris, overshadowing the Directory's internal fiascos.

## 13) Rise of Napoleon and the End of the Revolutionary Era

### 18 Brumaire (November 9, 1799)

Napoleon Bonaparte returned from military successes in Egypt and Italy with widespread popularity. Sensing the Directory's unpopularity, he aligned with key political figures to orchestrate a coup on **18 Brumaire Year VIII (November 9, 1799)**. Troops loyal to Napoleon took control of strategic points in Paris. The Directory collapsed, replaced by the **Consulate** with Napoleon as First Consul.

Many Parisians welcomed Napoleon's coup—desperate for stability and a strong leader who promised to preserve the revolution's core achievements while restoring order. Others lamented the demise of republican ideals. But the general sense was that a decade of revolutionary chaos required a unifying figure. Over time, Napoleon would become Emperor in 1804, effectively concluding the revolutionary experiment in pure republican governance.

### Paris at the Brink of a New Age

By 1799, Paris had seen monarchy abolished, a republic declared, terror unleashed, and multiple constitutions tried. The revolution's legacy in the city was immense:

- **End of Feudal Privilege**: Legally, all classes stood equal before the law (in principle), a stark contrast to pre-1789 status.
- **Transformations in Governance**: The city's councils, police, and administrative framework had been altered repeatedly, reflecting shifting ideologies.
- **Cultural Vibrancy**: Despite—or because of—upheaval, the city flourished as a site of artistic and intellectual dynamism.
- **Rise of Nationalism**: War and revolution fostered a patriotic identity, with Paris as the beating heart of France.

Stepping into the 19th century, Napoleon's reign would further reshape Paris, but the seeds of modernity—democratic aspirations, secular governance, and civic activism—were all sown during these revolutionary years. The illusions and achievements of 1789–1799 echoed long afterward, ensuring that Paris would remain a reference point for future struggles over liberty, equality, and the contours of political power.

# CHAPTER 15

## THE REVOLUTIONARY AFTERMATH – DIRECTORY, CONSULATE, AND THE RISE OF NAPOLEON

## Introduction

With the fall of Robespierre in 1794 and the end of the Reign of Terror, the French Revolution entered a new phase of reconstruction and political maneuvering. In the midst of war, economic troubles, and social unrest, Paris remained the central stage for power struggles. A new government, known as the **Directory**, attempted to stabilize the Republic—but was plagued by corruption, military pressures, and factional conflicts.

Out of this tumult emerged **Napoleon Bonaparte**, a young Corsican general who found immense popularity through battlefield successes. His coup d'état in 1799 replaced the Directory with the **Consulate**, ushering in years of significant but authoritarian reform. By 1804, Napoleon crowned himself Emperor, transforming the Republic into an empire—yet Paris remained both his power base and a showcase for his ambitions.

In this chapter, we follow the twists of the Directory's rule, the socio-political life of Paris during that period, and then the rise of Napoleon. We examine how the city responded to shifting alliances, foreign wars, and domestic transformations. By the end, it was clear that revolutionary ideals had given way to a new order—still shaped by the legacy of 1789, yet dominated by a single, towering figure.

# 1) The Aftermath of the Terror: Thermidorians and the Directory (1794–1795)

## Thermidorian Reaction in Paris

The fall of Robespierre (9 Thermidor Year II / July 27, 1794) ended the Reign of Terror. The so-called **Thermidorians**, a moderate-conservative coalition in the National Convention, took power. They dismantled the most extreme Jacobin institutions, closing the radical clubs and releasing political prisoners. Parisian society showed an almost abrupt shift from austere "Republican virtue" to more extravagant fashions and open enjoyment.

In the months following Thermidor:

- **Closing of the Jacobin Club**: Once a central force in Paris, it was suppressed. Remaining Jacobins struggled to keep influence through local "sections," but the new authorities cracked down, fearing further instability.
- **White Terror**: In some regions, supporters of the old aristocracy or moderate republicans committed reprisals against former Terror enforcers. In Paris, vengeance was more symbolic—destroying Jacobin emblems or harassing known Robespierrists—yet the city saw scattered violence.
- **Economic Hardships Continue**: Bread prices and inflation remained problematic. The poor demanded relief, and occasional riots flared. However, the Thermidorian Convention was less inclined to impose price controls, favoring freer market policies.

Despite these challenges, many Parisians welcomed a respite from incessant purges and a chance to rebuild normal life. Political clubs persisted but were forced to moderate their rhetoric, as the new authorities monitored any sign of resurgent radicalism.

## The Constitution of Year III (1795)

Fearing another period of dictatorial power, the Convention drafted a new constitution, completed in 1795 (Year III). It established:

1. **The Directory**: A five-man executive, each director holding power collectively to prevent another Robespierre-like figure.
2. **A Bicameral Legislature**: The Council of Five Hundred and the Council of Ancients.
3. **Property-Based Voting**: Rolling back the universal suffrage introduced during the radical years, restricting voting to wealthier male taxpayers.

This constitution attempted a balance between monarchism and radical democracy. In Paris, reactions were mixed. The well-to-do bourgeoisie appreciated the stability that property-based suffrage promised, while the sans-culottes—who had been powerful in

1793–1794—found themselves disenfranchised. Political energies thus shifted upward, favoring the propertied classes who now dictated the direction of the post-Terror Republic.

---

## 2) The Directory in Power: Unsteady Governance (1795–1799)

### The Birth of the Directory

In October 1795, the **Directory** took office. Right away, it faced threats from two sides:

- **Royalists** who hoped to restore the Bourbon monarchy and rallied around émigré plots.
- **Neo-Jacobins** who felt the revolution was betrayed by the property restrictions and demanded a return to egalitarian policies.

For Paris, which had seen so many political changes in a short span, the Directory era felt transitional. The new regime tried to maintain order by relying on the military, a reliance that would prove fateful.

### Economic and Social Conditions

By 1795, France was still at war with several European powers, straining finances. The Directory continued printing **assignats** (paper currency from revolutionary confiscations), leading to inflation. Parisians struggled under unstable prices, with bread and essential goods frequently in short supply or overpriced.

- **Speculators and Corruption**: Some individuals grew rich off army supply contracts and currency manipulation, fueling resentments among laborers.
- **Luxury Returns**: Upscale neighborhoods and salons re-emerged with flamboyant fashions. Balls known as **Bal des victimes**—where attendees wore mourning dresses or cut hair to mimic guillotine survivors—highlighted an odd mixture of tragedy and frivolity.
- **Police Measures**: To quell discontent, the Directory restructured the city's police apparatus. They suppressed insurrectionary sections and patrolled working-class districts closely. Radical clubs had little chance to reorganize without being harassed or shut down.

As 1796–1797 brought some military successes abroad (notably Napoleon Bonaparte's rising star in the Italian campaigns), the Directory gained a measure of prestige. But internal challenges—royalist plots, Jacobin revivals, and the regime's own divisions—kept Paris on edge.

**Political Instability: Coups and Riots**

The Directory faced a series of mini-coups, both from the left (e.g., the **Babeuf Plot** in 1796) and the right (royalist intrigues). **François-Noël Babeuf** and his supporters advocated a proto-communist "Conspiracy of Equals," aiming to abolish private property. They garnered limited support among the city's workers but were quickly suppressed.

Simultaneously, royalist sympathizers formed underground networks. In some elections, they won seats, prompting the Directory to annul results via "coup within the Republic." The best known was the **Coup of 18 Fructidor Year V (September 1797)**, where directors favorable to the left used the army to expel royalist deputies. Such actions eroded the Directory's democratic credibility. Parisians saw that, once again, military force overshadowed electoral choice.

---

## 3) Napoleon's Meteoric Rise and Paris's Fascination

**The Italian Campaigns (1796–1797)**

Into this scene stepped **Napoleon Bonaparte**, a brilliant general who, at age 26, led the French Army of Italy against Austria and its allies. His decisive victories brought territorial gains and restructured much of northern Italy into "sister republics" loyal to France. Through his official bulletins, widely reprinted in Parisian newspapers, Napoleon cultivated an image of a heroic liberator—transforming him into a popular icon.

In the capital, citizens devoured reports of Bonaparte's triumphs. War-weary Parisians found renewed national pride in his success. The Directory tried to keep him at arm's length, recognizing the threat of a charismatic general overshadowing the government. Nonetheless, his dispatches gave glimpses of an emerging statesman—Napoleon negotiated treaties, reorganized conquered lands, and lauded the virtues of French arms.

**The Egyptian Expedition (1798)**

Next, the Directory allowed Napoleon to lead an expedition to Egypt, hoping to strike at British trade routes and stoke French prestige. In May 1798, he sailed from Toulon with thousands of troops, eventually capturing Cairo. While the campaign's ultimate military success was mixed—Britain's navy under Admiral Nelson decimated the French fleet at the Battle of the Nile—the Egyptian adventure enthralled Parisians. Stories of pyramids, ancient ruins, and intellectual pursuits (Napoleon brought scholars to study Egyptian antiquities) gave the expedition an exotic allure.

However, as the Directory's domestic problems mounted, Napoleon sensed opportunity. Leaving his army in Egypt under subordinates, he secretly returned to France in October

1799. By then, the regime was widely disliked, and Bonaparte's reputation for decisive leadership seemed the cure for ongoing drift. Many Parisians were ready to embrace a strong figure who could end the political chaos and preserve the revolution's core achievements.

## 4) The Coup of 18 Brumaire (November 9, 1799)

### Planning the Overthrow

Napoleon found a network of co-conspirators: Emmanuel-Joseph Sieyès (a prominent Directory member), Talleyrand (former bishop turned diplomat), and others discontented with the Directory's failures. They planned a swift coup to topple the government and install a new executive framework.

Paris was carefully prepared: rumors circulated of a supposed Jacobin plot, justifying transferring legislative sessions outside the city center. Meanwhile, Napoleon's loyal soldiers and officers were stationed strategically around Paris. On **18 Brumaire Year VIII** (November 9, 1799), the legislature found itself surrounded by troops. Many deputies resisted, suspecting a coup, but Napoleon's brother Lucien, presiding over the Council of Five Hundred, manipulated events to label protesting deputies as agitators.

### Establishment of the Consulate

By the evening of 19 Brumaire (November 10), the Directory was abolished, replaced by the **Consulate** headed by **First Consul** Napoleon Bonaparte, alongside two nominal co-consuls (Sieyès and Ducos). Parisians were informed that this coup aimed to "save the Republic" from internal strife and looming anarchy. While some recognized it as a power grab, the general populace greeted the news with cautious relief.

The city's mood was hopeful. Napoleon promised stability, an end to partisan bloodshed, and moral reforms. Having just returned from famed campaigns, he was seen as a national hero. The press largely toed the new line—whether out of genuine optimism or fear. With the Directory gone, a more authoritarian but potentially dynamic regime took shape, anchored by the unstoppable will of Bonaparte.

---

## 5) The Consulate's Reforms and Napoleon's Consolidation of Power (1799–1804)

### Centralized Administration

Napoleon swiftly reorganized France's political institutions, harnessing many Revolutionary achievements (e.g., departmental divisions, secular bureaucracy) but infusing them with strong executive control. For Paris, this meant:

1. **Prefects and Sub-Prefects**: While these officials operated more visibly in provinces, their appointment from the center symbolized the monarchy-like concentration of power.
2. **New Municipal Arrangements**: The city's mayor and city council were placed firmly under the watch of the First Consul. Local elections were limited, ensuring a stable, compliant leadership.
3. **Police Reforms**: Napoleon expanded the role of the Paris police, led by Joseph Fouché, who used surveillance and a system of informants to suppress dissent.

The Consulate also maintained many Directory-era institutions like the Bank of France (founded 1800) to stabilize currency and credit. Paris's financiers and merchants appreciated this consistent economic direction—contrasted with the earlier chaos of revolutionary finance.

### The Concordat of 1801

Recognizing religious divisions since the Civil Constitution of the Clergy, Napoleon negotiated a **Concordat** with Pope Pius VII (1801). It acknowledged Catholicism as the religion of the majority of French citizens, while preserving religious freedom and state oversight. Churches in Paris reopened fully; exiled clergy returned. Many devout Parisians welcomed this measure, seeing it as a reconciliation with centuries of faith.

However, the state retained the right to appoint bishops, and Church lands confiscated during the Revolution were not returned. The Concordat thus satisfied moderate Catholics but angered some radical republicans who felt it compromised the principle of secular governance. Still, most Parisians appeared relieved by the end of open hostilities with Rome, hoping it would quell the lingering religious strife in the city.

### Napoleonic Code and Institutional Overhauls

Between 1802 and 1804, Napoleon presided over commissions drafting the **Civil Code** (later called the Napoleonic Code). It unified French civil law—abolishing feudal remnants, enshrining legal equality among men, and safeguarding property rights. In Paris, lawyers and jurists debated its articles intensively; printed copies sold widely, reflecting the public's curiosity about legal modernization. The code would become a cornerstone of French and even global law.

Parallel reforms reshaped education (lycées to train future officials), administration (merit-based appointments), and the judiciary. Many Parisians, especially the bourgeoisie, supported these rationalizing measures, which seemed to fulfill some Enlightenment aspirations for clarity and fairness, albeit under an authoritarian framework. Meanwhile, political liberties—like freedom of the press and assembly—remained severely restricted. Napoleon concluded that controlling public discourse was vital to maintaining order in the capital.

---

## 6) Napoleon Becomes Emperor (1804) and Paris's Imperial Ambitions

### The Coronation in Notre-Dame

By 1802, Napoleon secured the position of **First Consul for Life** via a plebiscite—reflecting a façade of popular approval. Two years later, maneuvering among elites and public acclaim set the stage for proclaiming him **Emperor Napoleon I**. On December 2, 1804, the coronation took place at **Notre-Dame Cathedral** in Paris, a grand spectacle with Pope Pius VII in attendance (though Napoleon famously crowned himself, symbolizing independence from papal authority).

Parisians reacted with a mix of awe and curiosity. This ritual marked a turn away from explicit republicanism—yet the city's inhabitants, tired of revolutionary upheaval, mostly celebrated the stability and grandeur the empire promised. Festivities across Paris showcased the new Imperial eagles, and official bulletins hailed Napoleon as the savior who continued the Revolution's core principles of meritocracy and national unity, now couched in imperial pomp.

**Imperial Projects and Monuments**

Napoleon believed that an imperial capital should reflect French glory. Major architectural and urban designs advanced:

- **Arc de Triomphe** (begun 1806): Intended to honor the Grand Armée's victories, situated at the western end of the Champs-Élysées. While construction took decades, Parisians saw the rising edifice as a statement of martial triumph.
- **Arc de Triomphe du Carrousel** (built 1806–1808): Near the Louvre, commemorating Austerlitz and other successes.
- **La Madeleine**: Originally planned as a temple to the Grand Armée, it was later converted into a church.
- **Improvements to Streets and Bridges**: Though overshadowed by military expenditures, Napoleon allocated funds for better paving and lighting in certain central arrondissements, seeking an orderly metropolis that befitted an empire.

For the city's populace, these monumental works instilled pride but also underscored heavy taxation and forced conscription fueling Napoleon's wars. Many families lost sons to ongoing European campaigns. Nonetheless, in the short term, the city basked in a sense of world-historical significance, hosting dignitaries, parades, and foreign delegations who recognized Paris as the heart of a continent-spanning empire.

---

## 7) Life in Napoleonic Paris: Society, Economy, and Culture

**Social Stratification**

Under Napoleon, the aristocracy reappeared in a novel form. The emperor bestowed noble titles—dukes, counts, barons—on generals, ministers, and supporters, creating an **imperial nobility** based on service and loyalty. Old Bourbon nobles who pledged allegiance to Napoleon often regained partial status. This emergent hierarchy resonated with Paris's bourgeoisie, who saw an opportunity for upward mobility if they performed well in administrative or military roles.

Common laborers, shopkeepers, and craftsmen found that daily life remained a challenge. War mobilization meant conscription, draining manpower from families. The cost of living was high in the capital, although wages for certain skilled trades rose with government contracts. Political clubs were nonexistent, ensuring little direct say in governance for the working class.

## Policing and Public Order

Police minister **Joseph Fouché** built an extensive network of spies in Paris, reporting on potential dissidents. Censorship of the press tightened further: only four newspapers were allowed, all supervised by the state. While some citizens grumbled about the stifling climate, many remembered the chaos of earlier revolutionary years and welcomed order. The regime's official bulletins promoted the emperor's achievements, overshadowing dissenting views.

Nevertheless, a thriving **underground press** and rumor networks persisted in the city's backstreets and cafés. Royalists conspired quietly for Bourbon restoration, especially after 1808–1809, when cracks in Napoleon's grand empire started appearing. Disenchanted republicans yearned for the lost days of 1792–1793, though few dared speak openly for fear of arrest.

## Cultural Patronage

Napoleon's court revived a degree of splendor reminiscent of Louis XIV. Opera, ballet, and art exhibitions found patronage from the Imperial household. Painters like **Jacques-Louis David**, once a revolutionary propagandist, now glorified the emperor's image in works such as *The Coronation of Napoleon*. Parisian salons re-emerged, though carefully monitored.

Scientific institutions flourished under the emperor's aegis, consistent with the Enlightenment tradition of rational progress. Polytechnique and other grandes écoles expanded to train military engineers, administrators, and scientists. Public lectures and demonstration experiments attracted crowds, albeit under the watchful eye of government censors. All these efforts reinforced an image of Paris as an enlightened imperial capital, bridging revolutionary legacies with monarchical grandeur.

---

# 8) The Wars Under the Empire and Their Impact on Paris

## Continental Dominance and Exhaustion

Throughout the first decade of the 19th century, Napoleon's armies triumphed in famous battles: **Austerlitz (1805)**, **Jena (1806)**, **Friedland (1807)**, and more. He created a network of satellite states—some ruled by his relatives. In the capital, repeated victory celebrations inflated national pride. Triumph arches, parades on the Champs-Élysées, and mass distributions of medals to returning troops fueled support.

But this success demanded conscription. Each year, more men were called to arms. Families in Paris parted with sons, uncertain if they would return. Wounded soldiers overwhelmed hospitals, and rumors of faraway battles circulated in cafés. By 1812, the empire stretched across Europe, but strains on manpower, logistics, and finances grew acute. The city's bread supply sometimes faltered when transport was disrupted by war.

**The Russian Campaign (1812) and Decline**

Napoleon's decision to invade Russia in 1812 proved catastrophic. The Grand Armée marched from victory to a Pyrrhic occupation of Moscow, only to retreat amid a brutal winter. The news of this disaster, when it reached Paris, shocked the populace. Although official bulletins initially downplayed losses, returning survivors told harrowing stories of starvation and freezing.

In 1813, European powers formed new coalitions against France. Defeats at Leipzig (October 1813) and elsewhere brought allied armies closer to French borders. Paris felt a sense of dread reminiscent of revolutionary times. Some saw the unraveling of Napoleon's empire as inevitable. Others still clung to the myth of his invincibility, hoping for a miracle. But by early 1814, enemy forces stood near the gates of the capital.

---

## 9) The Fall of Napoleon and the Bourbon Restoration (1814)

**Allied Invasion and Capitulation**

In March 1814, a coalition of Austrian, Prussian, and Russian armies advanced on Paris. With Napoleon away fighting, the city's defense fell to hastily assembled troops and National Guardsmen. Bombardment of Paris's outskirts caused panic. Royalists within Paris seized the moment to push for Bourbon restoration, while many city officials realized a prolonged siege could devastate the population.

On March 30–31, 1814, the allies entered Paris. The Senate, under Talleyrand's machinations, declared Napoleon deposed. When the emperor tried returning from Fontainebleau, it was too late. He abdicated on April 6, 1814.

**Arrival of Louis XVIII**

The victorious allies restored the Bourbon monarchy in the person of **Louis XVIII**, brother of the executed Louis XVI. Parisians greeted him with a mixture of curiosity and caution; some welcomed an end to constant war, while others lamented the collapse of the empire. The old fleur-de-lis flags replaced the tricolor, and royalists exiled for decades returned, seeking to reclaim positions and properties.

Napoleon was exiled to Elba, a small Mediterranean island. For the moment, the city's mood turned from imperial bombast to subdued relief at the prospect of peace. But the Restoration's reconciliation with revolutionary-era changes remained unsettled—posing questions about whether the monarchy would roll back the revolution's achievements or accept them in a new constitutional framework.

# 10) The Hundred Days and Napoleon's Final Defeat (1815)

### The Return from Elba

On February 26, 1815, Napoleon escaped Elba and landed in southern France. As he advanced north, troops sent to arrest him defected to their former emperor. His approach to Paris became a triumphant march, culminating in his return to the Tuileries on March 20, 1815, while Louis XVIII fled. Parisians, caught off guard, saw an extraordinary reversal in less than a year. Napoleon's return—known as the **Hundred Days**—reestablished the Empire, albeit briefly.

Napoleon quickly assured the nation he would rule as a constitutional emperor, promising freedoms and an end to war. But the European allies refused negotiation. By June 1815, Napoleon's final gamble at the Battle of Waterloo ended in defeat. The victorious allies marched on Paris once again.

### Second Restoration of the Bourbons

After Waterloo, Napoleon abdicated a second time, eventually surrendering to the British. The allies reinstalled Louis XVIII in Paris in July 1815. An air of exhaustion permeated the city. Many had hoped for a negotiated peace under Napoleon; others simply wanted stability, regardless of regime. Now, the monarchy was definitively back.

Royalist fervor flared, with reprisals against Bonapartist officials and supporters. Known as the "**White Terror**," this wave targeted those closely associated with the previous regime. Talleyrand again maneuvered to maintain France's basic institutional integrity under Bourbon rule, aiming to prevent the monarchy from unleashing a vengeful purge that might incite more chaos. Paris, battered by decades of upheaval, resigned itself to yet another political system, uncertain how deeply the Bourbons would alter the Revolutionary and Napoleonic legacies.

## 11) The Legacy of Napoleon in Paris

### Urban Transformations

Despite the empire's downfall, Napoleon left visible marks on Parisian architecture and infrastructure:

- **Arc de Triomphe du Carrousel**: Completed to celebrate early victories, it stood near the Louvre as a testament to Napoleon's ambition.
- **La Madeleine**: Its colonnaded facade, begun as a "Temple of Glory," eventually served as a Catholic church—symbolizing the blend of Napoleonic and traditional elements.
- **Bridges and Administrative Systems**: Napoleonic reforms continued shaping daily governance. Even after the monarchy returned, the city used the efficient systems for policing, prefecture administration, and central planning.

### Military and Administrative Culture

Napoleon's emphasis on merit influenced the capital's bureaucracy, which remained relatively open to talent—a stark shift from Bourbon nepotism of the past. Students at Polytechnique, the Ecole Normale, and other imperial schools carried on the rigorous, specialized education introduced during the Consulate and Empire. Intellectual life in Paris retained some of the impetus for rational administration, though overshadowed by renewed royal prerogatives.

### Cultural Memory

In the immediate post-war climate, references to Napoleon were suppressed by the restored monarchy. However, many Parisians quietly remembered the empire's glories—victories, code reforms, and modernization—and harbored nostalgic loyalty to the Bonapartist myth. Over time, these memories would resurface, playing roles in future rebellions and dynastic tensions. For now, under Bourbon rule, the official line dismissed Napoleon as an usurper who had brought ruin to France, ignoring how many had willingly embraced him for stability and national pride.

# CHAPTER 16

## THE RESTORATION AND THE SHIFTING POLITICAL LANDSCAPE

## Introduction

Following Napoleon's final defeat at Waterloo (June 1815) and his second abdication, the Bourbon monarchy was definitively restored in France. **Louis XVIII**, and later **Charles X**, sought to reestablish royal authority while selectively recognizing certain revolutionary and Napoleonic reforms. Yet Paris, exhausted by decades of upheaval, remained a tinderbox of conflicting aspirations: royalists clamored for the full return of the old ways, liberals defended constitutional principles, and Bonapartists dreamed of reviving the empire.

In this chapter, we explore the **Restoration era** (1814–1830) and the shifting political landscape that eventually led to another revolution in 1830. We examine how Bourbon kings tried to navigate a capital transformed by revolution—where new social classes, legal frameworks, and cultural expressions demanded acknowledgment. We will see how the monarchy's missteps alienated parts of the population, culminating in the **July Revolution**. Throughout, Paris served as the crucible, where insurrections broke out, intellectual circles debated, and the monarchy's success or failure was ultimately decided.

# 1) The First Restoration and the Hundred Days (1814–1815)

### Louis XVIII's Tentative Return

In April 1814, after Napoleon's abdication, the Bourbon family returned from exile. **Louis XVIII**, brother of Louis XVI, took the throne. He faced a delicate balance: large segments of French society had accepted Napoleonic institutions and did not wish to revert to complete pre-1789 tradition. Louis XVIII recognized this by issuing the **Charter of 1814**, which retained some features of the Napoleonic Code and confirmed property rights for lands confiscated during the Revolution (including those sold as biens nationaux).

For Parisians, who endured sieges and political reversals, the monarchy's reentry promised peace. However, royalist enthusiasm was tempered. Many remembered the Declaration of Verona (1795), in which Louis XVIII vowed to punish revolutionaries. Now, under pressure from Talleyrand and moderate advisors, the king took a more conciliatory tone—yet distrust lingered, especially among Bonapartists and liberals.

### Napoleon's Return and Second Abdication

When Napoleon landed from Elba in March 1815, Louis XVIII's supporters panicked. The king fled Paris as Napoleon advanced triumphantly. But after the defeat at Waterloo in June, the allies once more forced Napoleon to abdicate. Louis XVIII returned to the Tuileries in July 1815, initiating the **Second Restoration**.

Paris's reaction to these events was resignation—excitement about Napoleon's dramatic comeback had ended in disastrous war. This time, the victorious coalition demanded indemnities and stationed occupying troops around France. The city felt the humiliation of foreign soldiers on its streets, fueling resentment. Royalists unleashed the **White Terror**, persecuting Bonapartists, Republicans, and Protestants in some regions, though in Paris it was milder, focusing more on curbing political clubs and newspapers.

---

# 2) The Charter of 1814 and Bourbon Moderation

### Constitutional Monarchy Framework

Under the Charter, France became a **constitutional monarchy** with a bicameral legislature:

1. **Chamber of Peers**: Appointed by the king, often composed of aristocrats and former Napoleonic notables.
2. **Chamber of Deputies**: Elected by property-based suffrage, limiting the vote to about 100,000 wealthy men across France.

Louis XVIII tried to reassure the new elites that their revolutionary gains—like the Napoleonic Code—would be safe. Freedom of religion was proclaimed, though Catholicism remained favored. Property rights for those who acquired émigré lands during the revolution were upheld, mitigating fears of restitution demands.

**Paris and the "Ultras"**

Despite Louis XVIII's moderation, a faction of ultraroyalists (or **Ultras**) wanted a full return to absolutism. They distrusted the Charter, seeing it as a concession to revolutionary ideals. In Paris, Ultras formed clubs, distributed pamphlets, and pressured the Court for stronger measures against perceived enemies—Bonapartists, liberal intellectuals, Protestants, and all associated with the revolution.

For the city's bourgeoisie, stability and economic recovery took priority over ideological purity. Many wealthier Parisians supported the idea of a constitutional monarchy, hoping it would foster commerce, respect property rights, and avoid future revolutions. This moderate stance clashed with the Ultras' zeal, leading to political tension in parliamentary debates and street pamphlets.

---

## 3) The White Terror and Political Tensions (1815–1820)

### Purges and Reconciliations

Immediately after the Second Restoration, royalist authorities hunted down prominent Bonapartists responsible for the Hundred Days. Marshal Ney was executed, and others faced exile or lengthy imprisonment. Although some demanded a broader purge of revolutionaries, Louis XVIII tried to restrain extreme retribution, mindful that too harsh a crackdown could provoke unrest in Paris and beyond.

Nevertheless, sporadic violence flared, especially in southern provinces. In Paris, the monarchy aimed to portray itself as above vengeance. Official bulletins praised Louis XVIII's paternal clemency while also demonstrating that royal authority must be respected. This balancing act left both Ultras and liberals dissatisfied: Ultras felt the king was too lenient, liberals deemed him too reactionary.

### Police and Press Restrictions

To maintain order, the monarchy restructured Parisian police, granting broad powers to the prefect of police. Spies watched for seditious activity among Bonapartists or republicans. Royal censorship committees vetted newspapers, banning articles that criticized the Crown or advocated radical doctrines. Writers faced fines or prison for violating these guidelines.

Many liberals, including journalists and intellectuals in Paris, resisted quietly. They formed reading societies and circulated manuscripts critical of the monarchy.

Meanwhile, foreign ministers, especially from Britain and Austria, kept a close eye on the city—hoping France would not relapse into revolutionary chaos. Parisians learned to navigate these constraints, finding coded ways to express political ideas. Tension simmered beneath the surface, awaiting a spark to reignite open conflict.

## 4) Economic and Cultural Life in Early Restoration Paris

**Commerce and Recovery**

After two decades of near-constant warfare, the early 1820s brought some respite. Foreign troops withdrew, and trade routes reopened. Paris's ports on the Seine, commerce in Les Halles, and artisanal workshops revived. The wealthy bourgeois engaged in industrial projects—like textile mills in nearby suburbs—anticipating growth in a more peaceful era.

Luxury shops and cafés resumed flourishing along the boulevards, catering to aristocrats and affluent bourgeois. Meanwhile, the city's working classes faced low wages and rising living costs. Unemployment remained high in certain trades battered by the collapse of war-based production. Some migration from rural areas continued, crowding lower-income neighborhoods.

**Artistic and Literary Trends**

Artistic circles adapted to Restoration themes. While Napoleonic motifs went out of fashion, a new **Romantic** sensibility emerged—exemplified by writers like **Chateaubriand**, who merged Catholic royalist nostalgia with a passionate style, and painters like **Géricault** or **Delacroix**, who explored dramatic subjects. The monarchy sometimes patronized these artists for official commissions, though their works often contained subtle critiques or evocations of revolutionary energies.

The theater, especially the **Comédie-Française** and the **Odéon**, featured plays that navigated censorship by focusing on historical or mythical settings. Society dames hosted salons once more, but now with caution, aware that the monarchy's secret police kept watch for subversive talk. Culturally, Paris remained vibrant, yet an undercurrent of ambivalence about the Bourbon regime influenced the era's creative output.

---

## 5) The Assassination of the Duc de Berry and Political Shifts (1820)

### A Royal Tragedy

On February 13, 1820, the **Duc de Berry**, nephew of Louis XVIII and second in line to the throne, was assassinated by a Bonapartist fanatic as he left the Paris Opera. This event stunned the capital. The Ultras exploited it to demand harsh measures against liberals and Bonapartists, blaming them for fostering anti-royal sentiment.

The monarchy, already leaning to the right, used the assassination as justification to impose new laws restricting press freedom, dissolving liberal political clubs, and reinforcing censorship. Paris's liberal circles condemned the murder but protested the monarchy's overreach. Tensions escalated: a sense that Bourbon authority was sliding back into reactionary absolutism troubled moderate bourgeois who had hoped for balanced constitutional rule.

### Rise of the Ultras under Charles X

Louis XVIII, increasingly ill, ceded much influence to his ultra-royalist brother **Count of Artois**—the future Charles X. By 1824, when Louis XVIII died, Charles X inherited a kingdom whose political scene had polarized further. In Paris, liberal voices grew resentful of the monarchy's repressive tactics. This friction would intensify under Charles X's reign, setting the stage for another upheaval.

---

## 6) Charles X's Reign (1824–1830) and the Drive to Reassert Royal Power

### Royal Coronation and Aspirations

Charles X had himself crowned in a lavish traditional ceremony at Reims in 1825, openly reviving symbols of pre-revolutionary monarchy. Many Parisians viewed this as a theatrical attempt to restore anachronistic grandeur. The king championed indemnities for émigrés who lost property during the Revolution, enraging those who had purchased or benefited from such lands.

In the capital, resentment grew, particularly among the middle class. The government's stance against press freedoms and university autonomy sparked further dissatisfaction. While some conservatives cheered Charles X's forthright style, others perceived it as a dangerous denial of the post-1789 social contract. Napoleon's memory lingered as a possible alternative model of leadership, especially if Bourbon rule proved too backward.

**Conservative Policies and Liberal Opposition**

Charles X appointed **Jules de Polignac** as chief minister in 1829, an ultra-royalist who had lived as an émigré and was deeply out of touch with liberal circles. Polignac's government attempted to clamp down on free expression. In July 1830, it issued the **July Ordinances**—dissolving the newly elected Chamber of Deputies, restricting the press, and altering electoral laws to favor the aristocracy.

Paris exploded in fury. Newspaper owners refused to comply, continuing to print defiant editorials. Journeymen printers and students rallied in the streets, calling for the overthrow of tyrannical measures. As the monarchy miscalculated the city's temper, a short but decisive uprising unfolded, pushing the Bourbon line to the brink.

---

## 7) The July Revolution (1830) and the End of Charles X

**The Barricades in Paris**

On July 27, 1830, Parisians erected barricades across central districts—reminiscent of revolutionary episodes from 1789 and 1792. Workers, students, and middle-class liberals united in condemning the July Ordinances. Fighting broke out with royal troops. Over three days, known as the **"Trois Glorieuses"** (the Three Glorious Days), the city overcame the king's forces. Soldiers often sympathized with the protesters or simply refused to fire.

Charles X, alarmed, tried to revoke the ordinances too late. Popular insurrection had triumphed. On July 30, moderate deputies offered the throne to **Louis-Philippe**, Duke of Orléans, who claimed to be a "Citizen King" upholding a revised Charter. Charles X fled into exile. Once again, Paris had toppled a monarch and reshaped the nation's leadership, demonstrating that the capital's barricades remained a potent force for regime change.

### Aftermath and the July Monarchy

On August 9, 1830, **Louis-Philippe** was proclaimed "King of the French," not "King of France," implying a contract with the people. Parisians celebrated the victory, seeing it as a partial realization of liberal ideals. However, radical republicans and socialists felt the movement was hijacked by bourgeois interests. Indeed, the new regime, known as the **July Monarchy**, would soon face similar tensions over representation, workers' rights, and the role of the press.

Still, for the moment, the city rejoiced in toppling Charles X. This second Bourbon Restoration ended, capping an era in which royal authority tried to revert to old structures but was thwarted by an increasingly self-aware bourgeoisie and an emboldened urban populace. Paris's streets had once again proven decisive in altering the monarchy's fate, exemplifying the capital's unmatched power in France's evolving political landscape.

---

## 8) Social Transformations in Restoration-Era Paris

### The Emergence of a New Industrial Class

During the Bourbon Restoration, the seeds of early industrialization sprouted around Paris. Entrepreneurs established mechanized spinning or weaving plants in suburban areas like Rouen or Lille (though outside the direct city proper). Yet the capital still served as a hub for finance, distribution, and artisanal workshops. Wealthy bankers, many with Napoleonic or revolutionary backgrounds, financed canals, roads, and sometimes early rail prototypes.

The bourgeoisie dominated commerce, embracing new forms of capitalism. They looked to the monarchy for infrastructure improvements while insisting on lower taxes and fewer feudal remnants. This emergent business class helped shape city politics, balancing a desire for stability with liberal values such as property rights and freedom to innovate.

### Workers and the Growth of an Urban Proletariat

Paris's working classes, meanwhile, faced uncertain job prospects. Traditional guilds, weakened by revolutionary decrees, could not protect artisans from mechanized competition. Wages fluctuated with market conditions. Skilled laborers, such as printers or metalworkers, formed mutual aid societies, precursors to trade unions.

Political ferment among workers was sporadic but increasingly shaped by ideas of social equality. Secret societies, often influenced by Bonapartist or Jacobin nostalgia, emerged among younger laborers. They circulated pamphlets criticizing exploitation, hoping for a regime more responsive to the populace. The monarchy's periodic crackdowns on seditious gatherings exacerbated their sense of marginalization.

**Religious Renewal and Charitable Endeavors**

After decades of upheaval, Catholic institutions regained some ground under the Restoration. Churches refurbished damage from revolutionary desecrations, and priests resumed community roles. In Paris, philanthropic efforts expanded—religious charities aided the poor, sometimes supported by royal donations. However, divisions persisted. Some workers viewed the Church as aligned with the elites, while devout Catholics found hope in revived devotional practices and the monarchy's endorsement.

Protestants and Jews continued to exercise rights conferred during the Revolution, though they faced societal prejudice. The monarchy, officially Catholic, offered them partial tolerance, consistent with the Charter's spirit, but the "eldest daughter of the Church" sentiment often overshadowed genuine religious equality.

---

## 9) Cultural Vibrancy: Romanticism and the Arts

**Literary and Artistic Movements**

By the 1820s, **Romanticism** flourished. Writers like **Victor Hugo**, **Alfred de Vigny**, and **Alphonse de Lamartine** rebelled against classical constraints, championing emotional expression, medieval and exotic themes, and a focus on individual passion. In painting, **Eugène Delacroix**'s vibrant works mirrored these ideals, while **Antoine-Jean Gros** depicted Napoleonic legends infused with drama.

Paris's salons and theaters became battlegrounds for aesthetic debates: conservatives clung to neoclassicism, while romantics demanded liberation from formulaic rules. The monarchy tried to patronize the arts selectively—commissioning historical or religious subjects that upheld regal and Christian narratives. Nonetheless, a new generation of artists tapped into the city's restive spirit, forging innovative styles that shaped European cultural life.

**Music, Opera, and Public Entertainment**

The city's opera houses—such as the **Opéra de Paris**—hosted grand performances, financed partly by royal subventions. Composers integrated Romantic lyricism, featuring flamboyant costumes and large choruses. Concert halls emerged, allowing traveling virtuosos to dazzle Parisian audiences. The monarchy tolerated these amusements, seeing them as signs of civic prosperity and refinement.

Mass entertainment also included popular melodramas in less formal theaters, puppet shows in street fairs, and café-concerts. The city's nightlife thrived, despite strict policing. Aristocrats mingled with the bourgeois in luxurious gatherings, while workers found cheap amusements in rowdy taverns. This cultural dynamism contrasted with political tensions, demonstrating how art and leisure provided partial relief from the uncertainties of Restoration politics.

## 10) The 1830 Crisis and the July Revolution (Recap)

### The Trigger: July Ordinances

As Charles X embraced ultra-royalist policies, he alienated the moderate majority. The July Ordinances triggered immediate outrage in Paris:

- **Suppression of Freedom of the Press**: Journalists defied orders, printing fiery protests.
- **Electoral Reforms**: Favoring the aristocracy, drastically reducing the electorate.
- **Dissolution of the New Chamber of Deputies**: Undermining even the limited constitutional freedoms.

The monarchy underestimated the capital's reaction. Intellectuals, financiers, artisans, and students all resented the sudden power grab. On July 27, 1830, they erected barricades across central arrondissements, heralding an open insurrection.

### Triumph of the Barricades

For three days, fierce skirmishes erupted between insurgents and royal troops. Many soldiers sympathized with the crowds or deserted. By July 29, the Tuileries and the Louvre were in revolutionary hands. Charles X, lacking widespread loyalty, fled to Saint-Cloud and eventually into exile. The victory of the Parisian uprising forced constitutional liberals in the legislature to craft a new monarchy under **Louis-Philippe**—the "July Monarchy."

This second overthrow of the Bourbons in less than two decades illustrated Paris's unstoppable capacity to shape national destinies. The moderate-liberal elite, seeking order rather than a republic, installed the Duke of Orléans as King of the French. Some more radical revolutionaries lamented that the old monarchy was replaced by another crowned head, but the majority accepted the compromise, relieved to avert further chaos.

---

## 11) The Aftermath and Broader Implications

### A New Social Pact

The July Revolution launched the **Orléanist regime** (1830–1848). While this monarchy would itself face future unrest, it signified that any attempt to restore absolute monarchy was doomed in Paris's environment of vigilance and barricade tradition. The new charter recognized expanded suffrage (though still property-based), ended the most reactionary laws, and embraced the tricolor flag as France's national symbol.

For many middle-class Parisians, the regime offered opportunities to prosper without the fear of an Ultra crackdown. Political clubs revived, albeit under close scrutiny, and newspapers regained some freedom, fueling public debate. Worker issues, however, remained unresolved—wage laborers saw no fundamental revolution in their economic position. Tensions between the liberal bourgeois monarchy and popular aspirations for greater equality would soon resurface.

---

# CHAPTER 17

### THE JULY MONARCHY AND THE SEEDS OF FURTHER REVOLUTIONS

## Introduction

In July 1830, Paris once again served as the crucible for regime change. Angered by Charles X's autocratic July Ordinances, which curbed press freedoms and suffrage, Parisians took to the streets, erected barricades, and forced the king into exile. This short but decisive **July Revolution** ended the Bourbon Restoration and elevated **Louis-Philippe**, Duke of Orléans, to the throne. Styled the **"Citizen King,"** he promised a more liberal constitutional regime—a monarchy that would, in theory, cooperate with the growing bourgeois class rather than clamp down on modern freedoms.

Yet the **July Monarchy (1830–1848)** would be marked by contradictions. On one hand, it witnessed economic expansion, the continued rise of a wealthy industrial and financial bourgeoisie, and moderate civil liberties. On the other hand, its restrictive suffrage laws and cautious approach to political reform alienated workers, republicans, and other groups whose hopes for a more radical democracy remained unfulfilled. Over the course of Louis-Philippe's reign, social tensions in Paris steadily rose, fueled by cyclical economic crises, evolving labor demands, and new ideological currents—culminating in the revolution of 1848.

This chapter explores how the **July Monarchy** functioned in Paris, the social transformations underway in the capital, the cultural and intellectual climate, and the myriad ways in which disillusionment set the stage for yet another upheaval. By the time 1848 dawned, the city was once again on the verge of revolution—a revolution that would topple the Orléans monarchy and pave the way for France's second experiment in republican governance.

## 1) Louis-Philippe's Accession and the New Constitutional Framework

### A "Citizen King"

When Louis-Philippe was offered the crown by liberal deputies in July 1830, he accepted under the condition that he would reign as **"King of the French,"** not **"King of France."** The distinction implied a contract with the people, emphasizing that sovereignty resided in the nation rather than in divine right. He adopted the **tricolor flag**, symbol of the 1789 Revolution, in place of the Bourbon fleur-de-lis. For Parisians, these gestures suggested a more modern monarchy, perhaps bridging the gap between old aristocratic rule and republican ideals.

### The Revised Charter of 1830

Under the new regime, the **Charter of 1814** was amended to reduce royal prerogatives and broaden civil freedoms:

- **King's authority**: Still executive in nature, but tempered by an active legislature.
- **Chamber of Deputies**: Retained property-based suffrage, though the threshold was somewhat lowered, expanding the electorate slightly.
- **Press Freedoms**: Officially recognized in principle, though subject to government oversight.
- **Religious Toleration**: Confirmed the principle of freedom of worship, leaving behind the aggressive alliance with Catholic orthodoxy of Charles X's reign.

Many in Paris welcomed these changes, relieved to see a monarchy that at least symbolically aligned with liberal aspirations. Nonetheless, the new constitution did not grant universal suffrage or deep social reforms. The franchise was still heavily restricted to upper- and middle-class property owners—less than 200,000 voters nationwide, out of millions of adult men. This limitation soon became a flashpoint for discontent.

### Early Popular Support and Symbolic Gestures

In the first months of his reign, Louis-Philippe paraded through Paris on foot, sporting a plain frock coat and an umbrella, cultivating the image of a modest monarch in tune with bourgeois mores. He visited workshops, saluted the National Guard (staffed by middle-class citizens), and assured the crowd he had no illusions of absolute power. For a time, these gestures appeased many who feared a return to reactionary monarchy. The press largely celebrated this "Citizen King," although more radical newspapers demanded further liberalization.

## 2) Socioeconomic Developments: Industry, Finance, and Class Relations

### The Ascendant Bourgeoisie

The **July Monarchy** is often described as the "**bourgeois monarchy**," since it provided the best environment for the commercial and industrial elite to prosper. Under Louis-Philippe, Paris became a hub of **finance**, with the **Bourse** (stock exchange) flourishing. Banks and credit institutions proliferated, funding railways, mines, and manufacturing ventures across France. The city's wealthy financiers and entrepreneurs, many seated in the Chamber of Deputies, used government connections to secure favorable policies, like low tariffs on imported machinery or public works that spurred commerce.

Paris's boulevards saw an expansion of upscale shops, cafés, and commercial passages (arcades), symbolizing the newfound consumer culture. Middle-class families invested in real estate, building elegant apartment houses in neighborhoods close to the city center. Key examples included the **Faubourg Saint-Honoré** and the expanding districts around the **Grands Boulevards**, where new theaters and cafés attracted well-to-do patrons.

### Industrial Growth and the Urban Workforce

Simultaneously, new industries cropped up around Paris, often in suburban areas like **Saint-Denis**, **Aubervilliers**, or beyond. Textiles, metallurgy, chemicals, and later rail workshops employed a growing working class that commuted or migrated to the capital. The city's population surged, surpassing 900,000 by the mid-1840s. Neighborhoods near factories grew crowded, with cramped, unsanitary housing for laborers.

This nascent **proletariat** faced precarious employment and low wages, especially during economic downturns. Guilds, once abolished in the Revolution, had not been meaningfully restored, leaving workers vulnerable to exploitation. Strikes were rare and often met with swift police or National Guard intervention. Within Paris, the gap between bourgeois comfort and working-class hardship widened. This tension simmered, fueling demands for labor reforms—demands the monarchy largely ignored.

### Infrastructure and Public Works

The monarchy continued modest improvements to the city's infrastructure. Roads were paved or widened, and the first steps toward railroad construction took shape. In 1837, the **first railway line** connected Paris to Saint-Germain-en-Laye, foreshadowing a railway boom that would intensify in the 1840s. Louis-Philippe's government recognized the economic benefits of modern transport but balked at radical expansions, fearing the disruption large-scale transformations might bring.

Water and sanitation remained rudimentary, with minimal state intervention. Private companies sometimes managed water distribution in wealthier districts, ignoring poorer areas. Meanwhile, entrepreneurs opened new gaslight installations, illuminating select boulevards and theaters—enhancing the city's nightlife. Such partial modernization mirrored the monarchy's overall approach: gradual improvements shaped by business interests rather than far-reaching public welfare concerns.

---

## 3) Political Life and Factions in the July Monarchy

### The Orleanist Elite and Parliamentary Dynamics

Under the July Monarchy, political debate took place in the **Chamber of Deputies**, dominated by property-owning liberals known as **Doctrinaires**. Key figures included **François Guizot**, who believed in a narrow franchise restricted to the "most capable" citizens. They championed the monarchy's moderation, defending private property and incremental reforms. Guizot's famous statement—**"Enrichissez-vous!"** ("Enrich yourselves!")—epitomized this worldview: prosperity for the middle class would allegedly trickle down, stabilizing society.

A smaller group of more progressive liberals, like **Odilon Barrot**, pressed for expanded suffrage and free speech. They criticized government corruption and censorship. Meanwhile, **legitimists** (Bourbon supporters) refused to accept Louis-Philippe, labeling him a usurper, and stayed mostly out of official politics. Royalists occasionally plotted conspiracies, but the monarchy repressed them effectively.

### Republicanism and Bonapartism in the Shadows

Despite official acceptance of limited constitutional monarchy, underground republican clubs persisted in Paris. University students, radical journalists, and artisans formed secret societies—like the **Society of the Rights of Man**—aiming to overthrow the monarchy in favor of a republic. They circulated pamphlets praising 1792's republican triumph or condemning present inequalities. Government spies infiltrated these networks, leading to arrests and show trials.

Parallel to republican dissent was a lingering **Bonapartist** sentiment. Some veterans and middle-class admirers revered Napoleon's memory, hoping his nephew, **Louis-Napoleon Bonaparte**, might someday restore imperial glory. Though minor in the 1830s, these Bonapartists occasionally staged absurd conspiracies (like Louis-Napoleon's failed 1836 and 1840 coups), provoking a mixture of ridicule and alarm in Paris. Over time, as we will see in Chapter 18, Louis-Napoleon would become more significant, but for now, he remained a curious footnote.

## Censorship and Repression

Initially, Louis-Philippe's regime tolerated freer press laws than Charles X did. However, as criticism mounted, the king's ministers frequently invoked laws against "incitement" or seditious libel. Newspapers faced fines and closures if they published radical editorials or exposed governmental scandals. Street demonstrations by republican societies were swiftly suppressed by municipal guard forces.

The monarchy's reliance on repressive measures alienated some moderate liberals who had supported the July Revolution but now saw the new regime replicating old patterns of censorship. This disillusionment brewed particularly among students and skilled workers, who felt shut out from the promised "citizen" monarchy. Over time, each clampdown stoked resentments that would eventually explode in 1848.

## 4) Social Turmoil and the Rise of Workers' Movements

### Early Worker Associations

Amid industrial expansion, workers in Paris began forming **mutual aid societies** to address medical care, unemployment relief, and funeral costs—an embryonic form of labor organization. Although guilds remained abolished since the Revolution, some trades established "companionship" networks or "compagnonnages," preserving traditions of craft identity.

By the 1830s, more politically charged **workers' associations** emerged. Figures like **Flora Tristan** or **Auguste Blanqui** championed the idea that laborers must unite for political change. Secret printing presses produced pamphlets denouncing exploitation, highlighting cramped housing, and calling for universal suffrage as a means to achieve better conditions. The monarchy deemed these movements dangerously subversive, and the police frequently raided gatherings, arresting leaders.

**The Canut Revolts in Lyon and Echoes in Paris**

While the largest industrial unrest occurred in Lyon's silk-weaving district—where "canut" weavers staged revolts in 1831 and 1834 over wage cuts—the aftermath rippled through Paris. Many Parisians sympathized with the canuts, recognizing similar pressures of mechanization and employer dominance. Though Paris itself did not experience full-scale worker revolts in the early 1830s, smaller strikes occurred, fueling a sense that labor conflicts were becoming part of the national conversation.

The monarchy's response was typically repressive. Troops crushed strikes, framing them as threats to public order. In the Chamber of Deputies, few voices advocated for legalizing unions or implementing social legislation. Such official indifference to worker grievances contributed to deepening class polarizations—especially as the bourgeois elite prospered while real wages stagnated. Over the next decade, these tensions would intensify, setting the stage for major social unrest in 1848.

---

## 5) Foreign Policy, Colonial Expansion, and Public Opinion

**Intervention Abroad**

Under the July Monarchy, France pursued an active foreign policy designed to maintain a balance of power in Europe and secure overseas interests. One notable undertaking was the **French invasion of Algeria** in 1830, initially begun under Charles X but expanded greatly under Louis-Philippe. Official bulletins in Paris boasted of civilizing missions, but critics pointed out the brutal subjugation of local populations, forcing them off lands. Many Parisians, though, remained more focused on domestic issues than colonial exploits, seeing little direct benefit unless they were tied to trade or military careers.

Meanwhile, tensions with Britain periodically flared over colonial rivalries, though both powers generally avoided major conflict. Diplomatic incidents in Italy or Switzerland sometimes caused public debate in Paris, with liberal voices demanding support for nationalist movements abroad. The monarchy, however, trod carefully, seeking neither to antagonize the conservative Holy Alliance nor to spark internal turmoil by championing foreign revolutions.

**The Spanish Marriages Crisis and Diplomatic Setbacks**

One high-profile foreign policy blunder was the **Spanish Marriages** crisis of 1846, where Louis-Philippe arranged marriages that placed French influence in the Spanish royal family. Britain regarded this as a provocation, deepening Franco-British distrust. Parisians saw these dynastic intrigues as reminiscent of old-style monarchical plotting, tarnishing Louis-Philippe's reputation as a "modern" king. The fiasco reflected the monarchy's contradictory stance: upholding liberal constitutional rhetoric at home while engaging in realpolitik alliances reminiscent of pre-revolutionary Europe.

Such diplomatic missteps dented the monarchy's prestige, fueling cynicism in the capital. Some liberal newspapers lampooned the monarchy's nepotistic maneuvers, suggesting the Orléans line was less about citizen ideals and more about dynastic gains. Combined with domestic economic woes in the late 1840s, these foreign controversies heightened dissatisfaction, further discrediting the regime.

---

## 6) Cultural Flourishing: Romantic Paris in Literature and the Arts

### Romantic Triumph in Theater and Opera

Despite political tensions, the July Monarchy was a golden age for **Romanticism** in literature, arts, and music. The city's theaters—**Comédie-Française**, **Théâtre de la Porte Saint-Martin**, and others—hosted plays by **Victor Hugo**, **Alexandre Dumas**, and **Alfred de Vigny** that broke classical rules, emphasizing passion, medieval or exotic settings, and stirring dialogues.

Hugo's *Hernani* (1830) famously sparked the "battle of Hernani," where supporters and opponents of Romantic drama clashed in the theater. This cultural "battle" paralleled the political struggles in Paris: a younger generation demanding creative liberty vs. an older guard upholding neoclassical tradition. Over time, Romantic styles prevailed, shaping the city's literary tastes.

Opera also thrived, with **Gioachino Rossini** and **Gaetano Donizetti** drawing massive crowds. Parisians from various classes attended these grand performances, though ticket prices often limited poorer citizens to the cheaper seats. Meanwhile, more popular fare—vaudevilles, melodramas—found working-class audiences in smaller venues. Such entertainment offered an escape from political frustrations, even as it sometimes contained subversive undertones.

### Literary Salons and Emerging Critics

Salons hosted by figures like **Madame Récamier** or **George Sand** (though Sand herself was more progressive and sometimes scorned the idea of aristocratic salons) allowed writers, artists, and politicians to mingle, exchanging ideas on everything from feminism to social justice. The monarchy kept an eye on these gatherings, mindful that intellectuals could sway public opinion.

A new class of critics, published in journals such as *La Revue des Deux Mondes* or *Le Constitutionnel*, dissected theatrical productions and novels, shaping cultural discourse. Even as censorship threatened overt political commentary, literary criticism and indirect allegories flourished, gently mocking or praising the monarchy's stance on freedom. This synergy between art and mild dissent fed a broader consciousness that, while the city bristled with creative energy, the political system remained cautious and incomplete in fulfilling the revolutionary heritage.

---

## 7) The Economic Crisis of 1846–1847 and Mounting Discontent

### Agricultural Failures and Unemployment

Beginning in 1846, a series of poor harvests hit France, driving up food prices. Grain shortages caused bread costs in Paris to skyrocket. Working families, already spending a large portion of their income on food, faced hardship. Industrial layoffs followed as domestic consumption fell. The monarchy's reluctance to intervene fuelled anger among those who felt the government cared primarily for wealthy financiers and landowners.

In the capital, bread riots and local protests broke out. While not as large as earlier insurrections, these small disturbances reminded authorities of the city's explosive potential. The monarchy responded with limited charity efforts, establishing soup kitchens or job schemes. However, many saw these gestures as token, nowhere near addressing the structural problems. The press hammered the government for ignoring the root causes of poverty.

### Political Banquets and Calls for Reform

Because direct political gatherings were restricted, liberal activists invented **political banquets** as a workaround—ostensibly social dinners but actually forums for anti-government speeches. In 1847, these banquets spread across France, with major events in Paris drawing hundreds of attendees from the middle and working classes. Speakers demanded electoral reform—lowering property requirements to expand suffrage. Some pressed for an outright republic.

The monarchy frowned upon these gatherings, fearing they stirred revolutionary fervor. As banquets proliferated, the government tried to ban them, culminating in a standoff. By late 1847, the city braced for a showdown between liberal reformers, radical clubs, and a monarchy seemingly deaf to calls for broader democracy. Paris once again teetered on the edge of upheaval.

---

# 8) The 1848 Revolution in Paris: Overthrow of the July Monarchy

## The Banquet Canceled and the Barricades Return

In February 1848, the government forbade a scheduled reform banquet in the 12th arrondissement, pushing discontent to the breaking point. On February 22, Parisians took to the streets, chanting for "Reform!" Barricades reappeared, reminiscent of 1830. Students, artisans, and eventually National Guard units joined the protest. The monarchy, caught unprepared, resorted to calling in troops.

When troops fired on demonstrators near the Boulevard des Capucines on February 23, killing or wounding dozens, anger exploded. Insurgents looted armories, more barricades sprang up, and the city became impassable. Louis-Philippe hastily dismissed Guizot, hoping to appease the crowd, but it was too little, too late. On February 24, the king abdicated in favor of his grandson—yet the crowds demanded a republic. The Orléans family fled to England, and a **provisional government** proclaiming the **Second Republic** took power at the Hôtel de Ville.

Paris erupted in jubilation at dethroning another monarch via street action. Workers, students, and liberal deputies united under slogans of universal suffrage and "fraternity." The city's new provisional government quickly declared basic liberties, freed political prisoners, and set about organizing elections. It was a moment of euphoria, overshadowed by the daunting task of reconciling the diverse aspirations of the revolution's supporters.

# CHAPTER 18

## THE SECOND REPUBLIC, THE SECOND EMPIRE, AND HAUSSMANN'S PARIS

## Introduction

When Parisians overthrew the July Monarchy in February 1848, they proclaimed the **Second Republic**, embracing ideals of universal male suffrage, labor rights, and civic freedoms. Yet this republic quickly faced internal divisions—between moderates who prioritized order and radicals pressing for profound social change. Out of these tensions emerged **Louis-Napoleon Bonaparte**, nephew of Napoleon I, who skillfully navigated the era's politics to become President in 1848. By 1852, he declared himself **Napoleon III**, establishing the **Second Empire**.

Under his rule, Paris underwent a dramatic transformation, led by **Georges-Eugène Haussmann**, the prefect of the Seine. Haussmann's vast reconstruction carved wide boulevards through medieval districts, creating the modern cityscape still visible today. Simultaneously, the empire's authoritarian tendencies clashed with liberal demands, and foreign policy misadventures eventually undermined Napoleon III's regime. In this chapter, we explore how Paris changed under the Second Republic and Second Empire—politically, socially, and physically—and how those transformations set the stage for future upheavals.

## 1) The Second Republic (1848–1852): Birth, Hopes, and Conflicts

**Provisional Government and Universal Suffrage**

Upon toppling Louis-Philippe in February 1848, a provisional government led by figures like **Alphonse de Lamartine**, **Ledru-Rollin**, and **Louis Blanc** took charge. They proclaimed the **Second Republic**, swiftly issuing edicts:

1. **Universal Male Suffrage**: An unprecedented extension of the vote to all adult men, a radical break from property-based suffrage of previous regimes.
2. **Abolition of Slavery**: In French colonies, finalizing an issue that had lingered.
3. **Right to Work**: At least symbolic, responding to labor activists who demanded social measures.

Paris erupted in celebrations, with trees of liberty planted across neighborhoods. Workers hoped for immediate improvements—shorter workdays, guaranteed employment—while moderate republicans focused on establishing stable institutions. Meanwhile, socialist clubs gained visibility, advocating more sweeping economic reforms.

**National Workshops and Early Tensions**

Under the influence of **Louis Blanc**, the government created **National Workshops** to provide public employment for the jobless. Thousands of unemployed Parisians enrolled, clearing roads, digging ditches, or performing minimal tasks for a meager wage. Initially, these workshops served as a relief measure, but they soon became a financial burden and a political lightning rod for critics who decried them as socialist experiments.

Liberals and conservatives in the provisional government balked at rising costs. The city's bourgeois complained that their taxes funded idleness. The workers themselves found the tasks unfulfilling, with no clear path to career advancement. By mid-1848, Paris was brimming with tension—various clubs demanding radical changes, business owners worried about political chaos, and the government uncertain how to reconcile these pressures.

---

## 2) The June Days Uprising (1848) and the End of Radical Influence

**Dissolution of National Workshops**

In April 1848, France held the first national election by universal male suffrage for a Constituent Assembly. The results favored moderate republicans and conservatives more than socialists, reflecting provincial caution. Bolstered by this outcome, the Assembly decided to close the costly National Workshops in June, ordering unemployed workers either to join the army or relocate to rural areas for work relief.

This announcement triggered outrage in Paris. **Tens of thousands** of workers, feeling betrayed by the government they had helped install, took to the streets from June 23 to June 26. They erected barricades in neighborhoods like the **Faubourg Saint-Antoine** and the **Faubourg du Temple**, demanding a "social republic" that would guarantee their livelihoods.

**The Bloody Confrontation**

General **Louis-Eugène Cavaignac**, appointed with emergency powers, led government troops to crush the **June Days uprising**. The fighting was fierce, especially in eastern Paris. Artillery blasts and close-quarters combat left thousands dead or wounded. The insurgents' barricades eventually fell, and mass arrests followed. Many rebels were deported or imprisoned, effectively silencing the socialist wing of the revolution.

This event deeply scarred the capital. The violence overshadowed the idealistic fervor of February. Middle-class Parisians, alarmed by the specter of class warfare, supported the crackdown as necessary to protect property and order. Meanwhile, radical workers felt the Republic had betrayed them, sowing seeds of future antagonism. The June Days effectively ended hopes for a robust "social republic," steering the Second Republic onto a more conservative path.

---

**3) Emergence of Louis-Napoleon Bonaparte and the Presidential Election**

**Louis-Napoleon's Surging Popularity**

Amid the chaos of 1848, **Louis-Napoleon Bonaparte** returned to France after repeated exiles. A nephew of Napoleon I, he leveraged the Bonaparte legend, promising to restore national glory, champion popular sovereignty, and defend order. Although many in the Assembly distrusted him, the electorate found his name compelling—Napoleon's memory still loomed large, especially in rural areas and among some segments of Paris society disillusioned with other factions.

In the December 1848 presidential election, Louis-Napoleon won an overwhelming majority, defeating prominent republicans like **Cavaignac** and **Ledru-Rollin**. Paris itself showed strong Bonapartist support in certain districts, though the city's radical neighborhoods remained more skeptical. Nonetheless, the appeal of stability, the Napoleonic myth, and universal male suffrage catapulted him to the presidency.

**Policies and Maneuvers**

Once in office, Louis-Napoleon cultivated an image of paternal benevolence, visiting workers' quarters, sponsoring philanthropic projects, and hosting lavish receptions for the bourgeois elite. He also navigated political alliances carefully, isolating radical deputies and wooing moderates by pledging to safeguard property and resist extremist upheaval.

Simultaneously, he reorganized the city's police and municipal administration to ensure loyalty. The press found itself constrained by laws punishing insults or threats against the president. By mid-1851, Louis-Napoleon's ambition to extend his term beyond the four-year constitutional limit became evident—setting up a collision course with the conservative Assembly, which refused to amend the constitution for him. Tensions built ominously, hinting at a possible coup.

## 4) The Coup d'État of December 2, 1851, and the Birth of the Second Empire

### Seizing Power

On December 2, 1851—anniversary of Napoleon I's coronation and the Battle of Austerlitz—Louis-Napoleon staged a **coup d'état**. Troops loyal to him occupied strategic points in Paris, arrested opposition leaders, and dissolved the National Assembly. Official proclamations declared the constitution suspended, appealing directly to the people to legitimize a new regime via plebiscite.

Parisians awakened to posters announcing the dissolution of the Assembly, the restoration of universal suffrage, and calls for an orderly transition. While there was some resistance in working-class districts, widespread barricades did not materialize as in the past. Many city residents, weary of political gridlock, seemed resigned or even supportive of a strong figure promising stability and progress. The coup, though condemned by republicans as a betrayal, went unchallenged by large-scale insurrections in Paris.

**From Presidency to Empire**

After consolidating power, Louis-Napoleon sought to outdo the memory of his uncle. A subsequent plebiscite in December 1851 approved his extended authority, and in November 1852, another plebiscite sanctioned the reestablishment of imperial dignity. On December 2, 1852, he crowned himself **Emperor Napoleon III**, inaugurating the **Second Empire**. Official bulletins boasted that France had chosen order, glory, and national prosperity over the chaos of factional politics.

In Paris, daily life continued with minimal disruption, aside from heightened police surveillance. By retaining universal male suffrage (albeit under manipulative conditions), Napoleon III claimed a populist mandate. Over time, the new emperor would direct significant resources to modernize the capital, forging an ambitious plan that would reshape its very topography.

---

## 5) Napoleon III and Haussmann's Transformation of Paris

**Baron Haussmann: The Vision and Strategy**

In 1853, Napoleon III appointed **Georges-Eugène Haussmann** as the prefect of the Seine, giving him broad authority to remake Paris. Haussmann believed the city's medieval layout was unsanitary, congested, and prone to revolutionary barricades. Backed by imperial decrees and vast loans, he set out to:

1. **Cut Grand Avenues** through dense neighborhoods, linking major monuments and train stations.
2. **Construct Sewers and Water Systems** to reduce disease.
3. **Build Public Parks** like the Bois de Boulogne and Bois de Vincennes, offering green spaces for leisure.
4. **Enforce Uniform Building Regulations** for new facades and standardized floors.

Haussmann's plan was unprecedented in scale. Streets like **Rue de Rivoli** were extended, and new boulevards—**Boulevard de Sébastopol, Boulevard Saint-Germain, Boulevard Haussmann**—emerged, forming the backbone of modern Paris. Monuments such as the **Opéra Garnier** would arise in redesigned districts, symbolizing imperial splendor.

## The Impact on Parisians

Haussmann's renovation demolished entire neighborhoods, displacing thousands of working-class families who had resided in cramped but affordable quarters. Many moved to peripheral areas, fueling suburban sprawl. The new boulevards facilitated traffic flow, commerce, and policing—wide avenues could not be easily barricaded by revolutionaries.

Affluent Parisians gained elegant apartments along these shining boulevards, near fashionable cafés, theaters, and department stores. The city's aesthetic soared to new heights, adored by foreign visitors who marveled at uniform five-story stone buildings and tree-lined thoroughfares. Meanwhile, critics lamented the social cost: the old sense of community vanished for those uprooted by expropriations, and rising rents made central Paris increasingly bourgeois.

## Financing and Criticism

Haussmann financed these projects largely through municipal bonds and loans guaranteed by the imperial government. This system created heavy debt for the city, leading to allegations of corruption and profiteering by property developers. Many journalists and political opponents labeled Haussmann's approach "despotic"—an unaccountable use of eminent domain backed by the emperor's decree. Over time, resentment of mounting debts and high taxes brewed, but Napoleon III insisted that transforming Paris was crucial to symbolizing France's modernity.

# 6) The Social and Political Underpinnings of the Second Empire

### Authoritarian Liberalism

Though Napoleon III exercised authoritarian power—appointing senators, controlling the press, and restricting opposition—he also recognized the need for a certain liberal veneer. From the late 1850s onward, he gradually relaxed press laws, permitted workers' mutual aid societies, and encouraged open debate in a controlled fashion. The emperor called this **"liberal empire,"** attempting to appease both conservative supporters and the growing liberal middle class who wanted parliamentary influence.

In Paris, newspapers like **Le Siècle** or **La Presse** tested these new freedoms, cautiously criticizing government policy while praising the empire's modernization efforts. Opposition figures, including **Adolphe Thiers** or **Jules Ferry**, used legislative or journalistic platforms to push for constitutional evolution. Meanwhile, more radical republicans operated discreetly, mindful that open hostility could still provoke arrests.

### Workers' Conditions and the Emergence of Labor Activism

As industrialization advanced, factories employing hundreds of workers sprouted near the city. Some entrepreneurs introduced paternalistic measures—company housing, medical care—but wages remained low. Housing shortages forced laborers to share cramped apartments in older districts or newly built but substandard rentals at city fringes. The imperial police monitored any gatherings that hinted at unionization.

Nonetheless, labor activism gradually took root. Skilled workers formed associations, championing the right to strike. The regime allowed some strikes if they remained peaceful, seeing them as a safety valve rather than a direct political threat. The city's economy boomed, with rising consumer culture benefiting certain skilled artisans, yet many still struggled for basic security. This dynamic tension between imperial paternalism and working-class aspiration shaped the social fabric of mid-19th-century Paris.

---

# 7) Cultural Flourish under the Empire: Salons, Exhibitions, and Leisure

### The Imperial Court and High Society

Napoleon III and Empress **Eugénie** presided over an elaborate court life at the Tuileries Palace, mirroring a revived version of Napoleonic splendor. Aristocrats from old families mingled with newly ennobled financiers. Lavish balls and receptions marked the social calendar, often reflecting the empire's desire to impress foreign dignitaries. For the upper classes, Paris was a playground of grand hôtels, fashionable boulevards, and exclusive clubs.

## Artistic Innovation: Realism and Early Impressionism

Despite official preference for academic painting, new artistic movements blossomed in Paris. The **Realist** school, led by **Gustave Courbet**, challenged romantic and neoclassical conventions by depicting ordinary workers, rural scenes, and social realities. While the empire's official salons favored more traditional or patriotic art, younger painters found alternative venues to exhibit.

In the late 1860s, the seeds of **Impressionism** emerged among artists like **Claude Monet** and **Édouard Manet**—though they faced critical hostility at first. Manet's *Le Déjeuner sur l'herbe* (1863) and *Olympia* (1865) sparked scandal for their frank modern subjects. This clash between avant-garde creativity and conservative taste underscored a broader tension in the empire: a regime that encouraged modernization but remained uneasy about subversive expressions.

## Public Spectacles and Expositions

Napoleon III promoted grand exhibitions to display France's industrial might and cultural wealth. The **Exposition Universelle** of 1855 inaugurated an era of world's fairs in Paris, drawing millions of visitors to see machines, fine arts, and exotic displays from abroad. These events reinforced the city's reputation as a global center of progress, while fueling commerce in hotels, cafés, and shops.

Parisians enjoyed new leisure venues like the **Café-concerts**, the **Jardin d'Acclimatation**, or strolling along Haussmannian boulevards. Department stores such as **Le Bon Marché** (founded 1852) revolutionized retail, offering fixed prices and mass-produced goods. This consumer revolution exemplified the synergy between industrial capitalism and the empire's urban modernization.

---

# 8) Foreign Policy and the Empire's Challenges

## Crimean War and Italian Campaign

Napoleon III sought to affirm France's status in Europe through military engagements. The **Crimean War** (1853–1856) allied France with Britain against Russia, boosting the empire's prestige as a champion of the Ottoman Empire. Paris thrived on the jingoistic press coverage, celebrating victories like the siege of Sevastopol.

Then in 1859, France supported Piedmont-Sardinia against Austria in northern Italy, culminating in the battles of Magenta and Solferino. Parisians hailed these successes, yet some liberals criticized the empire's meddling, noting the cost in lives and finances. Meanwhile, Italy's unification later took on a momentum of its own, leaving Napoleon III uncertain about how to balance French influence with emergent Italian nationalism.

### The Mexican Adventure

A more disastrous foray was the **Mexican Expedition** (1862–1867), launched under pretexts of debt collection but really aiming to establish a pro-French monarchy under **Maximilian of Habsburg**. Although initially supported by conservative circles in Mexico, the experiment collapsed when Mexican republicans resisted. The withdrawal of French troops, pressured by the United States after the Civil War, led to Maximilian's capture and execution in 1867.

This fiasco tarnished Napoleon III's aura of invincibility. Parisians learned of mounting casualties and wasted resources. Criticism soared in newspapers that dared to question the empire's leadership. Coupled with the rising influence of **Prussia** in Europe, the empire's foreign adventures increasingly seemed risky and counterproductive.

---

## 9) Liberalization Attempts, Economic Downturn, and Opposition Growth

### Shifts towards a "Liberal Empire"

Facing criticism, Napoleon III introduced reforms in the 1860s, relaxing press censorship and allowing legislative corps more debate powers. He hoped to placate liberals and intellectuals in Paris, who demanded a constitutional monarchy or even a revived republic. Trade treaties, like the **Cobden-Chevalier Treaty** (1860) with Britain, lowered tariffs, stimulating commerce but also exposing French industry to competition.

New forms of political life emerged: the "**Belleville Radicals**," led by men like **Léon Gambetta**, championed universal suffrage and anti-clerical policies. Urban workers found it easier to hold small political meetings. The empire's loosening grip ironically fueled further demands for democratic representation. By the late 1860s, socialist ideas circulated more freely, culminating in more frequent strikes and the formation of embryonic labor unions.

### Economic Pressures

An economic downturn struck in 1866–1867, partially triggered by over-speculation, poor harvests, and reduced foreign demand. Layoffs in factories and a drop in public works spending left many workers precarious. The cost of living in Haussmannized Paris soared as new construction displaced cheaper neighborhoods. These stresses rekindled working-class grievances, which found resonance in newly emerging socialist clubs.

Many bourgeois also soured on the empire's heavy borrowing and the massive city debts accrued under Haussmann. Opposition newspapers hammered the government for corruption, nepotism, and reckless spending. Even moderate liberals saw the empire's liberalization as too slow or superficial. The stage was set for a potential crisis should a significant external shock occur—one that might unify the city's diverse opposition factions.

## 10) The Franco-Prussian War (1870) and the Empire's Collapse

### Prelude to War

Conflict with Prussia escalated in 1870 over the candidacy of a Hohenzollern prince for the Spanish throne. Napoleon III, maneuvered by his ministers, demanded guarantees that Prussia would not expand influence further. The resulting diplomatic fiasco, known as the **Ems Dispatch**, ignited nationalist fervor on both sides. On July 19, 1870, France declared war on Prussia, believing victory would rally Parisians behind the empire and secure Napoleonic prestige.

Instead, the French military found itself outmatched by the well-organized Prussian forces under **Helmuth von Moltke**. As news of defeats filtered back to Paris, the city's mood turned grim. Strains on supply lines and conscription mobilization added to a sense of desperation. By early September 1870, the catastrophic defeat at **Sedan** left Napoleon III captured, effectively destroying the empire's legitimacy.

### Uprising in Paris and the Proclamation of the Republic

When word of Sedan's disaster reached Paris, citizens erupted in indignation. On September 4, crowds stormed the legislative assembly, demanding an immediate end to the empire. Leading deputies, including **Léon Gambetta** and **Jules Favre**, proclaimed the **Third Republic** from the Hôtel de Ville. The empire that had shaped Paris for two decades collapsed within days, undone by foreign defeat.

Parisians prepared for a siege as Prussian armies encircled the city. The new republican government vowed to continue fighting, hoping to replicate the heroic resistance of earlier eras. Once again, Paris's political destiny took a radical turn: the city would soon endure blockade, hunger, and internal revolt, culminating in the **Paris Commune** of 1871. But first, the Second Empire ended as swiftly as it began, leaving behind a dramatically altered urban landscape and a populace hardened by repeated transformations.

## 11) Haussmann's Legacy and the Modernization of Paris

**Lasting Urban Accomplishments**

Though the empire fell in ignominy, Haussmann's renovation had permanently reshaped Paris:

- **Grand Boulevards**: The city gained a rational grid of wide thoroughfares, linking squares like **Place de l'Étoile** to **Place de la République**, facilitating both commerce and troop movement.
- **Sewer and Water Infrastructure**: Vast expansions in underground sewage networks improved public health, reducing epidemics of cholera that once ravaged cramped neighborhoods.
- **Uniform Architecture**: Distinctive Haussmannian buildings rose with regulated cornice heights and wrought-iron balconies, forging the elegant look that still defines central Paris.
- **Parks and Public Amenities**: The Bois de Boulogne, Bois de Vincennes, and smaller parks integrated green spaces into the urban environment, though primarily benefiting wealthier classes living nearby.

Despite fierce criticism of displacements and debts, subsequent regimes retained Haussmann's layout. Its symbolic value as a "City of Light," with grand vistas showcasing architectural harmony, endured. The empire's project thus bequeathed a physical map of modern Paris, integral to its global image as a center of beauty and order.

**Socioeconomic Stratification**

Yet the new boulevards and real estate developments also accelerated the exodus of lower-income residents from the center to outer districts. Wealthier families claimed prime central addresses, where rent soared. Such gentrification, a direct outgrowth of Haussmann's demolitions, sharpened class divisions. Over time, these patterns shaped suburban poverty belts that future planners would grapple with.

The city's commercial vibrancy thrived on tourism, leisure, and retail—an enduring economic engine. Department stores multiplied, giving rise to a consumer culture that would define the 20th century. However, the ephemeral illusions of empire overshadowed deeper structural issues: political representation, social welfare, and the precariousness of low-wage labor. These fault lines would soon erupt again, as the Third Republic and the Commune tested how Paris could balance modernization with egalitarian ideals.

# CHAPTER 19

## THE SIEGE OF PARIS AND THE PARIS COMMUNE (1870–1871)

## Introduction

In September 1870, following the defeat of Emperor Napoleon III at **Sedan** during the **Franco-Prussian War**, Parisians once again toppled an imperial regime. The French Second Empire collapsed, ushering in the proclamation of the **Third Republic**. Yet any hopes for immediate peace and stability were swiftly dashed: Prussian armies encircled Paris, laying siege to the city from September 1870 to January 1871. Over these months, Parisians endured hunger, bombardment, and frigid conditions, clinging to republican ideals in the face of adversity.

The humiliation of France was further compounded by internal political divisions. When the besieged city finally capitulated, the new republican government under **Adolphe Thiers** signed a harsh armistice with Prussia, prompting fierce indignation from many Parisians who saw the surrender as betrayal. Within weeks, the capital exploded in rebellion—leading to the short-lived but momentous **Paris Commune** (March–May 1871). This radical experiment in workers' self-government seized control of the city, defied the national government, and unleashed a violent showdown whose reverberations would echo for decades.

In this chapter, we trace the extraordinary events of the **Siege of Paris** and the subsequent **Paris Commune**. We look at how ordinary citizens coped with blockade and starvation, how political factions contended for influence, and how the Commune attempted a profound social and democratic reorganization—only to be crushed in a brutal finale known as **La Semaine Sanglante** (the Bloody Week). The city emerged from this crucible scarred, yet profoundly shaped by the memory of a fleeting but potent vision of popular power.

## 1) The Franco-Prussian War and the Collapse of the Empire

### From Euphoria to Disaster

When war broke out in July 1870, Napoleon III's government believed that swift victories would rally the nation and restore imperial prestige. Initial enthusiasm gripped Paris: patriotic processions, calls for volunteers, and illusions of a second Napoleonic triumph. Yet the French army proved unprepared, outmaneuvered by superior Prussian organization. Defeats followed in Alsace and Lorraine, culminating in the catastrophic surrender at **Sedan** on September 2, 1870, where Napoleon III was captured.

News of Sedan shocked the capital. On September 4, an enraged populace besieged the Legislative Body, demanding the end of the Second Empire. Deputies, led by figures like **Léon Gambetta** and **Jules Favre**, proclaimed the Third Republic from the **Hôtel de Ville**, forming a **Government of National Defense**. Many hoped France would regroup, but the Prussian forces advanced relentlessly. By mid-September, they began encircling Paris, severing railways and roads. The city braced for a siege that would test its resilience under desperate conditions.

**Government of National Defense**

The new republican authorities included **General Louis Jules Trochu** as military governor of Paris and **Gambetta**, who famously departed the city by balloon to coordinate resistance from the provinces. While intense patriotism roused many, the reality of a Prussian siege soon overshadowed ephemeral fervor. Parisians pinned hopes on relief armies from the provinces, but those armies struggled under chaotic mobilization, often failing to breach the Prussian lines. The city found itself alone, cut off from the rest of the country, determined to hold out whatever the cost.

## 2) The Siege of Paris: Day-to-Day Survival

**Encirclement and Bombardment**

By late September 1870, Prussian forces completed their ring around Paris. About two million inhabitants—citizens, refugees, the National Guard—found themselves under blockade. The city's massive defensive walls and forts forced the enemy to maintain a cautious distance, but Prussian artillery occasionally bombarded strategic points. Initially, shelling was light, but fear of heavier bombardment haunted the population.

Within Paris, rationing began. Bakeries limited bread, and prices soared. Meat soon became scarce. Zookeeper sources from the **Jardin des Plantes** described how exotic animals were eventually slaughtered for food—**elephant, camel, kangaroo**—a grim testament to desperation. Horsemeat became widespread. Black-market deals thrived, and the poorest starved as wealthier classes could still afford inflated prices.

**Adaptations and Morale**

Despite hardships, Parisians exhibited a spirited determination:

- **Hot Air Balloons**: Since telegraph lines were cut, balloons carrying mail and officials (including Gambetta) lifted off from the city to coordinate with the outside world. Return journeys by balloon or "balloon-post" were nearly impossible, intensifying the city's isolation.
- **Daily Life**: Schools often closed or converted into makeshift hospitals. Citizens formed volunteer brigades for relief. Women organized charitable soup kitchens.
- **National Guard Service**: The government armed thousands of men in the National Guard, hoping to defend ramparts and maintain order. Patriots pinned tricolor ribbons on ragged uniforms, rallying around the idea of a heroic last stand.

Public gatherings in clubs and café gatherings maintained morale, where radical orators promised eventual triumph if the city resisted long enough. However, as autumn passed into a harsh winter, coal shortages, malnutrition, and bleak news from failed provincial offensives eroded hope.

**Political Debates Inside the City**

Politically, factions vied for leadership. **Trochu** and moderate republicans tried to keep morale up while hinting at the possibility of honorable negotiations. More radical groups—**Blanquists**, **Jacobins**, **Socialist** clubs—demanded bolder military action and social reforms. They suspected the government might sell out the city to the Prussians for peace. Tensions rose between these radicals and the official government of national defense, foreshadowing deeper splits that would erupt after the siege ended.

---

## 3) The Armistice and Reactions (January 1871)

## The Final Assault and Capitulation

By January 1871, the siege had dragged on for over four months. Bombardment intensified, especially on the southern neighborhoods, as the Prussian high command sought to break Parisian resolve. Starvation loomed, with bread rations drastically cut and daily caloric intake at catastrophic lows for the poor. Horses, dogs, cats, and even rats were consumed on a widespread scale. Women and children suffered most, with infant mortality skyrocketing.

Facing the city's imminent collapse, **Jules Favre** and others in the government decided to negotiate an armistice. On January 28, 1871, they signed the **Armistice of Versailles**, halting hostilities and scheduling national elections to form a new government authorized to sign a final peace. Under humiliating terms, Prussian troops staged a brief symbolic occupation of certain city areas, though they avoided a full triumphant march down the boulevards to prevent further uprisings. This partial occupation stung Parisian pride, intensifying bitterness and fueling radical suspicion of national leaders.

### Elections and Growing Hostilities

In February 1871, nationwide elections returned a conservative majority to the new **National Assembly**, convened in Bordeaux. The majority favored an immediate peace with Prussia. Elected as chief executive, **Adolphe Thiers** began negotiating the **Treaty of Frankfurt**, ceding Alsace and parts of Lorraine and imposing steep reparations. Parisians, who had endured the siege, felt outraged by what they saw as capitulation and betrayal.

Meanwhile, discontent within the capital brewed. The National Guard, now composed largely of working-class and lower-middle-class men radicalized by the siege, bristled at disarmament plans. Many sections hoarded cannons purchased by public subscription. The National Assembly's removal to Versailles (rather than reestablishing itself in Paris) stoked fears that rural conservatives would impose reactionary policies on the city. Daily frustrations and the painful aftermath of siege conditions set the stage for an explosive confrontation.

## 4) The Road to the Commune: Conflicts Between Paris and Versailles

### The Cannons on Montmartre

The immediate spark igniting the Paris Commune came from a dispute over the **National Guard's artillery**. During the siege, Parisians had raised funds to buy cannons for defending the city. After the armistice, these cannons were stored in working-class districts like **Montmartre**. Thiers' government ordered the army to seize them, hoping to prevent further insurrection. On March 18, 1871, troops attempted a dawn operation to remove the cannons, but local crowds, including many women, blocked the effort.

Soldiers fraternized with citizens, refusing to fire. Two generals, **Lecomte** and **Clément-Thomas**, were captured and later executed by enraged guardsmen. This incident erupted into a broader revolt: the Thiers government fled to Versailles, leaving Paris effectively in the hands of the National Guard and radical leaders who declared the city autonomous. Thus began the **Paris Commune**—a dramatic experiment in workers' self-government.

### The Commune's Ideological Roots

The idea of a **commune** harkened back to revolutionary traditions of 1792 and 1848—local autonomy, direct democracy, social justice. Leaders included **Louis Auguste Blanqui** (though imprisoned at the time), **Eugène Varlin**, **Jacques Leon Clément-Thomas** (earlier killed), and a diverse array of Jacobins, Proudhonian mutualists, and international socialists. They all shared distrust of Thiers' bourgeois-led regime in Versailles, vowing to defend Paris's revolutionary heritage.

Committees formed across the city, organizing daily life: policing, welfare, and supply distribution. Many working-class neighborhoods enthusiastically supported the Commune, hoping it would realize long-postponed social reforms. Middle-class Parisians were divided—some saw the Commune as anarchy threatening property, others welcomed an alternative to Thiers' conservative assembly. The lines were blurred, but momentum lay with the armed National Guard and radical clubs championing a new social order.

---

## 5) The Paris Commune in Power (March–May 1871)

### Democratic and Social Measures

On March 28, 1871, the Commune was officially proclaimed at **Hôtel de Ville**. Members of the **Communal Council** were elected by universal male suffrage in each arrondissement. Though diverse ideologically, they quickly enacted progressive decrees:

1. **Separation of Church and State**: Nationalized church property, ended religious instruction in schools.
2. **Remission of Rent and Debts**: Suspended rent arrears from the siege, canceled interest on pawned items at the municipal Mont-de-Piété.
3. **Workers' Rights**: Encouraged cooperatives, allowed workers to take over workshops abandoned by owners.
4. **Equality and Social Freedoms**: Sought to eliminate class privileges, recognized unmarried couples' rights, advanced women's associations, though women's suffrage did not emerge.

Many Communards embraced a strong sense of local democracy: committees handled everything from food supply to public safety, often with chaotic overlap. The press flourished, with countless radical newspapers dissecting the new possibilities. City clubs held nightly debates, fueling an air of creative ferment.

**Internal Challenges**

Yet the Commune faced urgent military threats from Versailles, which massed troops for a counterattack. The city was short on supplies, and many administrative officials had left with Thiers. Some moderate Parisians were uneasy about the Commune's anti-clerical stance and seizing property. Rivalries among the Commune's factions—Blanquists demanding centralized revolutionary dictatorship vs. Proudhonians advocating decentralized worker-managed reforms—further complicated governance.

Still, the spirit of cooperation and the sense of forging a new social model energized many. Women's activism flourished, with figures like **Louise Michel** championing frontline defense and educational reforms. Street art, songs, and daily gatherings in squares broadcast the Commune's radical optimism, even as looming violence overshadowed the experiment.

---

## 6) The War Against Versailles and the Commune's Defensive Struggle

### Skirmishes and the Forts

Thiers' government condemned the Commune as an illegal insurrection. Adolphe Thiers secured an agreement with Prussia to release French prisoners of war, bolstering the army that he deployed against Paris. Fighting erupted at the city's perimeter. The Commune's defenders included experienced National Guardsmen from the siege, but they lacked centralized command. Meanwhile, Versailles artillery methodically pounded communal strongholds.

By April, **Fort Issy** and **Fort Vanves** fell, weakening the city's southern defenses. Communard generals, often amateurish, struggled to coordinate strategic offensives. Some attempts at negotiating or appealing to rural France for support failed; the provinces largely saw the Commune as an extreme Parisian revolt. Day by day, the numerical and logistical superiority of Versailles troops pressed closer.

**Diplomatic Failures and Radicalization**

The Commune tried to propose a decentralized republican model for all of France, hoping local communes elsewhere would rise in solidarity. Except for brief revolts in Lyon, Marseille, and a few towns, no widespread movement materialized. The national press outside Paris painted the Communards as violent fanatics bent on destroying property and religion.

Under siege once more, the Commune's radical measures intensified. Animosity toward the Catholic Church peaked, leading to hostages, including **Archbishop Darboy**, who were later executed. This tactic, intended as a bargaining chip to stop Versailles from executing captured Communards, backfired, heightening the enemy's resolve. Bitter factional disputes also flared within the Commune's leadership, sapping unity at a critical moment.

---

## 7) The Bloody Week (La Semaine Sanglante) and the Fall of the Commune

**Versailles Army Enters Paris**

On May 21, 1871, Versailles troops exploited a weakly guarded gate at **Porte de Saint-Cloud** to slip into western Paris. Over the ensuing week, street-by-street fighting engulfed the city. Communard forces erected barricades in working-class districts, hoping to replicate earlier revolutionary successes. But Versailles commanded overwhelming manpower and artillery. Scenes of chaos unfolded: burning buildings, final stands by Guard units, and reprisals on suspected Communard sympathizers.

The **Commune's leaders**, cornered, authorized desperate measures—some radicals proposed torching major monuments. Fires broke out at the **Tuileries Palace**, the **Hôtel de Ville**, and the **Palais de Justice**. While not all were systematically planned, this "**week of flames**" remains contested in historical accounts. The devastation symbolized the dying gasp of the Commune as well as the fury of the conflict.

**Brutal Repression**

Versailles troops, once victorious, executed many captured Communards on the spot. Summary courts condemned thousands more to prison or deportation. The final barricade fell on May 28 near the **Faubourg du Temple**, marking the end of the Commune. Historians estimate 20,000 to 30,000 Parisians may have perished in the fighting or in subsequent reprisals, with thousands more exiled to penal colonies like **New Caledonia**.

The scale of retribution horrified even some foreign observers, who likened it to a massacre. Yet the conservative classes across France cheered the suppression, seeing it as necessary to restore order. The Government of National Defense reconsolidated power. Paris was left traumatized. The city's radical ambitions lay in ruins. For years to come, talk of "Commune" evoked both heroic martyrdom among leftists and cautionary terror among conservatives.

---

## 8) The Aftermath and Significance of the Commune

### The "Black Memory" and Political Implications

In the wake of May 1871, the Third Republic—still in its infancy—governed with a wary eye on Paris. The Commune's legacy became a potent symbol for European socialists, anarchists, and communists who viewed it as the first workers' government in history. Karl Marx famously described it as the prototype of the "dictatorship of the proletariat," praising its democratic and egalitarian measures. In turn, conservatives used the Commune to demonize revolutionary socialism, referencing the atrocities of La Semaine Sanglante as justifiable retribution.

Within the city, the national authorities imposed strict surveillance. Commemorations or gatherings that honored the Commune's dead were banned. Families sought the remains of lost loved ones in mass graves, and the stigma of collaboration with the Commune made returning to normal life difficult. The massacre thus cast a long shadow, shaping the political culture of the new Republic. Meanwhile, a deep rift emerged between working-class neighborhoods and the republican government that had crushed them.

### Transformations in Republican Governance

Despite the violence, the Third Republic eventually stabilized. Monarchist attempts to restore a king fizzled out as divisions among royalists prevented a unifying candidate. Over time, republican leaders sought to distance themselves from the memory of the Commune's radicalism but also from the repressive stance of Versailles. Slowly, more liberal policies and expansions of suffrage emerged, albeit at a measured pace.

In Paris, reconstruction of burned areas advanced. **Hôtel de Ville** was rebuilt in a grand neo-Renaissance style, quietly omitting tributes to the Commune. The city retained the broad Haussmann boulevards, which ironically had not prevented the last-ditch barricades. The working classes, though decimated and demoralized, retained pockets of radical activism—commemorated in clandestine ceremonies at the **Mur des Fédérés** in **Père Lachaise Cemetery**, where many Communards had been executed. This site would become a pilgrimage spot for future socialists and trade unionists, linking the memory of 1871 with ongoing struggles for social justice.

---

## 9) Cultural and Social Legacy of 1870–1871

### The Siege in Memory and Art

The siege and Commune shaped the Parisian imagination for decades. Writers and artists produced accounts mixing heroism, tragedy, and bitterness. **Émile Zola**'s novel *La Débâcle* (1892) dissected the war's folly, the empire's downfall, and the trauma of occupation. Communard veterans, those who escaped execution or exile, penned memoirs defending the revolution as a legitimate workers' uprising undone by overwhelming force.

In popular culture, ballads and engravings depicted balloon flights from the besieged city, painting them as emblematic of French ingenuity under adversity. Satirical prints ridiculed the ineptitude of generals or the moral hypocrisy of wealthy families who ate lavishly while the poor starved. Over time, the city's resilience during the siege was folded into a broader narrative of French patriotism, overshadowing the humiliations of defeat.

### The Commune as Inspiration for Future Movements

Beyond immediate tragedy, the Commune's radical democracy and social measures inspired left-wing thinkers. Over the next half-century, socialist and anarchist organizations around Europe revered the Commune as a blueprint for proletarian governance. In Paris itself, clandestine circles kept the memory alive, culminating in annual tributes at Père Lachaise Cemetery after legal restrictions eased.

By the late 19th century, the growth of labor unions and socialist parties in France referenced the Commune's ideals. Figures like **Jean Jaurès** or **Paul Lafargue** championed democratic socialism, seeing 1871's events as a heroic but flawed attempt to reshape society. For them, the failure underscored the need for broader national support, disciplined organization, and a less confrontational approach. Yet the spirit of the Commune—its direct democracy, neighborhood committees, worker cooperatives—remained an enduring myth among revolutionaries well into the 20th century.

---

# CHAPTER 20

## THE LATE 19TH CENTURY – CULTURAL FLOURISH AND INDUSTRIAL CHANGES

## Introduction

By 1871, Paris had endured the siege, the trauma of the Commune, and a vicious crackdown by national forces. The city stood physically scarred—some districts still bore signs of bombardment, while the memory of mass executions and exiles weighed on its collective consciousness. Yet, remarkably, Paris rebounded over the next decades, affirming itself as a major hub of art, science, and industrial development. This era—from 1871 to the turn of the 20th century—saw the **Third Republic** consolidate power, forging new public institutions and hosting grand international expositions.

In this final chapter, we explore how the city navigated political consolidation after the Commune's defeat, how it recovered from war damages and repurposed Haussmann's modern infrastructure, and how it blazed a trail in cultural and technological innovation. The **Exposition Universelle** events (most famously in 1889 and 1900) showcased the city's self-image as the "Capital of the World," championing progress and the spirit of **la Belle Époque**. At the same time, we examine the underlying social dynamics that persisted—class tensions, labor struggles, and the seeds of new political currents like nationalism and socialism. By 1900, Paris was simultaneously a glittering metropolis of electric lights and grand boulevards—and a city grappling with the inequalities and political movements that would define the 20th century.

# 1) Post-Commune Governance: The Third Republic Takes Shape

### National Stability and Republican Institutions

In the immediate aftermath of the Commune, the **Adolphe Thiers** government, later succeeded by more enduring republican coalitions, worked to restore order across France. Though many had expected a monarchist restoration, internal divisions among royalists (Legitimists vs. Orleanists) blocked a unified candidate. Over time, **republicanism** gained acceptance as the default national framework.

Paris, which had historically driven radical change, found itself under tighter central control. The city's autonomy was curtailed by laws that limited municipal powers—fearing another insurrection. **Mayors** of each arrondissement were appointed by the state until 1882, and even then, central authorities heavily regulated municipal decisions. The government also reorganized the National Guard into smaller, more manageable units to prevent large-scale armed rebellions.

### Moral Order and the Legacy of Repression

The new republican regime took a firm stance against potential neo-Commune movements. Military tribunals continued sentencing suspected Communards or exiles well into the 1870s. Gradual amnesty laws eventually emerged, but the "moral order" approach shaped policy: a rejection of radical socialism and a promotion of Catholic-friendly moral values. Republican leaders such as **Jules Ferry** or **Léon Gambetta**, who had moderate liberal outlooks, championed secular public education and civil liberties while insisting on social stability.

Nevertheless, the city's population soared as rural migrants arrived, seeking factory jobs or domestic service. By the late 1870s, the Republican government's grip eased some of the anti-Paris prejudice, recognizing the capital's economic vitality. Political clubs reopened under scrutiny, and left-wing activism revived, although it avoided open calls for insurrection. Step by step, the Third Republic consolidated a parliamentary democracy, with universal male suffrage reaffirmed (women's suffrage remained decades away). Paris resumed its role as the nerve center of French politics—but now under a regime less prone to dramatic repressions, at least in normal times.

---

# 2) Economic Recovery and Industrial Dynamism

### Rebuilding and Infrastructure Extensions

After the Franco-Prussian War and the Commune, reconstruction accelerated. The **Hôtel de Ville** was rebuilt in neo-Renaissance style from 1874 to 1882, symbolizing municipal dignity. Burned-out blocks near the Tuileries were cleared or renovated, though the Tuileries Palace itself was left in ruins until its final demolition. The city also expanded rail lines and tramways to serve outlying districts, fostering suburban growth.

The **Haussmannian boulevards** remained the city's arteries, carrying omnibuses and carriages. Entrepreneurs capitalized on improved logistics to expand department stores—**Le Printemps** (founded 1865) and **La Samaritaine** (founded 1870, expanded later)—offering a shopping experience that combined convenience, fixed pricing, and spectacle. By the 1880s, these stores became tourist attractions, reflecting a booming consumer culture at the heart of the new republic.

**Industrial Growth and Modern Innovations**

France's industrial expansion in the late 19th century rested on steel, chemicals, and mechanized textiles. Paris served as a financial headquarters for these ventures, its banks underwriting ventures like the **Compagnie des chemins de fer**. Suburbs hosted factories making machinery, electric equipment, and scientific instruments. Inventors experimented with new forms of transport: early internal combustion engines, prototypes for motorized buses, and the first **Eiffel** engineering projects that would culminate in the iconic tower by 1889.

Meanwhile, electric lighting began to replace gas lamps in select neighborhoods, creating an aura of progress. The **Thomson-Houston** or **Edison** companies tested power grids. Though adoption was uneven, the city's bourgeois districts reveled in the novelty of electric arc lamps on certain boulevards. This synergy of commerce, finance, and engineering shaped a self-image of unstoppable modernization—a theme the Third Republic harnessed to legitimize its rule, contrasting with the gloom of the empire's collapse.

---

## 3) Cultural Renaissance: The Belle Époque Takes Root

### The Artistic Scene: Impressionism and Beyond

During the 1870s, a group of painters—**Claude Monet**, **Pierre-Auguste Renoir**, **Edgar Degas**, **Camille Pissarro**, and others—shocked the art establishment with their exhibitions, later labeled **Impressionist**. Rejecting academic rules, they painted modern life: sunlit streets, leisure activities, fleeting atmospheric effects. Critics at first ridiculed their "unfinished" style, but by the 1880s, Impressionism gained a dedicated following. Parisian cafés, the **Salon des Refusés**, and independent galleries fostered avant-garde expressions that eventually reshaped global art.

**Édouard Manet** bridged earlier Realism to this new wave, while **Mary Cassatt** introduced a female perspective, focusing on intimate domestic scenes. The city's brasseries in Montmartre or Montparnasse hosted nightly debates about technique and meaning in painting. By the 1890s, **Post-Impressionists** like **Paul Gauguin**, **Vincent van Gogh** (who spent formative years in Paris), and **Paul Cézanne** were extending the boundaries further—cementing the capital's reputation as the epicenter of innovative art.

### Literature, Music, and Entertainment

Beyond the visual arts, literary salons and publishing houses thrived. Authors like **Émile Zola**, champion of **Naturalism**, dissected social realities in sprawling novels—*L'Assommoir* (1877) or *Germinal* (1885)—depicting working-class struggles with unprecedented grit. **Gustave Flaubert**, **Guy de Maupassant**, and others propelled French literature to new heights, exploring bourgeois mores, psychological nuance, and moral ambiguities.

In music, the **Opéra Garnier** (completed 1875) stood as a temple of grandeur, hosting major productions. Composers like **Charles Gounod**, **Camille Saint-Saëns**, and **Jules Massenet** dominated the city's musical stage with lyrical, romantic works. Lighter forms—operetta and cabaret—flourished in venues like the **Folies Bergère** and the **Moulin Rouge**, captivating a broad audience with dance revues and comedic sketches. The nightlife in Montmartre blossomed, featuring cancan dancers and irreverent chansons—a vibrant subculture that expressed the city's taste for spectacle and novelty.

### The Rise of Mass Media

Newspapers proliferated, from serious political dailies like **Le Temps** and **Le Figaro** to sensational weeklies, echoing the public's hunger for current events and scandals. Advances in printing reduced costs, fueling the birth of mass-circulation press. By the 1880s, the penny press (petits journaux) reached lower-income readers, shaping popular opinion. This environment fostered more robust public discourse, albeit with the risk of sensationalism.

Political cartoons soared in popularity, lampooning politicians or depicting social issues in witty, often acerbic ways. The Third Republic, though generally supportive of freedom of expression, still enforced defamation and anti-blasphemy laws. Yet the overall climate was more liberal than earlier times, allowing fresh journalistic voices. In turn, illiteracy declined as state education reforms expanded, creating a more engaged citizenry that devoured news, arts, and entertainment.

## 4) The Third Republic's Political Trajectory: From Crisis to Consolidation

### The Moral Order Cracks and Republican Dominance

Adolphe Thiers, the provisional head of the new republic after the Commune's fall, soon fell out with monarchist deputies who wanted to restore the Bourbon or Orléans line. The so-called **"Legitimists vs. Orleanists"** disputes paralyzed the National Assembly. Eventually, in 1875, a series of constitutional laws—drafted by moderate republicans—cemented the **Third Republic** as the legal regime, though by a narrow vote.

Over subsequent years, republican factions consolidated power. Presidents like **Patrice de MacMahon** initially leaned conservative, but by 1879, republicans fully controlled parliament and forced a more liberal direction. Figures such as **Jules Ferry** championed free, compulsory, and secular primary education, weakening the Church's role. Slowly, anticlerical policies took root, including the expulsion of certain religious orders from teaching. For Paris, this signaled a final break from any revival of monarchy or Church supremacy.

### Opportunist and Radical Republicans

Inside the broad republican coalition, two main currents emerged:

- **Opportunists (Moderates)**: Led by men like **Gambetta** and **Ferry**, these politicians favored gradual reforms, a stable executive, and business-friendly policies. They embraced colonial expansion, seeing it as a mark of national prestige.
- **Radical Republicans**: More left-leaning, championing expanded welfare, secularization, and eventually universal male suffrage. Figures like **Georges Clemenceau** challenged paternalist or imperial policies, pushing for deeper social transformations.

Despite their differences, both factions agreed on preserving the Republic, preventing any Bonapartist or royalist comeback. Paris served as the stage for their parliamentary battles, with strong representation in the city's arrondissements. Local clubs and the daily press amplified these debates, ensuring that political life remained vibrant and often contentious.

## 5) The Age of Expositions and the Eiffel Tower

### The Exposition Universelle of 1878

Following the success of earlier world's fairs, the Third Republic hosted another **Exposition Universelle** in 1878. Set in the **Champ de Mars** and the **Trocadéro**, the fair showcased French industry, arts, and colonial products, reaffirming Paris as a global cultural capital recovering from war. Electric lighting, courtesy of Thomas Edison's inventions, dazzled visitors. The Trocadéro Palace, built for the occasion, served as a venue for concerts and scientific lectures.

Visitors marveled at exotic pavilions from French colonies, igniting new debates about imperialism. Parisians saw the fair as an image of national revival, burying memories of defeat and the Commune under a spectacle of progress. The city's hotels and cafés thrived, forging the notion that Paris was not only a political hub but also a tourist magnet for the curious and affluent.

### The 1889 Exposition and the Eiffel Tower

A decade later, the **Exposition Universelle of 1889** commemorated the centennial of the French Revolution—both celebrating the Third Republic's accomplishments and reaffirming the revolutionary heritage. Its centerpiece was **Gustave Eiffel**'s towering iron structure, **la Tour Eiffel**, rising over 300 meters on the Champ de Mars. Initially derided by some artists and intellectuals as a monstrous eyesore, the tower soon became a symbol of modern engineering triumph and Paris's futuristic spirit.

Visitors ascended the tower to behold panoramic city views, forging an instant tourist sensation. The fair also featured machinery halls, cultural exhibits, and amusements, drawing tens of millions of visitors. While conservatives lamented the tower's "subversion" of classical aesthetics, younger generations embraced it as a totem of industrial might and scientific audacity. Over time, the Eiffel Tower would become the emblem of Paris—a visible testament to the synergy of the Republic's ideals and cutting-edge technology.

### Late 19th-Century Urban Culture

The city's nightlife blossomed around major expositions. Electric street lamps extended business hours, fueling a café-concert boom. Cabaret culture soared in Montmartre, with venues like **Le Chat Noir** (founded 1881) featuring shadow plays and satirical songs. Toulouse-Lautrec's posters immortalized the cancan dancers of the **Moulin Rouge** (opened 1889), celebrating flamboyant popular entertainment. This mass entertainment coexisted with the refined world of opera, classical concerts, and academic salons, illustrating Paris's diversity.

Hence, by the final decade of the 19th century, Paris exemplified **la Belle Époque**, an era of optimism, artistic brilliance, and technological leaps. Yet, beneath the glow of expositions, the city still grappled with labor disputes, rising socialist movements, and mounting anti-Semitism and nationalism, foreshadowing new political storms in the coming century.

## 6) Social Struggles: Labor and Political Movements

### Workers' Organizations and Strikes

From the 1880s onward, industrial labor expanded around Paris, fostering a more cohesive working class. Although the Third Republic had legalized trade unions only in 1884, workers formed **syndicats** (unions) earlier in defiance of older restrictions. Sectors like printing, metals, and textiles led the way. Strike actions multiplied, demanding shorter hours, better wages, and safer conditions.

While the government typically avoided the brutal suppressions of earlier eras, it still deployed troops or police to quell large strikes, especially if they disrupted city life. Some in the Chamber of Deputies supported moderate labor reforms, while radicals advocated universal labor rights, cooperative enterprises, and social insurance. In Paris, union headquarters and workers' cafés became centers of political education, distributing socialist or anarchist pamphlets to an increasingly literate workforce.

### Socialist and Anarchist Currents

In 1882, the **Federation of the Socialist Workers of France** emerged, splitting between **Marxist**-inspired collectivists and **Blanquist** revolutionaries. By the 1890s, leaders like **Jean Jaurès** argued for a democratic road to socialism within the parliamentary framework, while anarchists like **Élisée Reclus** or **Jean Grave** championed direct action. A series of **anarchist bombings** and assassinations in the 1890s—tragically culminating in President Sadi Carnot's murder in 1894—provoked a fierce crackdown, with anti-anarchist laws muzzling radical presses.

Despite these tensions, the working class gained representation in municipal councils. In Paris, socialist candidates occasionally won local offices, particularly in the eastern arrondissements, highlighting a dynamic political shift. The memory of the Commune still inspired calls for social justice, though now channeled through union activism and parliamentary reforms rather than insurrectionary barricades.

---

## 7) Nationalism, Anti-Semitism, and the Dreyfus Affair

### Shifts in National Sentiment

Military defeat in 1870 and the subsequent drive for **revanchisme** (revenge) shaped France's political culture. Many demanded the recovery of Alsace-Lorraine from Germany, fueling nationalist sentiments that found expression in newspapers, patriotic leagues, and militarist education. In Paris, nationalist demonstrations sometimes turned hostile to foreigners, especially Germans or Italians. Yet, the city also boasted cosmopolitan enclaves, with visiting artists, students, and exiles adding to its cultural mix.

### The Dreyfus Affair (1894–1906)

A significant crisis erupted when Captain **Alfred Dreyfus**, a Jewish officer in the French army, was falsely accused of espionage for Germany in 1894. His secret court-martial and life sentence on **Devil's Island** triggered deep divisions. Nationalists and anti-Semites hailed his conviction, while intellectuals like Émile Zola (with his open letter "**J'Accuse…!**") argued it was a miscarriage of justice driven by anti-Semitism and a corrupt military.

In Paris, demonstrations split the city. Pro-Dreyfus liberals marched chanting for judicial revision, while anti-Dreyfus leagues smeared him as a traitor. Riots occasionally flared, and anti-Jewish violence rose. The affair lasted years, eventually culminating in Dreyfus's exoneration in 1906. This polarizing saga showcased the Third Republic's fragile institutions: while it eventually corrected the injustice, the ugly wave of nationalism and anti-Semitism shook Parisian society, revealing latent prejudices.

## 8) The 1900 Exposition and the Turn of the Century

### The 1900 World's Fair

Crowning the Belle Époque, the **Exposition Universelle of 1900** took Paris's self-promotion to new heights. Focused on the theme of "Evaluating the 19th Century and Celebrating the Future," it boasted pavilions for electrical technology, motion pictures (the Lumière brothers had debuted cinematic projections in 1895), and the first panoramic escalators. Millions of visitors thronged the **Grand Palais** and **Petit Palais**, newly built to house art exhibitions and industrial showcases.

The fair also introduced the **Paris Métro**: the first line opened in July 1900, revolutionizing city travel. Designed with elegant Art Nouveau entrances by **Hector Guimard**, the Métro symbolized cutting-edge engineering and artistry. It soon expanded across the city, weaving neighborhoods together and setting a model for future urban transit systems worldwide.

## 9) Cultural and Social Legacy of the Late 19th Century

### Architecture and Urban Aesthetics

Between Haussmann's legacy and subsequent expansions, late 19th-century Paris formed the classic urban landscape recognizable today: wide boulevards, symmetrical façades, iconic bridges, and iron landmarks. Art Nouveau motifs, championed by architects like **Hector Guimard**, introduced flowing lines in building ornamentation, Metro entrances, and interior design.

Simultaneously, the city's outskirts developed more factories, worker housing, and eventually modest "**cités**" that presaged future suburban sprawl. The tension between central bourgeois quarters and peripheral working-class zones was well established, a pattern that would intensify in the 20th century. Yet the overall effect was that Paris, with its 2+ million residents by 1900, had become a seamlessly orchestrated stage for modern life—magnificent in its public spaces, though not always equitable in its distribution of resources.

**Intellectual and Scientific Advancements**

The capital abounded in scientific achievements. The **Pasteur Institute**, founded by **Louis Pasteur** in 1887, advanced bacteriology and vaccinations, revolutionizing public health. Medical breakthroughs, alongside municipal improvements in water and sanitation, reduced epidemic outbreaks. Meanwhile, mathematicians and physicists lectured at the Sorbonne, forging new ideas in electromagnetism, thermodynamics, and eventually radioactivity (Marie and Pierre Curie discovered radium at the turn of the century).

Philosophically, the city hosted debates between positivists, neo-Kantians, and emergent sociologists like **Émile Durkheim**, who established sociology as an academic field. Paris's universities, academies, and intellectual journals formed a crossroad for global thinkers, from Spanish regenerationists to Russian revolutionaries in exile. The city's tradition of free inquiry, buttressed by the Third Republic's educational expansions, positioned it at the forefront of Western scientific and cultural discourse.

---

## 10) Conclusion

By 1900, Paris had traversed a tumultuous path from the last vestiges of Napoleon III's empire to the consolidation of the Third Republic. The city had seen war and siege, the fiery upheaval of the Commune, and a monumental reconfiguration under Haussmann. It hosted grand universal expositions that enthralled millions, showcasing electricity, engineering marvels, and a resurgent national pride. Culturally, it nurtured Impressionism, literary Realism, and an avant-garde spirit that would define modern art.

Yet, behind this cultural flourishing lay lingering social inequalities, memories of violent repressions, and the rise of new political ideologies—nationalism, socialism, anarchism—that would shape future revolts. The city's working classes, despite incremental improvements, remained largely on the economic margins, fueling demands for labor rights that were partially addressed but never fully resolved. Meanwhile, intellectual life soared, spawning breakthroughs in science and philosophy that reinforced the city's reputation as a beacon of progress.

**Paris at the dawn of the 20th century** was thus a paradox: an enchanting metropolis, an emblem of modernity with wide boulevards, electric lights, and cultural effervescence, yet also haunted by inequalities and the specter of further turmoil. The Third Republic persevered, forging a national identity that balanced conservative stability with liberal reforms, though always mindful of the city's capacity for upheaval. In the centuries to come, Paris's unique blend of revolutionary legacy, artistic innovation, and civic ambition continued to evolve—an ongoing story of transformation that built upon the decisive chapters recounted in this book.

# Help Us Share Your Thoughts!

**Dear reader,**

Thank you for spending your time with this book. We hope it brought you enjoyment and a few new ideas to think about. If there was anything that didn't work for you, or if you have suggestions on how we can improve, please let us know at **kontakt@skriuwer.com**. Your feedback means a lot to us and helps us make our books even better.

If you enjoyed this book, we would be very grateful if you left a review on the site where you purchased it. Your review not only helps other readers find our books, but also encourages us to keep creating more stories and materials that you'll love.

By choosing Skriuwer, you're also supporting **Frisian**—a minority language mainly spoken in the northern Netherlands. Although **Frisian** has a rich history, the number of speakers is shrinking, and it's at risk of dying out. Your purchase helps fund resources to preserve and promote this language, such as educational programs and learning tools. If you'd like to learn more about Frisian or even start learning it yourself, please visit **www.learnfrisian.com**.

Thank you for being part of our community. We look forward to sharing more books with you in the future.

**Warm regards,**
The Skriuwer Team

Printed in Dunstable, United Kingdom